Wittgenstein's Artillery

Wittgenstein's Artillery

Philosophy as Poetry

James C. Klagge

The MIT Press
Cambridge, Massachusetts
London, England

The MIT Press would like to thank the anonymous peer reviewers who provided comments on drafts of this book. The generous work of academic experts is essential for establishing the authority and quality of our publications. We acknowledge with gratitude the contributions of these otherwise uncredited readers.

This book was set in Stone Serif and Stone Sans by Westchester Publishing Services. Printed and bound in the United States of America.

Library of Congress Cataloging-in-Publication Data

Names: Klagge, James Carl, 1954– author.
Title: Wittgenstein's artillery : philosophy as poetry / James C. Klagge.
Description: Cambridge, Massachusetts : The MIT Press, [2021] |
Includes bibliographical references and index.
Identifiers: LCCN 2020036778 | ISBN 9780262045834 (hardcover)
Subjects: LCSH: Wittgenstein, Ludwig, 1889–1951. | Wittgenstein, Ludwig, 1889–1951—Literary style.
Classification: LCC B3376.W564 K533 2021 | DDC 192—dc23
LC record available at https://lccn.loc.gov/2020036778

10 9 8 7 6 5 4 3 2 1

publication supported by a grant from
The Community Foundation for Greater New Haven
as part of the **Urban Haven Project**

I don't try to make you believe something you don't believe, but to make you do something you won't do.

—Ludwig Wittgenstein, 1931

I believe I summed up where I stand in relation to philosophy when I said: one should really only do philosophy as poetry.

—Ludwig Wittgenstein, 1933 or 1934

Quite different artillery is needed here from anything I am in a position to muster.

—Ludwig Wittgenstein, 1947

Contents

Preface

In this book, I tell a story about how Ludwig Wittgenstein (1889–1951) came to care about the impact of his ideas on his students and readers and how he tried a "poetic" style of doing philosophy that could lead to the kinds of changes he sought. Although he did not ultimately think he was successful using this style, I examine various examples of this poetic style of writing that might serve Wittgenstein's purposes. This is what I call Wittgenstein's "artillery."

In writing this book, I have drawn on and significantly expanded earlier publications. Chapter 1 is based on "Wittgenstein and His Audience: Esotericist or Evangelist?" in N. Venturinha, ed., *The Textual Genesis of Wittgenstein's Philosophical Investigations* (Routledge, 2013, pp. 52–64). Chapter 2 is based on "Wittgenstein and His Students: 1929–1933," in D. Stern, ed., *Wittgenstein in the 1930s: Between the Tractatus and the Investigations* (Cambridge University Press, 2018, pp. 109–122). Chapter 3 is based on "Wittgenstein, Frazer and Temperament," in Lars Albinus, Josef G. F. Rothhaupt, and Aidan Seery, eds., *Wittgenstein's Remarks on Frazer: The Text and the Matter* (de Gruyter, 2016, pp. 233–248). I thank the editors and publishers for permission to draw on these works. In each case I have found a good deal to add. Chapters 5 and 6 were given trial runs at the Seventh and Eighth Regional Working Conferences on Wittgenstein, held in Morgantown, West Virginia, in October 2016, and Lexington, Virginia, in April 2018, respectively. I owe a great deal to this loyal band of Wittgenstein fans who live in my region of the country. Finally, I thank Nadia Hijab for permission to quote from her father's unpublished work.

I thank three anonymous referees from MIT Press, as well as those who have commented on earlier versions of particular chapters or the whole manuscript, including Lars Albinus, João José R. L. de Almeida, David Cerbone, Gabriel Citron, Cora Diamond, Mauro Engelmann, Christian Erbacher, Tom Gardner, Reza Hosseini, David A. Kessler, Nick Klagge, Karen Kovaka, Wilhelm Krüger, David Levy, William Lyons, Jakub Mácha, Elizabeth Malbon, Alfred Nordmann, Jim Peterman, Duncan Richter, David Stern, Béla Szabados, Tommi Uschanov, and Thomas Wallgren.

I began telling stories to children publicly as part of the Sunday school program at Blacksburg Presbyterian Church in the early 1990s. In 1997 I co-led an adult Sunday school class, Biblical Parables and Other Stories, with Larry Bechtel and Ann Shawhan. For several years now, I have told stories at the New River Valley Juvenile Detention Center as part of a regular program with other members of my church, Asbury United Methodist Church. I did not connect any of this with Wittgenstein's style until 2012, when Tom Gardner and I began talking with each other about our work. It was a surprise to find that his thoughts on the working of poetry and stories turned out to be just what Wittgenstein seemed to be looking for in his search for a poetic style of doing philosophy. Alois Pichler invited me for a month-long residence at the Wittgenstein Archive at Bergen in 2012, where I was required to give three talks. My thoughts about esotericism and evangelism came together for that occasion, and the book came to life from there.

I dedicate this book to my children, Meagan and Nick, who let me read to them until they left for college. Let us hope that stories will see us through.

Blacksburg, Virginia

April 2020, during the COVID-19 Pandemic and Seclusion

Abbreviations

Full details of the works referred to in this book are in the bibliography. However, I refer to the following works by Wittgenstein so commonly as to merit this list of abbreviations.

BB	*The Blue and Brown Books*
BT	*The Big Typescript: TS 213*
CV	*Culture and Value*, 1980/Revised edition 1998
GT	*Geheime Tagebücher: 1914–1916*
LC	*Lectures and Conversations on Aesthetics, Psychology and Religious Belief*
LFM	*Wittgenstein's Lectures on the Foundations of Mathematics: Cambridge, 1939*
LPP	*Wittgenstein's Lectures on Philosophical Psychology, 1946–47*
LW1	*Last Writings on the Philosophy of Psychology*, vol. 1
LW2	*Last Writings on the Philosophy of Psychology*, vol. 2
MS or **TS**	*Wittgenstein's Nachlass: The Bergen Edition* (for numbering of manuscripts and typescripts see G. H. von Wright, "The Wittgenstein Papers")
NB	*Notebooks: 1914–1916*
OC	*On Certainty*
PI	*Philosophical Investigations*
PO	*Philosophical Occasions: 1912–1950*
PPO	*Public and Private Occasions*
PR	*Philosophical Remarks*
RC	*Remarks on Color*
RFM	*Remarks on the Foundations of Mathematics*, revised edition, 1978
RPP1	*Remarks on the Philosophy of Psychology*, vol. 1

RPP2	*Remarks on the Philosophy of Psychology*, vol. 2
WA1	*Wiener Ausgabe*, vol. 1, ed. M. Nedo
WA2	*Wiener Ausgabe*, vol. 2, ed. M. Nedo
WA3	*Wiener Ausgabe*, vol. 3, ed. M. Nedo
WC	*Wittgenstein in Cambridge: Letters and Documents, 1911–1951.*
WLA	*Wittgenstein's Lectures: Cambridge, 1932–1935, from the Notes of Alice Ambrose and Margaret MacDonald*
WLL	*Wittgenstein's Lectures: Cambridge, 1930–1932, from the Notes of John King and Desmond Lee*
WLM	*Wittgenstein: Lectures, Cambridge, 1930–1933 from the Notes of G. E. Moore*
Z	*Zettel*

Introduction: Wittgenstein at War

When Austria-Hungary declared war on Serbia on July 28, 1914, setting off what would later be called the First World War, Ludwig Wittgenstein was in Vienna visiting his family. Due to his father's death in 1913, Ludwig was one of the richest men in Vienna—a distinction he did not want.

Ludwig had spent the previous year in Norway working alone on his philosophy. He had even begun planning an isolated cabin there to live in.[1] His first inclination now was to return to Norway—he had earlier been exempted from military service due to a double hernia. But when he discovered that travel was blocked, he volunteered for the army instead. No mention was made of his medical condition or his financial circumstances. Ludwig's sister wrote, "I know for certain that he was not motivated simply by the wish to defend his fatherland. He also had an intense desire to take something difficult upon himself and to do something other than purely intellectual work."[2] Ludwig himself called it "*eine Feuerprobe des Charakters* [a trial by fire]" (GT, 14; August 10, 1914).

Wittgenstein was inducted as a private on August 7 and assigned to an artillery regiment. He started a diary, immediately wondering, "Will I be able to work now?" (that is, on his philosophy), and acknowledging that he "felt the terrors of war."[3] But within two months, he had found a livable accommodation between philosophical work and war: "Hearing ongoing strong gun fire and seeing the shells exploding. I am in a very good mood.—! The most violent barrage all day. Worked a lot. At least I have *one* decent idea." And in fact, he soon employed the maneuvers of war as a metaphor for his work: "Did a lot of work still without success but with a lot of confidence. I am *laying siege* to my problem now" (GT, 28, October 9, 1914; and 33, October 24, 1914).

Wittgenstein liked this metaphor enough to keep using it over the next week: "Did a lot of work. Still laying siege to my problem, have already taken many forts," "I want to gather ALL my forces for the offensive," and, "Worked all day. Have desperately stormed the problem! But I will sooner leave my blood before this fortress than depart empty-handed."[4] From November into December he regularly commented on artillery fire in conjunction with the work he was accomplishing. Thirty years later, after his young friend Con Drury had participated in the D-Day invasion of France during the Second World War, Drury told Wittgenstein "how wonderful the sound of the big naval guns was when they opened up behind us." Wittgenstein replied, "Oh yes, I remember that well. Heavy artillery is a marvelous sound; there is nothing quite like it"[5] (presumably when it is your own).

When John Maynard Keynes wrote jokingly in a letter to him, "It must be pleasanter to be at war than to think about propositions in Norway. But I hope you will stop such self-indulgence soon," Wittgenstein replied, "You're quite wrong if you think that being a soldier prevents me from thinking about propositions. As a matter of fact I've done a good deal of logical work lately, and hope to do a good deal more soon."[6] Yet that winter and the following spring, after Wittgenstein had been transferred to an artillery workshop behind the lines and he was far removed from the shelling, his work lagged for months. He soon requested a transfer to the infantry, but this was ignored: he remained more useful at the workshop. In another conversation with Drury many years later, just before the D-Day invasion, Wittgenstein had advised, "If it ever happens that you get mixed up in hand-to-hand fighting, you must just stand aside and let yourself be massacred." Drury commented, "I felt that this advice was one he had had to give himself in the previous war."[7] We can be thankful this was never tested.

But by spring 1916, Wittgenstein finally managed to get assigned to an artillery regiment destined for the front. This time he "requested to be positioned at the observation post," and within days he was "shot at" (GT, 69; April 23 and 29, 1916). The next week, he took stock of his new situation: "Tomorrow perhaps I shall be sent out, at my own request, to the spotters. Then and only then will the war begin for me. And—possibly—life too! Perhaps nearness to death will bring light into my life. I am a worm, but through God I become a man. God help me. Amen" (GT, 70; May 4, 1916). Forward artillery observer is a notoriously dangerous assignment.[8]

Wittgenstein was well aware of the dangers, and even apparently sought them, but he also wondered, "Will I endure it??" (GT, 70; May 5, 1916).

He did. In the course of the remaining three years of the war, Wittgenstein won three medals for his bravery as a forward observer: Silver Medal for Valor, Silver Medal for Valor First Class, and Band of the Military Service Medal with Swords. Here is the report recommending his first decoration:

> Ignoring the heavy artillery fire on the casemate and the exploding mortar bombs he observed the discharge of the mortars and located them. The Battery in fact succeeded in destroying two of the heavy-calibre mortars by direct hits, as was confirmed by prisoners taken. On the Battery Observation Post, Hill 417, he observed without intermission in the drumfire, although I several times shouted to him to take cover. By this distinctive behaviour he exercised a very calming effect on his comrades.[9]

While Wittgenstein had personal and spiritual reasons for wanting a forward observer post, he also developed a far more practical interest in the effectiveness of artillery barrages. Following his first spell as a forward observer and the enormous strains of battle—"Colossal exertions in the last month. Have thought a great deal on every possible subject" (GT, 72; July 6, 1916)—Wittgenstein was withdrawn from the front to train as an officer. Battle had not prevented his philosophical work. In fact, reflections on his battlefield experiences in conjunction with his philosophical thoughts led to new ideas that would fill the end of his *Tractatus Logico-Philosophicus*.[10] Yet at the same time that Wittgenstein was working out new philosophical directions, he also took a very concrete step with regard to the battlefield. In autumn 1916, as his sister reported, "Ludwig made a donation of a million crowns for the construction of a 30cm mortar."[11]

After the war, Wittgenstein would take legal steps to sever himself from his inheritance, but in the meantime, he had a fortune at his disposal. At the start of the war, he made sizable charitable donations.[12] And in conjunction with his siblings and mother, he purchased large sums of war bonds on several occasions. In total, over the course of five years, Ludwig expended 2,335,000 Austrian crowns, roughly equivalent to 6.5 million US dollars in 2016 dollars.[13] The donation for the mortar alone would be equivalent to about $2,869,000 in 2016 dollars.

His sister's report about the mortar is regrettably brief, but we can make an educated conjecture about the details. Škoda Works developed the 305 mm mortar for production in 1911, and the Austro-Hungarian War Ministry ordered twenty-four of them. In 1916 the M-11 model was upgraded to M-11/16, which allowed a firing traverse of 360 degrees, and then upgraded again to M-16, which also had a longer barrel, a longer range, and a higher barrel elevation, and it was easier to transport. By the end of the war, seventy-nine of these three models of the mortar were in service, including only twenty-nine of the M-16 variety.[14] It seems quite likely that Wittgenstein acted when he did because of the prospect of the improved mortar. Given the rather small number of such mortars available, the addition of one, especially of the upgraded variety, would not be trivial.

As it turned out, the government never used the donated money. While his sister, in her later account, went on to chide Ludwig for the naiveté of his donation, my interest is not in the effect of the donation but in its intent.[15] Wittgenstein tried to invest in artillery that was more flexible, more accurate, and more powerful. As a spotter, these very things would matter greatly to him.

After the Soviet Russian government sued for peace in 1917 and a truce was declared on the eastern front in December, Wittgenstein was transferred to the Italian front. He continued to request an assignment in the infantry but was placed again as a forward observer in a Mountain Artillery regiment. After an extended leave over the summer during which he completed what was to become his book *Tractatus Logico-Philosophicus*, he returned to the front.

On September 22, Wittgenstein received the last of his three medals. But the collapse of the various allied forces led to chaos on the battlefield. While most Austro-Hungarian troops beat a hasty retreat for home, the artillery held out. Encircled by the Italians and short of equipment, Ludwig constructed his own mortar using an ancient technique: he wound bronze wire around a tree trunk of the same diameter as the shells and by means of an intense fire, fused the metal to form a gun barrel.[16] Resourceful, even to the end.

Despite the disastrous defeat, the war served an important purpose for Wittgenstein: "It saved my life; I don't know what I'd have done without it," he said.[17] And although the empire for which he fought had come to an end, Wittgenstein "continued to wear his uniform for many years after the war, as though it had become a part of his identity, an essential part, without which he would be lost."[18]

The military metaphors became rare in Wittgenstein's characterizations of his philosophical work for the next thirty-some years.[19] But the concern of the spotter, to see how effective the artillery has been and how it could be adjusted, the concern of the Viennese philanthropist, to provide the best artillery possible, the concern of the artillery lieutenant, to improvise artillery under difficult circumstances, would eventually show themselves in Wittgenstein's philosophical work as he gradually developed a concern for the influence of his ideas on his audience. Finally, in 1947, taking stock of this concern and his persistent attempts to meet it, his thoughts returned to the earlier metaphor: "Quite different artillery is needed here from anything I am in a position to muster."[20]

In this book, I tell the story of Wittgenstein as he became a *philosophical* spotter and how he struggled to find the right artillery to accomplish his philosophical purposes.

1 Wittgenstein and His Audience

On November 3, 1918, at the end of the war, Wittgenstein was taken captive by the Italians. He had sent off his completed manuscript to a prospective publisher while he was still on leave in August, but it would not be published for another three years. In the meantime, Wittgenstein shared the manuscript with various friends. Anyone who tries to read Wittgenstein's *Tractatus* is likely to be puzzled from the start:

> 1 The world is everything that is the case.
>
> 1.1 The world is the totality of facts, not things.
>
> . . .

These sound like pronouncements, yet did someone need to be informed of this? Had someone doubted it? What exactly is his point? Wittgenstein offers us no context for his claims, no way to orient ourselves. Perhaps this was not meant for me—as though I were reading a letter found in the attic of an old house I just bought. Wittgenstein's mentor, Bertrand Russell, worried: "I am seriously afraid that no one will see the point of anything he writes, because he won't recommend it by arguments addressed to a different point of view."[1]

Whom was Wittgenstein addressing with his writings? To engage Wittgenstein's philosophical work, it is important to consider this question. And once we consider the question, it becomes clear that the answer changed over time. Whom he was addressing in the *Tractatus* was different from the audience he was addressing in his later book, *Philosophical Investigations*, where he begins by retelling a story from St. Augustine. To appreciate the ways his target, and consequently his methods of hitting the target, changed over time, we must trace the development of Wittgenstein's work as both a writer and a teacher. While it is natural to look first at Wittgenstein's books, because they are more familiar, I contend that we must also appreciate Wittgenstein's work as a lecturer to fully understand his changing conception of his audience and his task. After rejecting the inheritance from his father, Wittgenstein determined to support himself—and the only way a philosopher can be self-supporting is by teaching. Wittgenstein taught well over forty courses at University of Cambridge from 1930 to 1947.[2] Teaching was a large part of his philosophical life, and it should not be surprising that it had an impact on his writing and his approach to philosophy. I make the case for this in chapter 2.

But in this chapter, I look at the bigger picture—how Wittgenstein's conception of his audience changed over time. Wittgenstein tells us a lot about his understanding of his audience, mainly in prefaces or drafts of prefaces that he wrote for his work. In describing his changing conceptions, I employ the terms *esotericist* and *evangelist,* which concern matters of audience. These terms have not generally been used in characterizing Wittgenstein; by using them, I place my discussion of Wittgenstein in a broader context that draws on a wider range of authors and audiences.

The English word *esoteric* comes directly from the Greek word *esoterikos,* which means inside the walls or belonging to an inner circle. An early use of the term applied it to the Pythagorean cult of fifth-century Greece, in which followers of the mathematician Pythagoras (c. 570–495 BCE) held certain metaphysical beliefs about the soul in common and withheld them from the public. Some few scholars (e.g., the so-called Tübingen school) claim that Plato wrote his dialogues for public (exoteric) consumption but reserved his own, esoteric, beliefs for sharing only with a limited group of followers, perhaps members of his Academy, and only orally, since he allegedly did not trust things written down.[3]

The distinction seems to be employed by Aristotle as well when he alludes to (his own) exoteric writings, which may be his legendary lost dialogues.[4] What is interesting about these allusions is that they imply that what we are reading by Aristotle are in fact his *esoteric* writings. And this fits with the requirement, which he sets out early in the *Nicomachean Ethics,* that his teachings are meant "for those who accord with reason in forming their desires and in their actions." He specifically declines to instruct the youth (whether young in age or in experience) who "lacks experience of the actions in life," "tends to follow his feelings," and "gets no benefit from his knowledge."[5] And near the end of the *Nicomachean Ethics*, he returns to this theme when he emphasizes that "the soul of the student needs to have been prepared by habits of enjoying and hating finely, like ground that is to nourish seed."[6] His articulation of this point in terms of the proper "student" supports the theory that what we are reading are (close to or based on) notes that Aristotle used at his Lyceum when literally lecturing to students.[7]

Similar issues of audience arise in the sayings of Jesus and the gospel writings that recount his life. Jesus regularly taught the crowds by telling parables. One of the first parables recounted in the Gospel of Mark is the parable of the sower (Mark 4:3–8). The story seems to directly address the question of audience:

> Listen! Imagine a sower going out to sow. Now it happened that, as he sowed, some of the seed fell on the edge of the path, and the birds came and ate it up. Some seed fell on the rocky ground where it found little soil and at once sprang up, because there was no depth of earth; and when the sun came up it was scorched and, not having roots, it withered away. Some seed fell into thorns, and the thorns grew up and choked it, and it produced no crop. And some seeds fell into rich soil, grew tall and strong, and produced a good crop.

As Jesus goes on to say (Mark 4:15–20), this represents the varying reception of his message. So the message is shared with all—the seed is sown in all directions, seemingly haphazardly—though it does not benefit all. This, at any rate, appears to be Jesus's intent.

But when the use of parables is explained, the gospel writers themselves offer a somewhat different take. Luke, for instance, adds, "His disciples asked Jesus what this parable meant, and he answered, 'The knowledge of the secrets of the Kingdom of God has been given to you, but to the rest it comes by means of parables, so that they may look but not see, and listen but not understand.'"[8] This is rather surprising and doesn't really make much sense, since parables seem designed precisely for their accessibility, especially to a crowd of peasants. But the gospel writers may have been trying in retrospect to create a sense that their readers were gaining privileged information.

The idea of a secretive message was reinforced by the discovery in 1945 (at Nag Hammadi, in Egypt) of ancient writings about Jesus. The Gospel of Thomas opens by describing "the secret words which Jesus spoke." This and other recently discovered writings have come to be called the "Gnostic" gospels, for those "in the know." They have provided fragments of views of

Jesus rather different (sometimes surprisingly so) from the picture found in the four canonical gospels of the Christian Bible.

So the idea of an esoteric message seems to be connected with the notion that certain things should or can be shared only with people who are especially deserving or able to appreciate the message. In recent work, the political theorist Arthur Melzer has contended that there are four categories of esoteric communication: (1) *defensive esotericism*, in which the author presents a message esoterically out of fear of persecution; (2) *protective esotericism*, in which the author conceals a message that may be dangerous to society; (3) *pedagogical esotericism*, in which the author presents a message in a way that only those who are suited to hear the message will best be able to learn it; and (4) *political esotericism*, in which the author presents a message in the service of new political goals.[9]

While these categories seem to cover a wide range of examples, it is not clear where Aristotle's lectures on ethics, the *Nicomachean Ethics*, should fit. Aristotle does not limit the students he addresses out of fear of persecution, the message is not dangerous to society, and it does not promote new political goals. While it is true that the students he chooses are most suited to hear the message, there is no indication that they can learn it better in this way. In fact, they are chosen only because they will be able to benefit from it, because they have acquired habits that will enable them to put his principles into practice. Melzer claims that Aristotle's *Ethics* and *Politics* "were beyond the reach of popular audiences only through their more advanced and exacting philosophical method."[10] But Aristotle makes quite clear that what distinguishes his target audience is their well-trained character, not their intellect. There would be no danger in others hearing the lectures; it would simply be a waste of their time because "the end is action, not knowledge."[11] Aristotle is simply not interested in those who cannot appreciate his work—cannot put it to work.

It would seem that we need another category of esoteric message. Perhaps we can call it (5) *concessive esotericism*, in which the author concedes or acknowledges that the message is not for everyone and yet is not bothered by that fact. There is no secretive intent or deeper purpose, but there is no concern to make the message accessible or useful to all. This notion should be familiar to college professors who teach introductory classes as well as advanced seminars with prerequisites. Advanced seminars would be what I am calling concessively esoteric.

With this understanding of esotericism in mind, let us return to Wittgenstein. In 1930, Wittgenstein drafted a passage he labeled "*Zu einem Vorwort* [Toward a Foreword/Preface]" for a book that he was working on:

> This book is written for those who are in sympathy with the spirit [*Geist*] in which it is written. This spirit is, I believe, different from that of the prevailing European and American civilization. The spirit of *this civilization* the expression of which is the industry, architecture, music, of present day fascism & socialism is a *spirit that is alien* [*fremder*] *and uncongenial* to the author. This is not a value judgement.[12]

Important parts of Wittgenstein's thought here are connected with his views, derived from Oswald Spengler, about the difference between culture and civilization.[13] Wittgenstein continues:

> Even if it is clear to me then that the disappearance of a culture does not signify the disappearance of human value but simply of certain means of expressing this value, still the fact remains that I contemplate the current of European civilization without sympathy, without understanding its aims if any. So I am really writing for friends who are scattered throughout the corners of the globe.
>
> It is all one to me whether the typical western scientist understands or appreciates my work since in any case he doesn't understand the spirit in which I write. . . . So I am aiming at something different than are the scientists & my thoughts move [*Denkbewegung*] differently than do theirs.

Wittgenstein later comments on these friends (January 18, 1931):

> If I say that my book is meant for only a small circle [*kleinen Kreis*] of people (if it can be called a circle) I do not mean to say that this circle is in my view the elite of mankind but it is a circle to which I turn . . . because they form my cultural circle, as it were my fellow countrymen in contrast to the others who are foreign [*fremd*] to me.[14]

Who were among the small circle of friends Wittgenstein had in mind? Likely he was thinking of friends in Olmütz, where he had been stationed for training to be an officer in the autumn of 1916 during the First World War: Paul Engelmann, Heini Groag, and Fritz and Max Zweig. In fact, when Engelmann himself described those friends in Olmütz, he referred to them precisely as a "*kleinen Kreis*."[15] Perhaps the circle would include also Moritz Schlick, Adolf Loos, Karl Kraus, Ludwig Hänsel, and Wittgenstein's sister, Hermine, in Vienna.[16] Among more current friends, perhaps Piero Sraffa and Raffaello Piccoli in England.[17] These were people Wittgenstein considered to be friends, peers, and sympathetic to him in some sense. They would understand him and know, as we say, where he was coming from. While they were not "scattered throughout the corners of the globe," they were at any rate scattered throughout the corners of Europe.

In contrast, when he speaks of the "typical western scientist," he has in mind a certain spirit that he imagines "the prevailing European and American civilization" to hold—what we might call a sort of "scientism": overvaluing the role and importance of science in society. G. H. von Wright has plausibly conjectured that Wittgenstein had Rudolf Carnap, and especially Carnap's "*Vorwort*" to his *Logische Aufbau der Welt,* in mind when drafting his own "*Vorwort.*"[18] But I think we can also plausibly take Wittgenstein's object here to be the mind-set that most of us now would hold. So Wittgenstein sees himself in the early 1930s as writing for a select group of people who would share with him a certain spirit that he imagines most people would not share. This shared spirit would allow them to understand him, unlike the general public, who would not. He concludes with a reflection on the Foreword:

> The danger in a long foreword is that the spirit of the book has to be evident in the book itself & cannot be described. For if a book has been written for only a few readers that will be clear just from the fact that only a few understand it.[19]

Wittgenstein famously insisted, over and over of certain of his works, that they would not be generally understood. This, I think, makes him an esotericist.

But Wittgenstein is not an esotericist in any of the four senses that Melzer laid out. Rather, his esotericism seems closer to that of Aristotle in his practical writings—he concedes that only a few will understand him. He is not intent on keeping his views from others, only that he does not expect them to understand or agree.[20]

This esotericism did not just take hold in 1930. He prefaced his *Tractatus* with similar thoughts: "Perhaps this book will be understood only by someone who has himself already had the thoughts that are expressed in it—or at least similar thoughts.—So it is not a textbook.—Its purpose would be achieved if it gave pleasure to one person who read and understood it." And the sheer difficulty of understanding the *Tractatus* made it natural to suppose that there was some esoteric intent.

A book on the *Tractatus* by Alexander Maslow, written in 1933 but not published until 1961, includes the following warning in its Introduction: "The *Tractatus* is in many of its passages so obscure that it would be impossible, I believe, to gather the fundamentals of Wittgenstein's view without some help from people who have been initiated into it directly by the author himself."[21] That is the essence of esotericism. This need for special insight, of a different sort, was asserted by another commentator, Roy E. Lemoine:

> The *Tractatus* is probably the most significant philosophical document since the *Critique of Pure Reason*, from which it is in some ways derivative; but it is much harder to read. Even Wittgenstein, as he stated in his foreword, was aware that perhaps only those who had thought similar thoughts would understand him. It may be that my contribution to the study of the *Tractatus* comes from the fact that my own background is different from that of most scholars and has some similarity to Wittgenstein's. I have been both a line officer and a chaplain, and I also served in a great war.[22]

The author's experience is supposed to account for the fact that his book "departs radically from the traditional interpretations of the *Tractatus*." I think Lemoine's take is accurate: understanding the *Tractatus* requires an understanding of its context—its logical background *and* its wartime background. Wittgenstein's wartime friend Engelmann claims that Wittgenstein's basic thoughts in the *Tractatus* "are incomprehensible" to ordinary readers "owing to the absence of the psychological conditions from which alone such thinking can spring and which must exist, though to a lesser degree, in the reader's mind as well."[23] This limits its audience significantly, and Wittgenstein realized and accepted that.

After the end of the First World War and the publication of his book, Wittgenstein trained as an elementary school teacher and taught in rural Austria for six years. He then lived in Vienna, assisting Paul Engelmann in the design and construction of a house for Wittgenstein's sister. During this time in Vienna, 1927–1928, he had occasional meetings with members of the Vienna Circle, especially Moritz Schlick, Friedrich Waismann, and occasionally others, such as Carnap and Herbert Feigl. Wittgenstein was somewhat reluctant to have such meetings, but eventually he consented to some. The circle members were interested in learning more about the *Tractatus*, which they had studied carefully, but, according to Feigl, "only on relatively rare occasions could we get him to clarify one or another of the puzzling or obscure passages in his work. . . . On occasion, he would read poetry to us (e.g., that of Rabindranath Tagore)."[24] When relating this latter fact McGuinness adds: "usually sitting with his back to the audience."[25] It is hard to imagine a clearer expression of an esoteric attitude.

Wittgenstein's attendance at a talk by the intuitionistic mathematician L. E. J. Brouwer in March 1928 sparked his interest in discussing philosophy again, and it led to continued meetings between Wittgenstein and Schlick, with Waismann present to record Wittgenstein's expositions or elaborations of his thoughts.[26] Carnap was excluded, presumably because his approach to the issues was so different. Carnap reports, "Although the difference in our attitudes and personalities expressed itself only on certain occasions, I understood very well that Wittgenstein felt it all the time and, unlike me, was disturbed by it. He [Wittgenstein] said to Schlick that he could talk only with somebody who 'holds his hand.'"[27] At Schlick's urging, Waismann's notes were meant to be shared with the other circle members as expositions of Wittgenstein's thoughts. Over the next few years, there were continued meetings between Wittgenstein and Waismann connected with plans for Waismann to cooperate with Wittgenstein in writing a book setting out Wittgenstein's ideas. But despite a great deal of effort on Waismann's part, these plans ultimately came to nothing.[28]

Wittgenstein returned to Cambridge in 1929, primarily at the urging of John Maynard Keynes, who reintroduced him to the Apostles discussion group.[29] The Apostles was a small, secret group of Cambridge men devoted to discussion of issues of human importance. For a time, it overlapped in membership with the Bloomsbury literary group. Wittgenstein never got on well with its members. It was here that he encountered the student Julian Bell. Based wholly or partly on Wittgenstein's interactions with the Apostles' group members, Bell wrote a satirical poem criticizing Wittgenstein's style of discussion. This portion of the poem highlights Wittgenstein's unconcern to influence or even consider the views of others:

> But who, on any issue, ever saw
> Ludwig refrain from laying down the law?
> In every company he shouts us down,
> And stops our sentences stuttering his own;
> Unceasing argues, harsh, irate and loud,
> Sure that he's right, and of his rightness proud.
> Such faults are common, shared by all in part,
> But Wittgenstein pontificates on Art.
> . . .
> Ethics, aesthetics, talks of day and night,
> And calls things good or bad, and wrong or right.
> The universe sails down its charted course,

> He smuggles knowledge from a secret source:
> A mystic in the end, confessed and plain,
> The ancient enemy returned again;
> Who knows by his direct experience
> What is beyond all knowledge and all sense.[30]

Bell presents Wittgenstein in 1929 as an esotericist.

When Wittgenstein began teaching in January 1930, his classes were small, and he published almost nothing (save for "Some Remarks on Logical Form").[31] It may have seemed from the outside as though his students were insiders, and his classes took on a reputation of being only for the select few. This secretive reputation seems well captured by the account in Alan Turing's biography of how Turing managed to get into Wittgenstein's class several years later, in the 1939 Lent and Easter terms:

> There were about fifteen in the class . . . and each had to go first for a private interview with Wittgenstein in his austere Trinity room. These interviews were renowned for their long and impressive silences, for Wittgenstein despised the making of polite conversation. . . . After they had talked about some logic, Wittgenstein . . . said that he would have to go into a nearby room to think over what had been said.[32]

Another student, J. L. Findlay, who attended classes in the following term in 1939, claimed that "Wittgenstein restricted attendance at his gatherings and access to his manuscripts."[33] But while this might have been the public reputation, I question the implicit suggestion that Wittgenstein allowed only certain people into his classes.

Wittgenstein's courses were almost always publicly announced in the *Cambridge University Reporter.* The only apparent exception was meetings in Lent and Easter, 1938. Redpath reports that "Wittgenstein had started lecturing that week, but didn't want too many people to come, and so the lectures were not 'open lectures', but for people Wittgenstein had 'decided on' to attend if they wished." But McGuinness explains that the lectures in these terms were unpaid and were not even official university classes.[34] And then also there is the famous case of the *Blue Book,* which was dictated to a select group of students in 1933–34 from a cancelled class that had apparently grown too large. Two announcements of his classes, for Lent 1930 (the first class) and Michaelmas 1931, in the *Cambridge University Reporter* noted that times were "to be arranged to suit the convenience of students, who are requested to call upon Dr Wittgenstein" at a specified place and time before the start of the term. While this could be the mysterious "private interview," it sounds more like a mere formality to facilitate scheduling.[35]

The only requirement I am aware of that Wittgenstein placed on students attending his classes was that they attend for the whole term.[36] He did not want casual visitors. As far as visiting professors from abroad, Malcolm mentions that Morris Lazerowitz had sought permission from Wittgenstein to attend his lectures in 1947–48, and Wittgenstein wrote back to grant it (though in the end, he resigned and never gave these lectures).[37] Perhaps such permission was appropriate for nonstudents, but there is no reason to suppose that Wittgenstein granted or withheld it selectively. As Douglas Gasking (who attended lectures in 1939) and A. C. Jackson (who attended lectures in 1946–47) wrote, "Anyone was welcome who seriously wanted to learn philosophy (and not just to hear Wittgenstein)."[38]

While the classes Wittgenstein taught were not large, he did teach at least one class each term, beginning in the 1930 Lent term and ongoing through the 1936 Easter term (and then again from Easter 1938 though Michaelmas 1941; a reduced schedule for Lent 1942 through Lent 1943; and a full schedule again from Michaelmas 1944 through Easter 1947).[39] These classes tended to have over a dozen attendees (including some dons), all of them self-selected rather than selected by Wittgenstein. This is an important fact because it means that Wittgenstein was addressing people whom he had *not* chosen. It is also important that Wittgenstein's classes were primarily discussions. They were sometimes announced as "lecture & conversation class" and sometimes simply as "conversation class" or "informal discussions." Although the discussions were often actually monologues, the reality is that Wittgenstein was faced with regular feedback—in either the form of questions from students, or unanswered questions posed by Wittgenstein, or the silence of incomprehension. In any case, Wittgenstein soon learned how attendees responded, or failed to respond, to his thoughts.

This put him in a very different situation from the one he imagined in the draft foreword quoted previously. Far from writing for the "small circle" of culturally sympathetic friends scattered around Europe, he was now faced with dozens of students, term after term, who were "foreign" to him—indeed, presumably of that "typical western" mindset.

At first, Wittgenstein thought that he could continue as before—as an esotericist. At the start of the Michaelmas term of 1930, for example, when he moved into new quarters, he reflected, "Writing this only to be writing something & to talk to myself. I could say: now I am finally alone with myself & must gradually get into conversation with me."[40] But as he came to know how these others thought and how that affected the issues he wanted to address, he began to identify thought patterns that ran contrary to his own (or, at any rate, to those he preferred), and he gradually began to address them. In stark contrast to Aristotle, who would lecture only to students whose habits were already trained to respond to reason, Wittgenstein now found himself lecturing to students whose habits of thought were resistant to his ways of thinking. He would no longer proceed esoterically.[41]

This transformation is a conjecture on my part, but it constitutes a central idea of this book. I examine the transformation as it occurs in his lectures in chapter 2 and as it occurs in his manuscripts in chapter 3. What transforms is Wittgenstein's concern for his audience. Until this point, which I date to roughly the first half of 1931, Wittgenstein was relatively unconcerned with his audience; afterward he is more concerned. He becomes a sort of philosophical "spotter," concerned with the effectiveness of his philosophical barrage. Soon he begins to think about what philosophical artillery would work best.

Wittgenstein expresses to himself this new concern to be understood this way in his diary in 1931: "I don't want happening to me what happens to some wares. They are lying on the display table, the shoppers see them, the color or the sheen catches their eye & they handle the object for a moment & then let it drop back on the table as undesired."[42] Notice how different this is from what he said in his draft for a foreword only one year earlier, quoted above: "It is all one to me whether the typical western scientist understands or appreciates my work." Six weeks later, Wittgenstein offers a different comparison: "Someone who teaches philosophy nowadays gives his pupil foods, not because they are to his taste, but in order to change his tastes."[43]

In notes by students from his lectures, it is not until the Easter 1931 term that he mentions things like being "tempted" to say certain things or think certain ways or the "resignation of temperament."[44] He begins to think about what might make it difficult to accept his views. In a diary entry at the beginning of the Lent 1932 term, Wittgenstein writes: "My main movement of thought is a completely different one today from 15 to 20 years ago. And this is similar to when a painter makes a transition from one school to another."[45] While this may just allude to the difference between his so-called early and later work, I'm not sure he would have said this even a year or two earlier. It is starting in 1932 that his mentions of temptation and other kinds of noncognitive factors become increasingly common. Wittgenstein is beginning to appreciate and engage with differing attitudes—to see what will hold the interest of the "shoppers." As Gasking and Jackson put it, in reflecting on Wittgenstein's later lectures, "Plainly he was sensitive to the kind of audience he had."[46] This became true in his teaching and in his writing.

The *Philosophical Remarks*, a manuscript from 1930 to which a later version of the above-quoted foreword was attached, hardly even alludes to issues of temperament. Wittgenstein only once mentions what "we are tempted to say."[47] And there are perhaps half a dozen other such confessions of noncognitive issues in *Philosophical Remarks*. Josef Rothhaupt argues, however, that these prefatory remarks were never intended for the *Philosophical Remarks* text that they are attached to by an editor. Rather, they are more likely intended for a selection of remarks that Rothhaupt labels the "Kringel-Buch."[48] A survey of the remarks intended for the Kringel-Buch, dating from 1930, shows the same result, only more clearly—that they do not consider or address wayward temptations.[49] They do not show a concern for the audience.

But when Wittgenstein comes to write the foreword for the *Philosophical Investigations* some fifteen years later, in 1945, he is explicitly no longer writing for the select few who think the way he does. About his thoughts: "I make them public with misgivings. It is not impossible that it should fall to the lot of this work, in its poverty and in the darkness of this time, to bring light into one brain or another—but, of course, it is not likely." Wittgenstein is pessimistic about how successful he might be, but his aim now is clearly to engage ways of thinking different from his own. So it is that in part I of the *Philosophical Investigations*, Wittgenstein provides us with a running commentary (of well over a hundred points) on what produces the philosophical confusions we get into and what the problems are with appreciating his resolutions. A survey of part I of the *Investigations* shows us that philosophical problems arise or remain because of these reasons:

1. What . . . forces itself on us, holds us captive, demands an answer, must be, leads us, we can't help, or no one would say (14 times)
2. What we are . . . tempted, seduced, bewitched, or dazzled by (19 times)

3. What . . . suggests itself, strikes us, occurs to us, or impressions we are under (7 times)
4. How things look to us (2 times)
5. What we find . . . surprising, convincing, senseless, ludicrous, sensible, or matter-of-course (8 times)
6. Our . . . compulsions, needs, urges, wants, tendencies, inclinations, expectations, or prejudices (28 times)
7. What we . . . notice, can get ourselves to think, can be satisfied with, only think of, overlook, don't realize, fail to see, or forget (14 times)
8. What we would like (6 times)
9. What we . . . are committed to, choose, decide, allow, or refuse (6 times)
10. How we . . . look at, or represent things (5 times)

These noncognitive tendencies in us can apply to a great variety of issues, leading to many different philosophical problems. The sum of such tendencies could be said to constitute a temperament—a spirit of the times. Wittgenstein is now spotting these characteristics and addressing them.

I conjecture that it was Wittgenstein's teaching in the 1930s that brought him to face and engage these differences and led him to try to address them. The *Blue Book*, which Wittgenstein dictated to selected students in 1933–34, already includes discussion of what we are tempted by (14 times); what we crave, incline to, tend toward, or are fascinated or preoccupied by (10 times); what we are dissatisfied with or contemptuous of (3 times); and what will break the spell. This shows a concern for how to address those who think differently. Elizabeth Anscombe recalls Wittgenstein's response in lectures in the fall of 1944—"Let me think what medicine you need"—and reports that "the 'medicine' was effective, and the story illustrates Wittgenstein's ability to understand the thought that was offered to him."[50] He would no longer approach things esoterically. Instead he was trying to figure out how to bring about the changes needed to appreciate a different way of viewing philosophical issues.[51] He had become an evangelist.[52]

Of course, *evangelism* has religious connotations, which I do not mean to invoke here. But the term still seems to me to be appropriate, because what Wittgenstein intended to bring about was not simply a change in beliefs. He saw the changes needed to go more deeply. In the opening lines of his "Philosophy" chapter in the so-called Big Typescript that he compiled in 1933, he wrote:

> The difficulty of philosophy [is] not the intellectual difficulty of the sciences, but the difficulty of a change of attitude. Resistances of the will must be overcome. As I have often said, philosophy does not lead me to any renunciation, since I do not abstain from saying something, but rather abandon a certain combination of words as senseless. In another sense, however, philosophy requires a resignation, but one of feeling and not of intellect. And maybe that is what makes it so difficult for many.[53]

What he has "often said" can't refer to anything other than his lectures, and the "many" for whom this is "so difficult" can only be his students. In a student's notes of Wittgenstein's lectures in Easter term 1931, we find the line, "Doing philosophy may perhaps mean resignation of temperament, but never of intellect."[54] His work, then, in the *Philosophical Investigations*, is to see how he might bring this resignation about. Since he articulated this goal in the 1930 draft as pertaining to the sort of "spirit" one has, it seems appropriate to use a term like *evangelism* after all.

How Wittgenstein went about his evangelizing is a question I address later in this book. I have emphasized that he was concerned with the noncognitive aspects of temptation and other attitudes toward the views in question.[55] I believe that this was motivated largely by his encounter with students. In the text of the *Philosophical Investigations* and the drafts leading up to it, Wittgenstein often expressed these temptations and other wayward tendencies in quotation marks or between dashes. Stanley Cavell has written, "The voice of temptation and the voice of correctness are the antagonists in Wittgenstein's dialogues."[56] And further research by David Stern has led him to identify a "commentator"—a third "ironic" voice—in addition to the voices variously identified as "narratorial," and "interlocutory."[57] There is no uniformity to how Wittgenstein expresses these voices, sometimes invoking "you," sometimes "I," sometimes "us." Jane Heal writes, "Sometimes it is part of a dialogue, in that it is directed at the interlocutor, while at other times it represents simply the flow of Wittgenstein's own ideas. . . . Some stretches can be read either way." But it is natural, once one has thought of the possibility, to read the conversation as one imitating a classroom discussion. Even if the voice of temptation had once lived in Wittgenstein's own head, Heal argues, he often "represents himself . . . as no longer impelled to say those things but rather as recognising sympathetically the impulse which another is there represented as experiencing."[58] Thus, the dialogical character of the *Investigations* seems plausibly derived from the classroom setting and aimed at diagnosing and treating the temptations of the wide variety of those present in that setting.[59]

How we conceive of the dialogical character of the *Investigations* could well depend on what sort of picture *of Wittgenstein* has "held *us* captive." If one is captivated by a picture of Wittgenstein alone at his desk, pen in hand, agonizing over a subject, then it is natural to think of the voices largely as expressions from within himself. But if one thinks instead of Wittgenstein in front of a classroom of students, chalk or poker in hand, then it may seem natural to think of the voices as arising from the discussions with students. Heal concludes that Wittgenstein "presents himself, pretty much throughout the *Investigations*, as having, to some extent at least, succeeded in escaping from the false pictures . . . and from which he hopes also to release his reader," and, I would say, his students. Isn't this how we sometimes think of ourselves in our role as teacher?

One of Wittgenstein's students from 1938, James Taylor, went on to graduate school in philosophy at the University of California at Berkeley. They corresponded, and in one of his letters back to Wittgenstein reporting on the department, he wrote (WC, 394; September 24, 1938): "I haven't done any missionary work yet." This would seem to imply that there was a common sense that something could now be accomplished, though surely the term *missionary* was a jest, whether it originated from Wittgenstein or from Taylor. But the term *missionary* does clearly convey a sense of being among those who are quite different in important ways—and wanting to do something about it. It evokes the image of an evangelist.

When Taylor mentioned the missionary work, he confessed, "Am quite aware I'm not good enough to."[60] What did Wittgenstein think that he could accomplish as the missionary preaching against the idols? Discussing in 1946 an upcoming Joint Session of the Mind Association and the Aristotelian Society meeting, Karl Britten described how Wittgenstein "railed against professional philosophers, mourned the present state of philosophy in England and asked: 'What can one man do alone?'"[61] By now it seems that Wittgenstein—the voice crying in the wilderness—finally felt that he had failed. This sense of failure is already evident in the 1945 preface quoted above and even in a 1938 draft preface: "I don't dare to hope that it should fall to the lot of this inadequate work to throw light into this or that brain, in our dark age."[62] But he is, according to these prefaces, trying to evangelize.

During the break before Easter term 1947, what would turn out to be his last term teaching, Wittgenstein reflected on the difficulty of trying to change people's philosophical views by writing or arguing (April 13–14, 1947): "It is as though I wanted to change men's and women's fashions by talking." Perhaps recalling his 1931 strategy to deal with common philosophical problems by erecting "signposts . . . to help people past the danger points," he now reflects, "My warnings are like the posters at the ticket offices at English railway stations 'Is your journey really necessary?' As if anyone reading that would say to himself 'On second thoughts, *no*.'"

> The philosopher says "Look at things *like this*!"—but first, that is not to say that people will look at things like this, second, he may be altogether too late with his admonition, & it's possible too that such an admonition can achieve absolutely nothing & that the impulse towards such a change in the way things are perceived must come from another direction. . . .

The diagnosis he proposes sounds positively political: "It is not by any means clear to me that I wish for a continuation of my work by others, more than a change in the way we live, making all these questions superfluous."[63]

Wittgenstein finally quit teaching in 1947. He explained his resignation to his friend Oets Bouwsma as necessary to finish his book, but also as a result of pessimism about his role as a teacher.[64] He told Drury in 1949, "My thinking is not wanted in this present age, I have to swim so strongly against the tide. Perhaps in a hundred years people will really want what I am writing."[65] And in a draft of yet another prefatory comment (January 8, 1948), he wrote, "With repugnance I hand over the book to the public. The hands in which it will fall are mostly not the ones in which I like to imagine it. May it, I wish, soon become entirely forgotten by the philosophical journalists, and thus perhaps remain preserved for a better kind of reader."[66] Here we find him jettisoning his evangelism and apparently returning to esotericism; his audience is not "the public" or even the "philosophical journalists" but "a better kind of reader" who presumably understands what he is up to. His audience for now is really just himself: "Almost the whole time I am writing conversations with myself. Things I say to myself tête-à-tête."[67] At most he now awaits "a change in the way we live, making all these questions superfluous."

When Frank Ramsey met with Wittgenstein in 1923, after the publication of the *Tractatus*, to discuss the book with him, he discovered this same sort of orientation to the future—esoteric but without an existing inner circle. Ramsey wrote to his mother (September 20, 1923), "His idea of his book is not that by reading it anyone will understand his ideas, but that some day someone will think them out again for himself, and will derive great pleasure from finding in this book their exact expressions."[68]

My conjecture is that the writing he did once he lost faith in and gave up his teaching may sometimes show a move away from addressing the non-cognitive aspects of temperament as they bear on philosophical puzzles.[69] But this is an issue for another occasion.

At the start of this chapter, I posed the question, "Whom was Wittgenstein addressing in his writings?" My answer to the question led me to contrast an esoteric and an evangelistic attitude to this issue. If we ask whether Wittgenstein is an esotericist or an evangelist, my answer is, "Both—first one, then the other, and then perhaps the first again." If I am right about the transitions I have outlined, then this would provide a basis for another way of talking about stages in Wittgenstein's philosophy. Initially scholars distinguished between an early and a late Wittgenstein, based primarily on the differences of method and of substance in the *Tractatus* and then the *Investigations*. That approach has been criticized from two directions, some adding a third, "middle," Wittgenstein (and even a fourth, post-*Investigations*, Wittgenstein), others wanting to reestablish a unity all along. The grounds for making or denying stages have been somewhat unclear and, indeed, variable.

My suggestion is not wholly separate from these, but asks us to focus on whom Wittgenstein takes himself to be addressing and how, and what he is trying to accomplish. From this point of view, the *Tractatus* and the work of the early 1930s is esoteric, the work from mid-1931 or so becomes evangelical until he loses confidence in his approach around the time he quit teaching in 1947, and then again perhaps becomes esoteric. These stages do not involve sharp dividing lines and do not fit with previous maps of the stages, but they do focus attention on issues of importance to us and to Wittgenstein. In particular, they draw on Wittgenstein's own ways of characterizing what he was doing. Finally, they offer an agenda for looking at Wittgenstein's work in ways that have not so far received much attention. In that respect, I hope that this may be a fruitful idea for future work.

One implication of my stages is that most of what is familiar to us in Wittgenstein's later philosophy, especially part I of the *Philosophical Investigations*, falls into the evangelical stage. While this is a new term of description, it helps to focus our attention on what Wittgenstein was trying to do and how he was trying to do it. I think it is important to see that he took evangelism seriously, even while he did not see how to succeed and eventually admitted failure. It is important because proponents of Wittgenstein's views too often proceed as though his views and arguments should take hold just as a result of being presented, and resistance can be addressed by louder or clearer restatement of the views.[70]

I would label this approach the rationalistic fallacy. It mistakenly supposes that what Wittgenstein is primarily trying to accomplish is to establish belief in a conclusion through a reasoned argument. It ignores Wittgenstein's repeated insistence: "I don't try to make you *believe* something you *don't* believe, but to make you *do* something you won't do."[71] Like G. E. Moore's so-called naturalistic fallacy, it is not really a fallacy in reasoning but a mistaken belief. Nevertheless, it emphasizes the mistake even while it mischaracterizes it. Defenders of Wittgenstein, and even interpreters, look for arguments for positions. But that is not exactly how Wittgenstein saw it.

Wittgenstein writes (April 13–14, 1947), "Quite different artillery is needed here from anything I am in a position to muster. Most likely I could still achieve an effect in that, above all, a *whole lot* of garbage is written in response to my stimulus & that *perhaps* this provides the stimulus for something good. I ought always to hope only for the most indirect of influences."[72] Of course, then we would want to ask *who* is writing the "garbage." Perhaps that was all the Wittgensteinian publications! And then, what is the "something good" that may come from it? New polemical arguments? No—more likely something else. He calls it an "indirect" influence. But what is that? We come back to this in chapter 5.

2 Wittgenstein and His Students

Wittgenstein's return to Cambridge in January 1929 was announced by John Maynard Keynes: "God has arrived. I met him on the 5.15 train."[1] His return was motivated by the feeling that he had more to say about philosophy, including the topics of the *Tractatus*. He began meeting with Frank Ramsey on a regular basis for conversation, and in his notebooks, he began reworking and eventually rethinking his views on a number of topics. If he was to continue his research at Trinity College, he would need a PhD. The *Tractatus* was deemed suitable as a dissertation, but he would have to be examined on it. An examination was scheduled in June with Bertrand Russell and Moore designated as the examiners. Russell had this to say about the examination: "The Viva on the *Tractatus* ended amicably with Wittgenstein putting an arm on each of the examiners' shoulders and saying 'Don't worry, I know you'll *never* understand it.'"[2] In any case, he passed.

That same summer, William Empson invited Wittgenstein to speak to a student group, the Cambridge undergraduate Heretics Society.[3] On November 17, 1929, he delivered a talk entitled "Ethics."[4] A student described the setting that evening: "The Heretics were an enormous crowd meeting in the Conservative Clubs with a terracotta bust of Disraeli on the mantelpiece."[5] That Wittgenstein did not have high hopes for this occasion is indicated by the letter he sent to his Austrian friend Rudolf Koder (November 1929): "I myself shall give a lecture this Sunday and it weighs on me because I am sure that almost no one will understand me [*mich so gut wie niemand verstehen wird*] & yet I promised to give it. I feel pretty bad."[6] In the lecture Wittgenstein discusses ethics and value in ways that are compatible with the viewpoint of the *Tractatus*, except for the fact that he is, after all, *talking* about them.[7]

The lecture ends with Wittgenstein waxing eloquent: "My whole tendency and, I believe, the tendency of all men who ever tried to write or talk Ethics or Religion was to run against the boundaries of language. This running against the walls of our cage is perfectly, absolutely hopeless. Ethics so far as it springs from the desire to say something about the ultimate meaning of life, the absolute good, the absolute valuable, can be no science. What it says does not add to our knowledge in any sense. But it is a document of a tendency in the human mind which I personally cannot help respecting deeply and I would not for my life ridicule it."[8]

Apart from some information about the society itself and several of the previous speakers, nothing further has been known about this occasion. But Max Black was one of the students in attendance, and he recalled the event in an interview in 1987:

> It was done under the auspices of the Heretic Society, and at that time there was a lot of interest among Cambridge philosophers in verifiability . . . and there was a little local slogan or jargon—"What would it be like if it were not?" So that if something came up and it was thought to be violating the principle of verifiability, a flippant question would be "What would it be like if it were not?" . . . Well Wittgenstein gave a talk about the Tractatus. . . . It was a large audience . . . and then there was a question period and somebody in the audience, an undergraduate, stood up and said "Dr. Wittgenstein, in the Tractatus you say that the world is everything that is the case. What would it be like if it were not?" Laughter from the audience. Wittgenstein was absolutely furious. He was striding off the stage, and he had to be forcibly held back and be persuaded that the man in question would apologize and there was no malice behind it.
>
> Rosenbaum: What was the lecture like?
>
> Black: I can't recall it. But I do know that he was in many ways a very difficult person.[9]

Here, I believe, we have Wittgenstein's first formal encounter with undergraduates. Obviously there were no "good old days" when undergraduates were properly respectful. The disrespect in this case is especially noteworthy after Wittgenstein had just concluded the lecture by insisting on his own respect for the attempt to talk about ethics.[10]

Despite the absurdity of the situation Black describes, there is some sense to it as well. Though the undergraduate questioner perhaps did not intend it, the question does pose a fair challenge to Wittgenstein. According to the *Tractatus*, propositions lack sense if they are not descriptive of the world. Verificationists suppose that it would make a difference in the world if a descriptive proposition were made false. The question implies that the propositions of the *Tractatus* are not descriptive, and hence lack sense. This question presses the issue of proposition 6.54, of how the *Tractatus* can survive its very own standards. The student question pursues a legitimate issue; Wittgenstein reacts with anger. This will not be unique.

A month before his lecture to the Heretics, on October 16, 1929, the Faculty Board of Moral Science at Cambridge had resolved that Dr. Wittgenstein should be invited to give a course of lectures to be included in the lecture list for the 1930 Lent term.[11] Wittgenstein was asked under what title his course should be announced and, after a long silence, he replied: "The subject of the lectures would be philosophy. What else can be the title of the lectures but Philosophy?"[12] And so they were. Wittgenstein continued lecturing at Cambridge on a fairly regular basis, except for various leaves of absence, through the 1947 Easter term.

In chapter 1, I proposed that Wittgenstein's interactions with students at his lectures were relevant to important changes in his approach to writing philosophy. For instance, I think that the presence of the so-called interlocutor (or interlocutors) in the *Philosophical Investigations* owes something to the ways in which Wittgenstein came to see the need to address and influence contrary points of view. This is something that he resolutely did not do in the *Tractatus*. But once he began to teach, it was an issue he encountered on a regular basis. Along with this change, he also began to think about what makes it difficult to change our philosophical views, which he attributed to temptations, inclinations, and other noncognitive factors.

The idea that Wittgenstein's students influenced him and his writing style might seem implausible. Wittgenstein's forceful personality, certainly on display in Black's anecdote, may seem impervious to such influence. And Wittgenstein's students have sometimes had a reputation as a small group of select disciples who simply and unquestioningly accepted what the charismatic Wittgenstein propounded. Based *not* on attending lectures but on a modest acquaintance with Wittgenstein, the literary critic F. R. Leavis judged:

> Wittgenstein's discussions were discussions carried on *by* Wittgenstein. I say this with confidence, though I was never present when he was observed to be in action in professional company—in the company of philosophers and philosophy students. . . . I don't question that now and then some especially gifted, well-equipped and determined person did succeed in breaking into the battle and

> maintaining for a while something in the nature of an exchange. But what one has seen written and heard said a good many times seems to me well-founded: that the wonder and the profit for the lecture-audience lay in the opportunity to witness the sustained spontaneous effort of intellectual genius wrestling with its self-proposed problems.[13]

Leavis thought Wittgenstein was a bad influence on students because of his mesmerizing effect. But apart from his own judgment, he also claims to be representing an opinion expressed "a good many times."[14] J. N. Findlay, who first met Wittgenstein briefly in February 1930, described his effect this way:

> I . . . found him . . . of a quite unbelievable personal beauty, such as might be attributed to the Apollo one visits at Olympia, or to the Norse Sun-god Baldur. . . . As the extreme beauty of Wittgenstein is not often spoken of, it seemed fit to mention it here: certainly it contributed, even if unconsciously, to his immense influence at Cambridge.[15]

So it would seem natural to turn to the Cambridge lectures, which Wittgenstein began offering in the 1930 Lent term. Lectures were held once a week—Mondays at 5:00 p.m.—lasting for about an hour, in an ordinary lecture room in the University Arts School. The first class meeting was on January 20—the day, as it happened, after Frank Ramsey's death. Discussion class, lasting at least two hours, was Thursdays at 5:00 p.m. Wittgenstein always had a blackboard at both lectures and discussions and made plenty of use of it.[16] Classes in later terms followed a similar pattern.

The first meeting of the class was described by a student, Arthur MacIver:

> Wittgenstein had already begun to lecture when I got to the room in the Arts School, but I took no notes to-day and found it rather distressing to listen, for the poor man was terribly nervous and I thought at first that he would not spin out the hour; how he will conduct a discussion I cannot imagine, for the audience fills the room but consists, I should think, very largely of the curious, who will have nothing to say for themselves.[17]

Within two weeks, however, Wittgenstein had gotten his bearings. MacIver continues: "I thought him very much better than he has been in the past—very much more sure of himself and of the thread of his argument—and I was able to take quite a lot of notes" (235).

To see what Wittgenstein's interactions with students were like, we must consult the notes that various students and auditors managed to take of those lectures. From the early 1930s, we have G. E. Moore's summary and report of the lectures from 1930 to 1933, which he published in the mid-1950s; we have published notes from John King and Desmond Lee of lectures from 1930 to 1932; and from Alice Ambrose of lectures from 1932 to1935.[18] More recently, we have the original and very full notes from Moore, from which he had extracted his summaries.[19]

When we read the lecture notes previously available, however, one thing that stands out is that there is almost no interaction with students recorded. The one exception to this is in Moore's summary of the lectures where he reports, "[Wittgenstein] said that the student who had asked him whether he meant that the meaning of a word *was* a list of rules would not have been tempted to ask that question but for the false idea (which he took to be a common one) that in the case of a substantive like 'the meaning' you have to look for something at which you can point and say 'This is the meaning.'"[20] In Moore's full notes, this occurs on April 28, 1933: "If I say meaning of a word is *determined* by its grammar—by rules, I've been asked do I mean that the meaning is a list of rules. Of course, not. You wouldn't be so tempted to ask the question whether I do, unless you supposed that when you have a substantive 'the meaning' you have to look out for something at which you can point & say 'this' is the meaning."[21] While the previous class meeting (April 24) does include a discussion of meaning as use, there is no specific question of this sort noted. (Of course, the question could have been asked outside class.)

While this is an isolated example, it is an important one. The following November, when Wittgenstein set out to record the current state of his ideas, he dictated them to a small group of students, the result of which came to be called the "Blue Book." The opening paragraphs of this dictation address this very topic about meaning, including this parenthetical remark: "(We are up against one of the great sources of philosophical bewilderment: a substantive makes us look for a thing that corresponds to it.)" (BB, 1). Where better for Wittgenstein to have learned about philosophical bewilderment than from his students? In this case, it was a student from the previous term.

I scrutinized Moore's full notes with the expectation that here we would find the interactions with students that I imagined. But to my surprise, very little interaction with students is recorded in these notes. While students are occasionally mentioned, usually in examples of one sort or another, interventions by students are hardly noted until the 1933 Lent and Easter terms.[22] Perhaps Leavis was right.

There are various possible explanations for this. Wittgenstein's teaching was initially arranged to be an hour lecture on Mondays and a longer discussion later in the week. Moore decided to take notes only during the lectures and not during the discussions, so Moore did not note the occasions specifically intended for student participation. When Wittgenstein cancelled the lectures and held only discussions during the Michaelmas term of 1931 and the Lent term of 1932, Moore took no notes at all. And in the Easter term of 1932 and then all the terms of the following academic year, 1932–33, Wittgenstein no longer distinguished between lecture and discussion, and Moore took notes of all the class meetings.[23]

One might then suppose that during Wittgenstein's lectures, for which Moore *was* taking notes, there would be no student interventions, these being reserved for the discussion meeting later in the week. But this was not in fact true. Arthur MacIver was a visiting student at Cambridge who attended only the first term of lectures that Wittgenstein gave, in Lent 1930. He did not take extensive class notes, but he recorded in his diary comments about the classes he attended. They give a livelier sense of what happened in class than do Moore's notes.[24] Regarding the lecture on February 17, 1930, MacIver records:

> Wittgenstein was speaking to-day of the illegitimacy of calling anything a "thing" or a "number" or speaking of the number of things or numbers[.] I was pleased to see him in conflict with the mathematicians over transfinite numbers, but for the rest all this argument from a symbolic logic which I cannot accept leaves me cold.[25]

This is not much to go on, but it happens that the mathematicians mentioned who raised this question about transfinite numbers included Max Black. In the 1987 interview Black recounts the following:

> In the class, he could become very angry if one did the wrong thing. And on one occasion I thought he was really going to blow me up because he was talking about numbers, and as it quite often happened, there was a long pause when he was just thinking of something or other, nothing happened, and then he started again. I asked him, very wrongly as it turned out, whether what he was saying about integers would apply to transfinite numbers as well. And he got very angry.
>
> Rosenbaum: Why?
>
> Black: Because he wasn't interested in transfinite numbers, and I was just sort of pursuing a red herring. With idiots to work with, what can you expect? I believe it's just a rage, and I thought this was it and I was going to be thrown out, but he didn't.

> Rosenbaum: Did he throw people out of class?
>
> Black: Oh, yes. He would expel them, if they were really stupid.
>
> . . .
>
> He didn't throw me out, and on some other occasion, he did talk about transfinite numbers. It wasn't that my idea was all that stupid; it's just that he wasn't thinking about it. He could get very angry. So I had the great distinction of being one of the very few people that he ever got angry with. Well, publicly angry with, at any rate. He did do some strange things.[26]

Clearly this is the occasion that MacIver has described in his diary. In MacIver's description of the discussion class at the end of that week (February 20), he reports: "The discussion looked at the beginning as if it was going to be run entirely by the mathematicians, Braithwaite and Du Val and Guest and Black talking a lot about prime numbers and various people's theorems."[27] So there was a group of students who had a mathematical background, who took issue with Wittgenstein, and not only in discussion classes.[28] In a diary entry a year and a half later, Wittgenstein wrote: "The best prepared these days for the study of philosophy are students of physics ~~(Not of mathematics)~~ Due to the evident lack of clarity in their science their understanding is more loose than that of the mathematicians who are stuck in their self-assured tradition."[29] This "self-assured tradition" may be just what gave them the courage (or stubbornness) to take issue with Wittgenstein. While Leavis and others may have been right about Wittgenstein's "numbing effect" on some students, it clearly was not true of all of them—particularly the mathematicians.

When we turn to G. E. Moore's full notes for the lecture class on February 17, 1930, we find only this relevant remark: "There can be no definition which applies to both transfinite and finite cardinals."[30] While that does capture the point that Wittgenstein makes in response to Black's query, it leaves out a lot: the extended silence that preceded the claim, the fact that the issue was raised by a student's question, any sense of conflict in the class, and Wittgenstein's angry reaction to Black and his question.[31]

This issue turns out to be an important one for Wittgenstein. The possibility that "[what] he was saying about integers would apply to transfinite numbers as well" is the core of the view that infinite sets are just like finite sets, only (much) larger. This view has a very natural attraction to it, which Black expressed, and apparently others in the class supported. While we do not know the details of the discussion on February 20, we can imagine that the distribution of prime numbers might constitute a case in point.

The "various people's theorems" were doubtless the prime number theorems about the distribution of primes developed by Jacques Hadamard and Charles de la Vallée-Poussin, based on work of Bernhard Riemann.

The easiest example of this issue to imagine is based on the question of whether there is a series of four consecutive 7's in the decimal expansion of π—an example Wittgenstein used (with slight variations) many times over the years. The ratio of the circumference to the diameter of a circle is represented by π: 3.1415926. . . . It turns out that this ratio is an irrational number that cannot be captured in a finite number of decimal digits—thus, the ellipsis at the end. If you continue the expansion of the decimal to 25 places, you will find two consecutive 3's. With modern computing power, it has been possible to expand the decimals to many trillions of places. While the discovery of four consecutive 7's would resolve the question in the affirmative, what, if anything, could resolve the question in the negative—that there are not four consecutive 7's? If the question were asked about a rational number with a finite expansion, then an answer, positive or negative, would simply depend on inspection of the expansion.[32] But the deeper issue is not, What would *resolve* the question in the negative? but What, if any, state of affairs could make it the case that there were *not* four consecutive 7's? It is natural to imagine that "there is" a determinate "full" expansion of π that could theoretically be inspected, by God if not by us. And that is what might lead one to suppose that what applies to the finite case might apply to the infinite case as well. Bertrand Russell endorsed this way of looking at things when he supposed that our limitations, compared to God, made it merely "medically impossible" for us to inspect the infinite decimal expansion.[33]

By the time of the *Philosophical Investigations*, this natural thought has been turned into a "curious argument" voiced by the interlocutor (§352): "'In the infinite expansion of π either the group "7777" occurs, or it does not—there is no third possibility.' That is to say: God sees it—but we don't. But what does that mean?—We use a picture: the picture of a visible series, the whole of which one person [God] can survey and another can't." This thought is embodied in a picture. The picture is subjected to an extended discussion in the (notebooks that were compiled as) *Remarks on the Foundations of Mathematics*, where it is called "a false picture," a "misleading *picture*," and a "squint-eyed way of putting things."[34] All of these characterizations show the temptation to misunderstand the nature of infinity as Wittgenstein saw it.[35]

Wittgenstein's angry reaction to Black seems significant. Black supposes Wittgenstein's anger was provoked because "he wasn't interested in transfinite numbers" and "he wasn't thinking about it." But that doesn't seem to account for Wittgenstein becoming "very angry" (which Black says three times) and calling Black an "idiot" (or for throwing people out of class). More plausible, to my mind, is that Wittgenstein is confronted by a different way of thinking that he is not prepared to address. In fact, after Wittgenstein's initial lecture on January 20, he wrote to himself (in code): "Held my first regular lecture today: so, so. I think that it will go better next time.—if nothing unforeseen [*unvorhergesehenes*] comes up."[36] It seems that Wittgenstein feared the unforeseen right from the start—and that is exactly what came up four weeks later, on February 17. Wittgenstein reacted with anger.

This marks, I believe, the *beginning* of a transition from writing for himself to concerning himself with how his views are received—by his class, in this case, and ultimately by his readers. In chapter 1, I characterized this as a transition from esotericism to evangelism. Teaching students at Cambridge introduced the challenge of transcending esotericism with its attendant reaction of angrily dismissing other perspectives.

Maurice Cornforth, one of the students in 1930, also contradicted the idea, in a memoir for another student, David Guest, that Wittgenstein's students in 1930 were simply passive listeners:

> A circle of young students quickly gathered around [Wittgenstein], and both David and I belonged to that circle. We used to sit at Wittgenstein's feet, drinking in his new ideas, and at the same time we argued furiously, both with him, and with one another. This went on for a whole year.[37]

My point is not that Wittgenstein's students changed his mind about issues, but that they at least sometimes, in important ways, shared *their* mind with Wittgenstein and that this became important in his process of how to address issues.

In the first two events I have related, from 1929 and 1930, in which a student raised an unforeseen question, Wittgenstein reacted in anger. But as the later 1933 example about the "list of rules" of meaning shows, Wittgenstein eventually took these questions as expressions of a frame of mind or a perspective that differed from his, and they deserved a response.[38] I imagine that he gained a sense of equanimity about contrary ways of thinking about issues as he came to label them as "pictures" and "temptations" and began to address them as such in his writings.

In 1933, when Wittgenstein was writing his first extended reflections on the nature of philosophy, in his chapter, "Philosophy," in the so-called *Big Typescript*, he opened as follows:

> Difficulty of philosophy not the intellectual difficulty of the sciences, but the difficulty of a change of attitude. Resistances of the will must be overcome.
>
> As I have often said, philosophy does not lead me to any renunciation, since I do not abstain from saying something, but rather abandon a certain combination of words as senseless. In another sense, however, philosophy requires a resignation, but one of feeling and not of intellect. And maybe this is what makes it so difficult for many. It can be difficult not to use an expression, just as it is difficult to hold back tears, or an outburst of anger//rage//.[39]

While Wittgenstein does not indicate when he has "often said" these things or for whom it is "so difficult," it seems likely that he is referring to his classes and his students. Indeed, R. D. Townsend's notes for Easter term, 1931, include the following: "Doing philosophy may perhaps mean resignation of temperament but never of intellect."[40] It soon becomes part of Wittgenstein's philosophical method to address rather than anathemize such views. Black's conflation of finite and infinite becomes for Wittgenstein a picture that tempts us and that we must give up. He will eventually try to help us do that.

I have here described one student intervention and followed out its effects through Wittgenstein's writing and lecturing, but it was not unique. MacIver's diary for the very next lecture meeting (February 24, 1930) records: "Wittgenstein was very confused in this lecture to-day, just as he was on Friday night, and things were made worse when he came again onto the octahedron of colours and people began to interrupt from the body of the room—first a strange man who sat in the front row and then Guest and Du Val."[41] When we turn to Moore's full notes for this lecture, we do find a discussion of the octahedron of colors, but no mention of questions, interruptions, or confusion.[42] So in certain ways that are important, especially interactions with students, we cannot take Moore's notes as a complete guide to the lectures under examination.

That Wittgenstein did not want a complete record of what happened in lectures is indicated by the following incident, reported by Theodore Redpath, from 1935:

> [There was a student who] knew shorthand, and he asked Wittgenstein if he might take down in shorthand what was said and, after Wittgenstein had vetted

> it, have it circulated to whomever Wittgenstein thought fit. Apparently Wittgenstein agreed to this, and [the student] came a couple of times or so and took the proceedings down in shorthand and then typed them out. Unfortunately, I gather, he badly misjudged Wittgenstein's reaction to the typescript. Apparently he thought that Wittgenstein was so honest that he would want everything he said to appear in the draft submitted to him, and so the typescript included a good sprinkling of the oaths of which Wittgenstein characteristically delivered himself when he lost the thread of his thought or felt baffled and unable to proceed. [The student] never appeared again, and I heard that Wittgenstein had been wild with anger and submitted the delinquent to a far from gentle dressing down.[43]

In this case, the issue concerned Wittgenstein's language, but we can imagine the same would be true of his anger and his extended silences.

I do not mean to fault Moore (or other note takers) for not recording outbursts or student interactions.[44] Moore was concerned to record Wittgenstein's thoughts; he did not set out to give a full account of the lecture experience. Nevertheless, we have independent evidence that such student interactions did occur and had an impact. If I am right, these student interactions led Wittgenstein toward a style of writing that culminated in the *Philosophical Investigations*.

In Moore's full notes for the academic year 1932–33, there are well over 120 instances where Wittgenstein is reported to preface comments with endless variations of "it will be said," "suppose one wanted to ask," "people will say," "you may answer," "suppose somebody says," and so on. All of these prefixes couch the discussion in the subjunctive mood.[45] That is, they present ideas for consideration rather than as assertions. They create a hypothetical conversation—a sort of dialogue.

Whether these phrases report things that have arisen from class discussion or not is impossible to tell, though we now know they do at least sometimes. A comparison with the *Philosophical Investigations* is instructive. In addition to the numerous well-known places where the interlocutor speaks in quotation marks or within dashes, there are also many dozens of places where Wittgenstein uses these same phrases: "one might ask," "you may say," "someone says to me," "one might object here," "suppose it were asked." So by 1933 Wittgenstein had begun to think in his lectures in the dialogical fashion later exhibited in the *Philosophical Investigations*.

It is also instructive to compare notes of Wittgenstein's lectures from the early 1930s with those from later courses.[46] Student questions or comments are noted much more often in Wittgenstein's lectures on the foundations of mathematics in the 1939 Lent and Easter terms.[47] In the course of those thirty-one lectures, eleven students are mentioned by name as engaging in discussion with Wittgenstein on over one hundred occasions.[48] While there was no apparent discussion during the first lecture, Casimir Lewy made a comment during the second lecture, and then this opened the floodgates.

By far the most vocal participant in 1939 was Alan Turing, the famous logician and mathematician, who joined in the discussion in the second lecture and offered over a third of the comments all told. When he ceased attending, after the twenty-seventh lecture, there appears to be no more discussion. This continues the tradition of the mathematicians being the most provocative participants in discussion.

One of the students, and note takers, in 1939 was Norman Malcolm. In his memoir of Wittgenstein, he characterized those class meetings as follows:

> It is hardly correct to speak of these meetings as "lectures," although this is what Wittgenstein called them. For one thing, he was carrying on original research in these meetings. He was thinking about certain problems in a way that he could have done had he been alone. For another thing, the meetings were largely conversational. Wittgenstein commonly directed questions at various people present and reacted to their replies. Often the meetings consisted mainly of dialogues.[49]

Malcolm's reflection puzzles me. The fact that the meetings were "conversational" and mainly "dialogues" seems to undermine Malcolm's claim that "[Wittgenstein] was thinking about problems in a way that he could have done had he been alone."

In fact, Turing's interventions occasionally surprise Wittgenstein and to a certain extent steer the discussion.[50] The issue of whether a contradiction might lead to a "bridge falling down" is a case in point. Wittgenstein decides to devote the next class to this question, and at another point he decides to hold off on discussing an issue because Turing is not present.[51] Wittgenstein attends not only to what others think, but why they do so, and what it would take to address their concerns. He is being an evangelist.

While some interpreters, such as Malcolm, might wish to downplay the role of student interaction in Wittgenstein's thinking, it becomes only more apparent in later years.

3 Wittgenstein at Work

Two weeks after Wittgenstein returned to do philosophical work at Cambridge, he got down to business. He began keeping a hardbound 8-by-10-inch notebook, gray covers with a burgundy spine, of his personal (for a short time) and his philosophical thoughts, much as he had at the start of the First World War. On February 2, 1929, he records personal reflections: "Back in Cambridge. Very strange. Sometimes it seems to me that time has gone in reverse," as well as philosophical ones: "Is a space conceivable that contains only all rational but no irrational points?"[1] He kept filling these pages, and additional similar notebooks, over the next year. A year later, during Easter break between Lent and Easter terms in 1930, Wittgenstein wrote to Moore:

> I am in Vienna now, doing the most loathsome work of dictating a synopsis from my manuscripts. It is a terrible bit of work and I feel wretched doing it. . . . My plan is to go and see [Russell] in Cornwall on the 22nd or 23rd of April and to give him the synopsis and a few explanations.[2]

The resulting typescript was shared with Russell and then with the mathematician J. E. Littlewood, who had both been asked by Moore to offer reports on Wittgenstein's work. Later in the year Wittgenstein cut up portions of the typescript, reorganized and pasted them into a minute book, and eventually gave that to Moore as a keepsake.[3]

This process set the pattern for how Wittgenstein proceeded for the next dozen years or more—hand-written manuscript notebooks, condensed into dictated typescripts, and reformulated through cut-and-pasted revisions. In his will, Wittgenstein designated three of his student friends to edit and publish his work as they saw fit, but as André Maury has reminded us, "Wittgenstein's main editor was himself."[4]

What Wittgenstein would write about in his manuscript notebooks varied quite a lot. He was interested in addressing the problems of the *Tractatus* in new ways, and he had conversations with members of the Vienna Circle, Ramsey, Piero Sraffa, and Moore in which he developed new philosophical ideas. Wittgenstein was an avid reader, though not generally a reader of philosophy. He read widely and, when he liked an author, deeply. He sometimes took authors as springboards for his own philosophical reflections: Augustine's *Confessions* for the opening of the *Investigations*, and William James's *The Principles of Psychology* and Wolfgang Köhler's *Gestalt Psychology* for his lectures in the 1940s, for example.[5]

Wittgenstein especially enjoyed reading passages from books aloud with friends. This was a way to pass the time in prisoner-of-war camp after World War I, where they read aloud selections from Augustine, the Bible, Tolstoy's *Gospel in Brief*, Dostoevsky's *House of the Dead* and *Crime and Punishment*, *Tristram Shandy*, Weininger's *Sex and Character* and *On the Last Things*, and numerous Austrian authors.[6] He continued this practice when he taught elementary school in rural Austria, reading *Brothers Karamazov* aloud to the village priest.[7] And once back in Cambridge, he read Prescott's *History of the Conquest of Mexico* with Drury and Skinner and, most famously, Sir James Frazer's *The Golden Bough: A Study in Magic and Religion*.

Frazer's book is a wide-ranging comparative study of magic and religion from a modern perspective. Drury recounts the experience from 1931:

> Wittgenstein told me he had long wanted to read Frazer's *The Golden Bough* and asked me to get hold of a copy out of the Union Library and read it out loud to him. I got the first volume of the full edition and we continued to read from it for some weeks. He would stop me from time to time and make comments on Frazer's remarks. He was particularly emphatic that it was wrong to think, as Frazer seemed to do, that the primitive rituals were in the nature of scientific errors.[8]

Not only did Wittgenstein make comments to Drury, but he began to write about Frazer, putting his remarks in the dark green hardbound manuscript notebook he was working in at the time. Between June 19 and July 6, 1931, Wittgenstein made entries that pertained to Frazer, but often to other topics as well—understanding, meaning, complexity, intention.[9] This was now the sixth hardbound notebook that Wittgenstein was filling with his thoughts since returning to Cambridge, and when he was in Vienna in the middle of August 1931, he began the process of dictating another synopsis of his work thus far, covering the notebooks since his previous synopsis.[10] In a portion of this synopsis of about ninety typed pages so far, he takes manuscript entries pertaining to Frazer spread over several weeks and brings them together, deleting some and reorganizing others, amounting to some thirteen pages. Wittgenstein showed this typescript to Waismann when he was in Vienna, and Waismann reported (on September 21, 1931): "The sentences are quite higgledy-piggledy [*ganz kunterbunt*—disorganized?]. They are meant for Wittgenstein who will carry them with him to England, in order to continue working on them. They are an extract from his manuscript books (90 pages so far)."[11] In other words, they were still very much a work in progress.

As before, Wittgenstein later used this typed synopsis as a source for further work, using many of the passages as part of an enormous summary of his views—untitled by Wittgenstein, but known to his editors as "The Big Typescript."[12] That contained just a few passages pertaining to Frazer, some not even selected by Wittgenstein for the synopsis. The rest of the Frazer passages from 1931 lay undisturbed for three decades, until well after Wittgenstein's death.[13]

Editing the Text

Rush Rhees was one of the three students Wittgenstein designated to edit and publish his work after his death. In 1962 Rhees was examining the manuscripts from the early 1930s when the remarks on Frazer caught his attention, but in another context. In a series of lengthy letters to G. H. von Wright (another of the designated editors) he wrote:

> I am enclosing a copy I typed (badly) of some remarks Wittgenstein makes in the course of the last 123 pages of Manuscript Volume VI [MS 110], during June and July 1931. If we are looking for the origin of the use of "language games" as a philosophical method, then I think that one source or one influence was this reflexion on the analogy of metaphysics and magic, and on Frazer's misunderstanding of the magic about which he was writing.[14]

Rather than having interest in their own right, Rhees sees the remarks on Frazer more as an illustration of Wittgenstein's more important reflections on language games and the nature of metaphysics. Consequently, he is not inclined to publish them on their own:

> I am uncertain what should be done with the remarks about magic and Frazer. I think they ought to be published, and I do not think they should be published by themselves—since this would give rise to queer sorts of misunderstandings.[15]

Then he comes up with the idea of publishing them in combination with some other shorter works:

> I had been thinking of a smallish volume which might include this [lecture on ethics] together with the remarks on Frazer, for instance (which were written about a year later), and . . . it might include some of the later scattered remarks upon religion and upon "value." . . . On the other hand, I do not see just where the notes on Frazer, for instance, could be published *unless* it were in a volume of this sort.[16]

In fact, when Wittgenstein talked about Frazer over the course of several of his course lectures in Easter term of 1933, they were, in that context, intermixed with comments about religion, ethics, and aesthetics.[17] So Rhees's idea for "a smallish volume" has some basis. Yet in the end, Rhees opted to publish the remarks on Frazer on their own. This turned out to be a popular decision, as Wittgenstein's remarks on Frazer are among the best-known and most widely read of his writings by nonphilosophers—anthropologists, social scientists, and religious scholars.

Rhees culled Wittgenstein's remarks that constitute part I of his so-called Remarks on Frazer's *Golden Bough* from a lengthy typescript by Wittgenstein, labeled TS 211, and from a hand-written notebook, labeled MS 110. Wittgenstein created TS 211 by selecting and reorganizing passages from a series of such hand-written notebooks (MSS 109, 110, 111, 112, 113, and 114).[18] While he made comments about Frazer's writings in notebooks, typescripts, and lectures, he never set out to write a "work" on Frazer. However, his comments had sufficient interest and presumably unity that Rhees did create a "work" out of Wittgenstein's remarks about Frazer, in the sense that he published them as a separate chunk of material.[19]

There are at least six published versions of this work: Rhees's original German edition published in 1967, an English translation by A. C. Miles and Rhees published in 1971, a bilingual book edition that Rhees edited and published in 1979, an English translation by J. Beversluis published in 1979, a German edition published by J. Schulte in 1989, and a bilingual edition published by J. Klagge and A. Nordmann in 1993.[20] That there are these versions would not bear mentioning if it were not that the editions differ in notable ways.

But first, the similarities. The work begins with consecutive passages from nine pages (pp. 313–321) of TS 211 (PO pp. 118–top paragraph of 132). Then Rhees inserts two paragraphs from earlier in TS 211 (pp. 281–282) before returning to the earlier series (p. 322) for two paragraphs (PO, middle of p. 132). At this point (marked by " * * * " in PO, p. 132), Rhees turns to five paragraphs from even earlier in TS 211 (pp. 250–251) before returning to two later paragraphs (p. 281) in TS 211. That completes the remarks drawn from the typescript. Now (marked by " * * * " in PO, p. 134) Rhees adds remarks from the hand-written manuscript (MS 110) from which the typescript had been drawn: four paragraphs come from pp. 253–254 and later on p. 255 (PO, pp. 134–136), then Rhees finishes part I with eight consecutive paragraphs from pp. 297–299. Rhees leaves out one passage from p. 259 of MS 110 in which Frazer is specifically mentioned. Rhees neither notes nor explains his failure to include this fairly obvious passage in the later published editions.[21] It is not necessary for readers to follow all these transitions, only to know that they exist.[22] They indicate the great extent to which this "work" is the construction of an editor.[23]

Now, the differences. For reasons never explained, Rhees cut out the last six paragraphs of part I in the 1971 English translation.[24] This cut was maintained in his bilingual book edition. The Beversluis translation restores the cut paragraphs. The Schulte edition, while claiming (p. 141) to follow the original 1967 edition, in fact continues the deletion of the six paragraphs. The Klagge and Nordmann edition includes the paragraphs but marks them in square brackets.[25] The deleted paragraphs are textually continuous with the preceding paragraphs in the source manuscript (MS 110, pp. 297–299), topically continuous with the preceding paragraphs, and interesting in their own right.

Rhees's editorial work has provided students of Wittgenstein with many worthwhile texts, not the least of which is the text under consideration. They include the *Philosophical Remarks*, *Philosophical Grammar*, "Notes for Lectures on 'Private Experience' and 'Sense Data,'" "The Language of Sense Data and Private Experience," "Cause and Effect: Intuitive Awareness," and "Eine Philosophische Betrachtung." In each case Rhees has found ways to present interesting texts that address salient issues of philosophical interest. He has gotten us to see Wittgenstein as addressing circumscribable topics when there would otherwise be only continuous notebooks of Wittgenstein's remarks that are hard to enter and harder to survey. One might say that Rhees has served us some bite-sized and appetizing pieces of Wittgenstein's work. This has served the necessary and useful purpose of making parts of Wittgenstein's work accessible and even popular.[26] Wittgenstein's remarks on Frazer are certainly among his works most widely read by those outside philosophy.

But many of Rhees's editing projects have been questioned for their scholarly integrity, often for their seemingly arbitrary and unexplained decisions. The best-known of these controversies concerns the book *Philosophische Grammatik*, which Rhees edited and published in 1969. In the course of preparing an English translation of this, Anthony Kenny traced the textual sources for this edition in TS 213 and various later revisions that Wittgenstein made.[27] After examining possible reasons for various of Rhees's editorial choices, Kenny comments, "It cannot be said that the published version of the *Philosophical Grammar* results from any systematic application" of possible criteria. Three chapters from TS 213 are omitted altogether, including a lengthy discussion of the nature of philosophy.[28] "Any reader of the Big Typescript cannot help but find it strange that the omission of these important and fascinating chapters from the published *Grammatik* is not only not justified in the editorial note, but not even mentioned there." Kenny concludes, "The most prudent editorial policy would have been to print the original Big Typescript as it stood rather than to seek for a definitive revision of it."[29]

In *Philosophical Occasions*, Nordmann and I contributed to the debate over Rhees's editing by publishing an expanded edition of "Notes for Lectures on 'Private Experience' and 'Sense Data,'" reprinting the missing "Philosophy" chapter from the Big Typescript, and calling Rhees's editorial posture "almost authorial."[30]

In a letter written in 1977, Rhees responded to criticisms of his editing by invoking the charge that he and the other executors received from Wittgenstein in his Will: "I intend and desire that Mr Rhees, Miss Anscombe and Professor von Wright shall publish as many of my unpublished writings as they think fit." Rhees explained that what he saw "fit" required him to exercise his judgment, which he did: "In any editing I have done I have asked again and again what Wittgenstein would have wanted. This has guided me in what I have decided to leave out and in what I have decided to include."[31] He has, in essence, assumed an *almost authorial* editorial policy, as we claimed. And he based this on not only Wittgenstein's own trust but on the experiences that led to that trust. He had "known Wittgenstein for some time (I knew him pretty well for 15 years) and having been with him while he was working on and revising his manuscripts—having seen him cut out certain things (sometimes to my bewilderment) and change the order of passages . . . remembering *especially* the reasons he often did give for cutting out, revising and shortening . . . so that I could see something of the same way of working and the same standards in some of the crossings out and revisions in the manuscripts."[32]

Here, in defense of his authorial editing, Rhees calls on what Wittgenstein had once termed "imponderable evidence." Wittgenstein wrote in 1949:

> I tell someone that I have reasons for this claim or proofs of it, but that they are 'imponderable.'" There are certainly spheres in which this is appropriate. "Well, *for instance*, I have seen the look which one person has given another. I say 'If you had seen it you would have said the same thing.' . . . An important factor here is that we learn certain things only through long experience and not from a course in school. How, for instance, does one develop the eye of a connoisseur? . . . A connoisseur couldn't make himself understood to a jury, for instance. That is, they would understand his statement, but not his reasons. He can give intimations to another connoisseur, and the latter will understand them.[33]

Unfortunately, this leaves Rhees making the circular claim that connoisseurs will agree with him because those who do not agree with his judgments are, by definition, not connoisseurs.[34]

The fact that Wittgenstein's literary "executors" (those named in his will) exercised iron control over his papers until they were microfilmed in 1967, and considerable control even after that, fueled suspicion that they wanted their claims to special insight to go untested.

This danger is illustrated by the unfortunate fate of an alternative edition and translation: *Ludwig Wittgenstein: Remarks on Frazer's Philosophical Anthropology*, prepared by Kenneth Ketner and James Eigsti. The translation was presumably begun in the late 1960s, when Rhees's German-only edition was published, and completed only in 1972, after Rhees's translation had been published. This new edition had a more complete selection of passages, including extensive excerpts from the Frazer material Wittgenstein was reacting to, as well as a superior translation. Ketner, though a Peirce scholar with a PhD in philosophy, also had an MA in folklore and was interested in placing Wittgenstein's work in relation to the anthropological and religious studies fields. In a rejection letter that academic scholars (at least of my generation) will recognize as only too familiar, Anscombe unhelpfully pronounces that "your work is just not good enough for us to authorize its publication."[35] While Ketner emphasizes the scholarly value of the more careful editing and the academic value of alternative translations, it is hard to avoid the thought that Rhees did not accept the attempt to present the material in a way that emphasized its interest for anthropologists or accept having his editorial judgment questioned. After further inquiries and unhelpful replies, the matter was dropped and the manuscript was never published.

This is the kind of thing that gave the executors a bad name. Jaakko Hintikka articulated this concern in 1991:

> An unhealthy climate has been created among those who are aware of the importance of the *Nachlaß* [Wittgenstein's unpublished writings] but are without easy access to [it]. . . . Some of the very same persons responsible for the editing of Wittgenstein have also been engaged in interpreting his philosophy. They have therefore placed themselves in the precarious position of being in control of other scholars' access to materials in the light of which their own interpretations are to be judged and which could conceivably prove some of these interpretations wrong. For their own sake, it is to be hoped that the present untenable situation will soon be resolved so as to clear up unnecessary suspicions and rumors of their motivation and comportment.[36]

The "untenable situation" was finally resolved by the release in 2000 of the CD-ROM of Wittgenstein's papers in facsimile with diplomatic and normalized text transcriptions, known as the Bergen Electronic Edition.[37]

But as Rhees said, his editing was only an attempt to mimic the sort of editing that Wittgenstein himself often did. Wittgenstein created TS 211 from his hand-written manuscripts, and the process is itself instructive in his handling of passages relevant to our discussion.

If we take the sentence, "Frazer's account of the magical and religious views of mankind is unsatisfactory,"[38] to be the beginning of the core of Wittgenstein's remarks on Frazer, we can see that Wittgenstein decided that the five sentences that had led up to this sentence in the manuscript should be deleted. He marked the five sentences in the manuscript with "ʃ" for "*schlecht*" or "bad." These are, nonetheless, commonly included in the editors' prefaces to publications of Wittgenstein's remarks on Frazer.[39]

Instead, in the typescript, Wittgenstein took five sentences that had been composed earlier in the manuscript, reordered them, and placed them before the sentence in question, constituting a sort of introduction—"One must start out . . ."—to his core remarks on Frazer.[40] We will return to these, but let us begin by examining Wittgenstein's core remarks.

Error and Satisfaction

Wittgenstein begins by saying, "Frazer's account of the magical and religious views of mankind is unsatisfactory: it makes these views look like *errors* (*Irrtümer*)." In fact, Frazer specifically talks of "our predecessors . . . and . . . their errors." And he characterizes these errors as being "hypotheses . . . which a fuller experience has proved to be inadequate."[41] While Frazer talked mainly about ancient or so-called primitive practices, his discussion was applicable to any religious practices, and Wittgenstein took the discussion this way: "The religious actions, or religious life, of the priest-king are no different in kind from any genuinely religious action of today, for example, a confession of sins."[42] For Wittgenstein, what is at stake is the nature and status of religious belief and practices generally: Are they such as to be vulnerable to modern scientific discoveries, as Frazer seems to suppose, or do they have a dignity and worth that is independent of modern scientific discoveries? Without himself espousing religious beliefs here or engaging in religious practices, Wittgenstein nonetheless endorses their dignity and independence from science.

However, six years later, while Wittgenstein was living alone in Norway and after he had endured six months of literal winter darkness, he had his own religious crisis, which can be traced in his diary entries at the time. On March 20, 1937, he records his agony: "There is *no one* here: & yet I speak & thank & petition. But is this speaking & thanking & petitioning an *error* [*Irrtum*]?!" And three days later he continues: "Help & Illuminate! But if I believe something tomorrow that I don't believe today, I was not therefore in an error [*in einem Irrtum*] today. For this 'believing' is not *holding an opinion*, after all."[43] Wittgenstein comes to eventually and explicitly identify with the objects of Frazer's criticisms.

In his 1931 remarks on Frazer, Wittgenstein offers a test for whether a religious practice, or indeed any other practice, is predicated on something that could turn out to be erroneous:

> It can indeed happen, and often does today, that a person will give up a practice after he has recognized an error on which it was based. But this happens only when calling someone's attention to his error is enough to turn him from his old way of behaving.[44]

Wittgenstein claims this can and often does happen today, but does not go on to give examples.

One of Wittgenstein's later discussions of this sort of issue is about ascribing responsibility for actions in his "Lectures on Freedom of the Will." One might think that our practice of ascribing responsibility for actions depends on a factual claim that our actions are not determined. In that case, if we were to discover that indeterminism were false, then the practice could be interpreted scientifically and would in this case be predicated on an error. As is typical in his lectures, he does not offer a clear-cut position, but consider the following comments:

> I can't see why they should not have held that a human being is responsible, and yet held that his decisions are . . . determined. . . .
>
> It seems as if, if you are very strongly impressed by the responsibility which a human being has for his actions, you are inclined to say that these actions and choices can't follow natural laws. Conversely, if you are very strongly inclined to say that they do follow natural laws, then you are inclined to say "'I can't be made responsible for my choice." . . .
>
> Would it be unreasonable to think that the actions of a human being follow natural laws, but never the less hold him responsible for what he does? . . .
>
> I wanted to say that if really someone could perform this calculation (of what he was going to do), I don't see why we shouldn't still hold him responsible.
>
> "To understand all is to excuse all." "If you understood the workings of his mind and understood all the circumstances as well as you understand a piece of machinery you wouldn't hold him responsible for his actions." I would say: "how do you know?" It doesn't follow . . . [45]

So he contemplates someone who holds that our practice of ascribing responsibility for actions depends on those actions not being determined, or following natural laws, as a piece of machinery. But he thinks we would not have to give up that practice—we would not be unreasonable to maintain the practice even so. Wittgenstein ends up treating this case similarly to the way he proposes to treat the ceremonial practices that Frazer considered.[46]

I have not been able to think of a passage where Wittgenstein discusses a person giving up a practice because it is seen to depend on an error. But one example that comes to mind is the practice of using dowsing sticks (or divining rods) to discover water or minerals underground. In this case, it seems clear that the practice presupposed a factual claim—that certain sticks or people using sticks can find water or minerals at a rate far better than chance. This practice arose in the sixteenth and seventeenth centuries in the absence of other reliable means for finding these valuable resources. It wasn't long before doubts arose about the reliability of this practice, and in fact numerous careful tests over the centuries have disproven its reliability. It would seem to be a good example of the kind of practice for which Frazer's attitude would be appropriate.[47]

Since Wittgenstein claims that such cases "can indeed happen" and often do "today" but doesn't offer examples, it seems worth setting out some other possible contemporary practices for reflection. While Wittgenstein has not said what he means by a "practice," I think the following cases might qualify (others might offer different examples or analyze these cases differently):

A. Inflicting capital punishment for certain kinds of murder

B. Shaming obese people

C. Eating meat

D. Giving IQ tests

The question is whether we can find a factual claim that underlies each practice ("on which it was based") that might turn out to be false, and whether the discovery and acknowledgment of such an error would lead to a change or rejection of the practice ("turn him from his old way of behaving"). In each case a factual claim that might be thought to underlie the practice could be:

A′. Capital punishment (significantly) deters future murders.

B′. Obese people can control their weight by choosing to eat less, or healthier, food.

C′. Eating meat is necessary for a healthy diet.

D′. There is a (strong) correlation between IQ tests and performance in other ways.

We can certainly imagine cases in which the practice (or a particular person's engagement in the practice) in question is based on the truth of the factual claim offered. It will inevitably be difficult to determine whether the practice is always and only based on the offered claim.

But assuming these claims do underlie the practices, the question then is: What would happen if a practitioner were to learn that the claim was false? Would this be enough to lead to the rejection (or modification) of the practice? If so, then we could say that the practice had been predicated on an error (that the practitioner was "in error") and that the practice (erroneous or not) could be "interpreted scientifically."[48] In each case this question must be settled on an individual basis: What would it take for a given person (or set of people) to give up or modify a practice?

In the case of capital punishment, the practice might well continue if there were additional independent reasons for it, such as retribution. A given person might well continue eating meat if they considered meat to be especially tasty. Perhaps most practices that we are familiar with are supported by multiple reasons, so there is not some single or easily isolated basis for the practice. But, and this is the relevant scenario, if there are cases where the practice is given up or modified, then we can say that the practice was vulnerable to "the facts" and potentially erroneous. Clearly there are cases that fit this description.[49] Perhaps the practice of gay conversion therapy would be one. After significant questions about its effectiveness, and indeed even its harmfulness, this practice has been largely abandoned and is even legally banned in some places.

If the practice withstands the acknowledged refutation of the underlying claim, then either there is another underlying claim or the practice is not vulnerable to the facts and is not the sort of thing that can be called an error (as practiced by that person or set of persons).[50] If we suspect another underlying claim, we can repeat the process. In principle, this process of isolating grounds and then imagining them to be false can ultimately determine if a practice is empirically vulnerable. In practice, it is unlikely we will be able to assert that we know and have considered all the potential underlying claims.[51]

After setting out this test, Wittgenstein claims, "But this is not the case with the religious practices of a people and *therefore* there is *no* question of an error."[52] In light of his proposed test, this amounts to the claim that there is no set of empirically testable claims that are such that if they were all shown to be false, then the practitioner would give up the religious practice. Frazer supposes that there *are* such empirically testable claims such that if the religious practitioner knew they were false, the practitioner would give up the practice *and* that the practitioner simply did/does not realize the falsity.[53] This is what leads Wittgenstein to pretend that Frazer would call these practices "sheer stupidity."[54] It is Frazer's condescending tone that most irks Wittgenstein.

But where Frazer goes wrong, according to Wittgenstein, is in his supposition that there must be an underlying basis, an explanation, for religious practices: "The very idea of wanting to explain a practice—for example, the killing of the priest-king—seems to me wrong [*verfehlt*]." And: "I believe that the attempt to explain is already therefore wrong [*verfehlt*]."[55] Wittgenstein attributes this desire for an explanation to the kind of "people who think as [Frazer] does" and what he calls "a tendency in ourselves."[56] Whether or how Wittgenstein thinks we can change this tendency is a question we return to below.

In place of offering an explanation of religious practices, what Wittgenstein proposes is that we simply *describe* them, because explanation "is only *one* way of assembling the data—of their synopsis. It is just as possible to see the data in their relation to one another and embrace them in a general picture."[57] In Wittgenstein's typescript, this leads to mention of the now-famous notion of a perspicuous representation (*übersichtlichen Darstellung*).[58] This, he thinks, can be an adequate substitute for explanation: "One must only correctly piece together what one *knows*, without adding anything, and the satisfaction being sought through the explanation follows of itself. . . . Here one can only *describe*."[59] We might even say that this perspicuous representation is itself a *sort of* explanation (though not a historical or causal explanation). In this (minimal) sense of "explanation," Wittgenstein writes that "this is precisely the explanation wished for; that is, the explanation which resolves this particular difficulty."[60] According to Wittgenstein, simply bringing things into connection with one another provides "of itself" "the satisfaction being sought."

One might wonder whether Wittgenstein is right that "the satisfaction being sought through the explanation follows of itself" from a perspicuous representation. In Wittgenstein's lectures two years later, when he talks about Frazer and Frazer's concerns, he says, "What satisfies my puzzlement about Beltane [festival], is not [the] kind of causal explanation which Frazer gives—which is a hypothesis; but simply describing lots of things more or less like Beltane."[61] So the descriptive approach satisfies Wittgenstein. But he has acknowledged that the desire for something more, for a causal or developmental explanation, is a "tendency in ourselves"[62] and in "people who think as [Frazer] does." So it seems that such people (including "us") will in fact *not* likely find the satisfaction that Wittgenstein himself claims to find. It may well be "wrong [*verfehlt*]" of us to want more, but it does not follow that we thereby *stop* wanting more, even when we are told it is wrong and that Wittgenstein himself *needs* no more. In discussing the general problem of wanting an explanation in place of a description, Wittgenstein admits, in another context, "The difficulty here is: to stop."[63]

The issue here is really a noncognitive, temperamental one: What can we be satisfied with? And (how) could Wittgenstein influence what it takes to satisfy us?

Wittgenstein's Introduction

Wittgenstein placed the five sentences that stand at the beginning of his remarks on Frazer (as edited and published by Rhees) in the typescript he dictated. The first four can be seen as an overview of how to address the problems already raised in this chapter and that are to follow in Wittgenstein's own typescript:

> One must start out with error [*Irrtum*] and convert [*überführen*] it into truth.
>
> That is, one must reveal the source of error, otherwise hearing the truth won't do any good. The truth cannot force its way in when something else is occupying its place.
>
> To convince someone of the truth, it is not enough to state it, but rather one must find the *path* [*Weg*] from error to truth.[64]

I believe these sentences characterize roughly the situation described in the previous section of this chapter and in Wittgenstein's core remarks on Frazer as follows.

Frazer and those like him are in "error" because they ask too much by insisting on an explanation (or on a *causal* explanation). The "truth" is that a perspicuous representation of the practice and its surroundings is satisfactory. But hearing this truth will not do any good if one already has these erroneous expectations. To convince Frazer and those like him of this truth, it is not enough to state it. One must find a path—a *way* to get—from the erroneous expectations to a place where one can be satisfied with a description. One must find a way to convert Frazer and those like him to a different way of thinking.

Wittgenstein offers no path, no answer, here. But that is not surprising, since this is a problem he struggled with for many years. What is noteworthy is that he was able to formulate the problem in this way at this point. The problem is not one of stating the truth but one of converting the misguided. I suggested in chapter 1 that it was roughly during early

1931 that Wittgenstein began to appreciate the need to address those with a temperament different from his own. This is an early and clear-cut case of that.

While the problem Wittgenstein is trying to formulate here is a real one, his formulation is problematic in this context. In particular, his use here of the word *Irrtum* and its cognates is problematic.[65] In the core remarks, he criticizes Frazer for attributing errors (*Irrtümer*) to primitive believers. But in the introductory sentences, he is not talking about *those* kinds of errors. In the core remarks, Wittgenstein does address the kind of challenge he raises in the introductory sentences, but in the core remarks, he generally calls the attempt to explain religious practices "wrong [*verfehlt*]."[66] In fact, in some of the manuscript notes that Wittgenstein deleted in creating TS 211, he would talk of rectifying a "philosophical mistake/wrong [*philosophische Fehler*]."[67] So he had the terminology at hand, and it would have made more sense to use some cognate of *Fehler* to characterize the misguided, wrong-headed, position Wittgenstein identifies in the introductory sentences. In the brief account that Drury gave of his reading of Frazer with Wittgenstein, quoted above, Drury (presumably loosely quoting Wittgenstein) makes the distinction clear in English: "He [Wittgenstein] was particularly emphatic that it was *wrong* to think, as Frazer seemed to do, that the primitive rituals were in the nature of scientific *errors*" (italics added). This is a good way to make Wittgenstein's point.

Furthermore, the contrasting terminology of "truth" is misleading because it is too cognitive for the issue that is raised by the core remarks and in the introductory remarks. If the issue at stake really were (simply) one of *truth*, then it should be enough to state it and give one's reasons. But it is clear that this is not enough in the case at hand. And the imagery of struggle in the introductory sentences suggests a noncognitive issue is at stake: "The truth cannot force its way in when something else is occupying its place" in the mind-set of the believer.

This struggle is clearest in the need to "*überführen* [convert]" the error into truth. But the situation described pertains more to the *holder* of the belief than it does to the *object* of the belief. As Wittgenstein says: "To convince *someone* of the truth, it is not enough [italics added]." So, it is not really a matter of converting the error into a truth but of converting the misguided believer. This would seem to call for something closer to *bekehren*, which describes a (possibly religious) conversion. One wants to find a *way* for the *person* to move from one state to the other.[68] This suggests the need for an evangelist.

This issue in the core remarks is how to get Frazer and those who think like him (i.e., us) to be satisfied with a synoptic description of a religious practice rather than seeking a causal explanation. This will require some kind of conversion, for it is a noncognitive matter of temperament: What will I be satisfied with? In the remarks on Frazer, it comes down to this: How can Wittgenstein cure a "narrow spiritual life" that is unable "to conceive of a life different from that of the England of his time"?[69] But in many contexts, throughout much of his philosophizing, Wittgenstein became concerned with this kind of challenge—that issues he cared about came down to a matter of temperament . . . —and how was he to change people's temperament?

Apparently sensing the enormity of the task that lay ahead of him, Wittgenstein decided not to offer class lectures in the upcoming Michaelmas term of 1931. He wrote to Moore as follows: "Now do me a favour: I don't intend to give any formal lectures this term as I think I must reserve all my strength for my own work. I will however have *private* (unpaid) discussions with students if there are any who want them."[70] This then turned out to be an especially fertile time in Wittgenstein's thinking.

Already Wittgenstein had hoped that a synopsis of phenomena might accomplish what he wanted. At some points, he thought a process of philosophical therapy was called for. At other points, he felt philosophy should be written poetically. But he was taking seriously the challenge to influence how (other) people think about issues. He had become an evangelist.

In November 1931, Wittgenstein reflected in his diary on Kierkegaard's methods and characterized Kierkegaard's concerns in a way similar to his own introductory comments on Frazer.[71] Finally, in 1947, he threw up his hands in frustration, exclaiming: "Quite different artillery is needed here from anything I am in a position to muster."[72] But the remarks on Frazer provided one of the first, clearest, and best-known contexts in which Wittgenstein came to see his philosophical challenges in this way.

Perhaps it was prophetic, then, that the last of the five introductory sentences is, "I must plunge into the water of doubt again and again." Wittgenstein never did find a satisfactory way of bringing about the conversion that he sought.

4 Wittgenstein's Methods and Aims

When Wittgenstein began to lecture at Cambridge for the first time, in Lent term of 1930, he opened with a brief methodological remark: "Philosophy is the attempt to be rid of a particular kind of puzzlement. This 'philosophic' puzzlement is one of the intellect and not of instinct."[1] And over the course of that term and the next, he addressed issues such as the nature of propositions, representation, logic, infinity, generality, and mathematics. By the beginning of the Michaelmas term, he felt he could announce: "There have been great philosophers; but now for the first time, there can be skillful ones. . . . Philosophy is reduced to a matter of skill." He admitted, "It's very difficult to acquire any skill. You can't acquire it by hearing lectures: only way is to discuss." But still: "the method is found."[2]

In the previous chapter, we saw the emergence of his synoptic method, in which he would provide a perspicuous representation (*übersichtlichen Darstellung*) of relevant phenomena to get us to see something in the right way. The idea is to provide a context in which a philosophical confusion or perplexity would be reduced or disappear.

For instance, to use the issue from the previous chapter—our understanding of so-called primitive magical practices—Wittgenstein's proposed solution is to describe those practices in the context of other modern social practices with which we are more familiar rather than to compare them with modern scientific explanations that seem more successful. In this way, we change our context for the phenomena, and we see it as a different kind of thing—a ritual rather than a mistaken explanation with misguided expectations. Philosophy thus "leaves everything as it is" (PI §124), only modifying our way of looking at, our way of seeing, things.

Wittgenstein invents fictional scenarios for a similar purpose—to offer them as "objects of comparison" (see PI §130) for philosophically puzzling phenomena. If the fictional scenarios are philosophically transparent and are interestingly similar to puzzling phenomena, then they help create a context that allows the initially puzzling phenomena to be seen in a new way. While Wittgenstein used this approach throughout his later philosophizing, he began to see its limitations, as I have conjectured.

A good example of his struggling with the method's limitations comes fifteen years later. Wittgenstein began his course of lectures in Michaelmas term 1946 by asking, "What is thinking?" In a series of class lectures later in the term, he imagined a tribe that has been enslaved, and "we the conquerors have a theory that they feel no pain" or have no "feelings," but we want them to work for us, so we teach them our language, including "psychological verbs." In class on December 2, he reflected on the purpose of this case. Here are notes from four students of the same point in the lecture:

> Edwards (p. 31): "It may be asked why fictitious cases are used. I use them to make people change the way they look at real cases, to make them compare other things than those they usually do. We asked the question: What is thinking? And it vanished when we no longer sought comparison with phenomena or 'happenings' hidden from us. In this way our old concepts may be changed."[3]
>
> Geach (LPP, 43): "You may ask [what] is the point of considering an admittedly fictitious tribe. The point is that we may be led to compare the real phenomena with the fictitious and so conceive them in different ways from the common. E.g. we need no longer compare thinking to something going on 'inside', 'in a hidden place.'"
>
> Shah (LPP, 168): "In a way I tried to change your point of view: look at it this way. Ultimately we considered the soul-less tribe. It is pure fiction. What is it for? It is a waste of time. What can one do by doing what we did? This: the way in which people look at the non-fictitious case can be changed. We are inclined to compare some phenomena with something: I ask you to compare them with something else. The question vanished when we classified phenomena *not* with something happening. We change the concept we have. Whether it is important or not is another matter."
>
> Jackson (LPP, 285): "I have been trying to change the point of view. Everything is of the form 'Look at it this way'; 'Compare it to this and not to that.' The question 'What is thinking?' vanishes when we cease to compare the phenomena concerned with phenomena happening inside things and hidden from us."[4]

The point was to find a way to get us to "cease to compare the phenomena concerned with phenomena happening inside things and hidden from us." This is done by creating a new comparison set—a new context. Wittgenstein thought this could be accomplished with fictional cases as well as real ones. We are "inclined to" make certain comparisons, but Wittgenstein will "ask you" to compare them with something else: "Look at it this way."

But the interesting question is whether this method is effective in achieving the goal—in this case, apparently, to get us to cease asking, "What is thinking?" Wittgenstein asserts that it is effective: "The question vanished." That seems to be wishful thinking on his part . . . , at least if the question's "vanishing" implies that people *stop asking* the question. And, indeed, he claimed "to make people change the way they look at real cases, to make them compare other things."[5] But it is unclear that this has happened or will happen reliably. "The difficulty here is: to stop."[6]

In Wittgenstein's work with Friedrich Waismann (in 1932–1933) to write an account of his new and evolving thoughts, Wittgenstein was apparently very confident of this method:

> If we offer an analogy to our language as the solution to a philosophical problem, we are always exposed to the danger of being misunderstood: it is as if, with our admission that the investigated game is only *similar* to our language, we had conceded that we had not solved our original problem at all, but outlined only the solution of a similar problem. But we are not dealing here with an *explanation* of phenomena; it is not that I wanted to explain one phenomenon and have in fact explained another one similar to it, but rather that I remove the disquiet [*Beunruhigung*] that looks like a problem by juxtaposing with it a number of similar cases. It is remarkable that the mere bringing together of cases calms disquiet.[7]

Not long after, Wittgenstein reflected deeply on the question of reliable success and failure in a dictation (or perhaps a lecture—it is not clear) from February 5, 1934, in notes taken by Francis Skinner:

> Suppose Miss Ambrose is troubled by some philosophical problem, can I remove her trouble in spite of herself? Suppose someone says I have never removed his troubles. Is this something damning? (If you wanted an addition done, I could do your addition for you and remove your trouble.)
>
> I don't think this is any argument against what we do. It is only an argument against what I do as far as the particular person's trouble is concerned. I may not be able to remove his trouble. The trouble shows in that he can't ask a question—it consists in not being able to ask a significant question. If like a doctor who describes the symptoms of an illness, I would say he can't ask a significant question but does ask a question. When the trouble is removed, the question has not been answered but he ceases to ask it. What must you give a person that he no longer has the temptation to ask such a question?
>
> I may not give the right analogy.

> I may give the right analogy but the person may not be able to overlook or survey what I give him.
>
> I haven't succeeded, but it does not mean what I have done is absurd.
>
> I may give lots of descriptions of meaning, but the person may not have it ready.
>
> How far does the thing I do compel you to remove your doubts? It just can't.
>
> Sometimes the thing I do will work, and sometimes it won't work. Can I bring it about that you, whenever you are in a new trouble, can remove it yourself?
>
> This depends partly on the imagination. What does for a trouble I have depended on for me to get rid of it? [*sic* ?]
>
> It may be that the right picture comes into my mind.
>
> If I can't answer it, it may happen that I shall never be able to answer.
>
> The more pictures you have had, the less likely you are to be in a hopeless muddle.
>
> I can only make it more [*sic*—less?] likely.
>
> The sort of question which arises now may arise anytime again. It will arise as long as you are caught in your form of expression.
>
> The puzzle is a sort of misunderstanding and the word which solves it may never be found.[8]

That is the question: "What must you give a person that he no longer has the temptation to ask such a question?" This is a question Wittgenstein did not ask in 1930 but did come to ask in the course of his ongoing teaching. (I provide this extensive passage because it shows Wittgenstein so seriously concerned with the problem of how to get his points across.)

Wittgenstein's focus was on this exact question in a class in 1944. Elizabeth Anscombe reports, "At another point I came out with 'But I still want to say: Blue is there.' Older hands smiled or laughed but Wittgenstein checked them by taking it seriously, saying 'Let me think what medicine you need.'" At this point Wittgenstein introduced an imaginary situation: "Suppose we had the word 'painy' as a word for the property of some surfaces." Anscombe reports that "the 'medicine' was effective, and the story illustrates Wittgenstein's ability to understand the thought that was offered to him in objection."[9]

This anecdote illustrates two points: that Wittgenstein saw the need to address philosophical problems in an ad hoc fashion that depended on the individual and that doing so required the individual to confess her or his views honestly. Wittgenstein emphasized the need for an ad hoc approach in his elaboration of the fly-bottle example: "First of all, it is not at all clear that this will help every fly. What happens to work with me doesn't work with him (Prof. Moore)—works with me now, and may not work with me tomorrow."[10] As for the honesty, Wittgenstein made this point in a dictation to Skinner later that same month in 1934:

> There is one [piece of] advice I can give you. If you think about philosophical problems and you are up against expressing a particular idea in your mind, be honest and say what your particular idea really consists in.
>
> If you wanted to express your idea of the number three, and you have often before your mind's eye three fingers, then don't be ashamed of admitting this. These crude things are enormously important.
>
> Why shouldn't one be honest?
>
> It wants a particular technique to really definitely get hold of that crude picture which is really wanted. As soon as you have got it, things seem alright.[11]

In a notebook in 1947 Wittgenstein wrote: "*Don't for heaven's sake*, be afraid of talking nonsense! Only don't fail to pay attention to your nonsense."[12] And then at a discussion in Oxford not long after, Philippa Foot reported: "Wittgenstein interrupted a speaker who had realized he was about to say something that, although it seemed compelling, was clearly ridiculous, and was trying . . . to say something sensible instead. 'No,' said Wittgenstein, 'Say what you *want* to say. Be *crude* and then we shall get on.'"[13] But, again, Wittgenstein seems to be overly optimistic when he says, "As soon as you have got it, things seem alright."

While Wittgenstein sometimes makes it sound as though *he* can figure out how to address a person's problem, other times the burden is seen to be on the person with the problem. Kierkegaard, in Johannes Climacus's *Concluding Unscientific Postscript*, wrote, "It is thus left to the reader himself to put two and two together, if he so desires; but nothing is done to minister to a reader's indolence."[14] And in a letter to Russell from Norway in 1913, discussing "Notes on Logic," which he dictated for Russell, Wittgenstein expressed frustration: "If you thought about it for a bit you could discover it for yourself. . . . I beg you to think about these matters for yourself: it is INTOLERABLE for me, to repeat a written explanation which even the first time I gave only with the *utmost repugnance*."[15] He returned to this thought much later, in a notebook in 1948: "Anything the reader can do for himself, leave it to the reader."[16]

This notion that a person must articulate and endorse her or his own confusions, and that the problem is ultimately left to the reader connects with the idea that philosophy is a sort of therapy. Wittgenstein in fact was more specific on occasion. In the so-called Big Typescript, dated 1933–1934, Wittgenstein writes: "Indeed, we can only convict someone else of a mistake if he acknowledges that this really is the expression of his feeling. . . . For only if he acknowledges it as such, *is* it the correct expression (Psychoanalysis.)"[17] In his notebook in 1938, Wittgenstein returns to this thought: "I'm not teaching you anything; I'm trying to persuade you to do something. What we do is much more akin to Psychoanalysis than you might be aware of."[18] But on the other hand, Malcolm reports (from 1946–1947) that Wittgenstein was "angered" by "the suggestion that in his conception, philosophy was a form of psychoanalysis," which Malcolm "heard him explicitly attack, on two occasions, as based on a confusion. 'They are different techniques,' he had said."[19] By the time of the *Philosophical Investigations*, Wittgenstein opts for the more general characterization: "There is not a single philosophical method, though there are different methods, different therapies, as it were" (PI insert between §§133 and 134).

Perhaps Wittgenstein's closest acquaintance with therapy was the spiritual therapy that he practiced on himself. In January 1937, after returning to Norway from Vienna and England, where he had attempted to set himself on a different course by making confessions to a number of people from his past and present, he records in his diary a running commentary on his spiritual struggles. He records in considerable detail his attempts to deal with his own obsessions with vanity, pride, hypocrisy and self-deception, and other unnamed temptations in the context of his struggles with (lack of) religious belief. While this is not surprising to those who are familiar with Wittgenstein's life, what is striking is that he uses methods on himself that he also used in treating philosophical problems. Here are some parallels:

Change how you live:

Diary entry for February 4, 1937 (MS 183, p. 161; PPO, 169): "I may well reject the Christian solution of the problem of life (salvation, resurrection, judgement, heaven, hell) but this does not solve the problem of my life, for I am not good & not happy. I am not saved. And thus how can I know what I would envision as the only acceptable image of the world order if I lived differently, lived completely differently. I can't judge that. After all, another life shifts completely different images into the foreground, *necessitates* completely different images. Just like trouble teaches prayer. That does not mean that through the other life one will necessarily change one's *opinions*. But if one lives differently, one speaks differently. With a new life one learns new language games."

Notebook entry for August 27, 1937 (MS 118, p. 17r; CV, 27/31): "The solution of the problem you see in life is a way of living which makes what is problematic disappear."

Notebook entry for May 30, 1938 (MS 121, pp. 27r-v; RFM, 132): "The sickness of a time is cured by an alteration in the mode of life of human beings, and it was possible for the sickness of philosophical problems to get cured only through a changed mode of thought and of life, not through a medicine invented by an individual. Think of the use of the motor-car producing or encouraging certain sicknesses, and mankind being plagued by such sickness until, from some cause or other, as a result of some development or other, it abandons the habit of driving."

Change your surroundings:

Diary entry for February 19, 1937 (MS 183, p. 181; PPO, 189): "One could say, after all, 'Take some medicine (or search for some) so that the idea of this dependency goes away.' And I could imagine, of course, that it will go away. Also for example through a change of surroundings. And if one told me that I was sick now, this is perhaps also *true*. But what does it say?—This means, after all: '*Flee from this condition!*' And assume it ceased right now and my heart ceases to look into the abyss, able to direct its attention to the world again,—but this doesn't answer the question what I am supposed to do if that does not happen to me (for it doesn't happen through my wishing it)."

Diary entry for March 18, 1937 (MS 183, pp. 217–218; PPO, 225–227): "You have an incorrect concept when you get angry with fate. You should rearrange your concepts."

Recall from above: "another life shifts completely different images into the foreground, *necessitates* completely different images." (PPO, 169)

Recall from above: "We are inclined to compare some phenomena with something: I ask you to compare them with something else." (LPP, 168)

Don't explain; describe:

Diary entry for February 19, 1937 (MS 183, p. 183; PPO, 191): "Call it a sickness! What have you said by that? *Nothing*. Don't *explain*!—*Describe*! Submit your heart & don't be *angry* that you must suffer so!"

PI §109: "All *explanation* must disappear, and description alone must take its place."

Diary entry for February 21, 1937 (MS 183, p. 195; PPO, 203): "May gloom, the feeling of misery, somehow cleanse while I am writing all this!"

Alfred Nordmann, who translated this diary, comments (PPO, 6), "Instead of trying to express what he feels, he offers descriptions of his feelings."

While Wittgenstein is trying to treat himself, he is also offering treatment for philosophical problems:

Diary entry for February 8, 1937 (MS 183, p. 163; PPO, 171): "But now nothing is more important than making clear to ourselves which phenomena, which simple home-spun cases are the original picture of this idea. That is: When you are tempted to make general metaphysical statements, ask yourself (always): What cases am I actually thinking of?—What sort of case, which conception do I have in mind here? Now something in us resists this question for we seem to jeopardize the ideal through it: whereas we are doing it in order to put it in the place where it belongs. For it is supposed to be a picture with which we compare reality, through which we represent how things stand. Not a picture by which we falsify reality."

So when, in reply to Russell's question, "Are you thinking about logic or about your sins?" Wittgenstein replied, "Both," the answer didn't apply just in 1912 when he gave it, but still in 1937.[20] The difficulty of actually getting the problems to disappear, whether they be personal or philosophical, continued to nag him throughout his life—not only the problems but the inability to resolve them.

In 1950, in conversations in Oxford, Wittgenstein's friend Oets Bouwsma mentioned that he had been reading Dostoevsky's *Notes from Underground*. Wittgenstein "had read them a few years ago but he did not know what to make of them. He was puzzled that a man who could so clearly see and understand his own humiliation should not change."[21] One could say the same about Wittgenstein's own troubles.

It is notable that Wittgenstein's characterization of philosophy as a skill drops out of Wittgenstein's comments after the 1930 lectures—not that there was not a skill to creating helpful synopses for philosophical puzzles but that this was only a part, and perhaps the easier part, of the problem. The idea that "the method is found" seems simplistic.

The reason is brought out by Plato and his experiences with his friend and mentor Socrates. Socrates had a method too—the elenctic method. Socrates sought to show that people were confused about important matters by leading them to articulate their beliefs and then showing that the person's beliefs were inconsistent in some way. (*Elenchus* means refutation.) Socrates assumed that this would lead to a change in some of those beliefs and a consequent change in behavior. Socrates treated people as though to change them, all he had to do was deal with their beliefs. This is clear in his trial, when he refuses to put on an emotional display for the jurors (*Apology* 34c) and instead responds to the charges against him by cross-examining his accusers (*Apology* 24d)—trying to show that their beliefs were inconsistent. We can suppose he was successful in this, but it was not sufficient to save his life. One moral that Plato drew from this is that one needs to address the whole person—intellect *and* emotions. Thus it is that in the *Republic*, for example, he is concerned about training children from the start (maybe even for as long as fifty years!—*Republic* 540a), and he defines the just soul as one with a proper balance of reason, spirit, and appetite (*Republic* 441d-e). This goes well beyond the slogan of Socrates that "virtue is knowledge."

Aristotle, who also learned from Socrates's experience, sees the problem in a slightly different way. For Aristotle, the virtuous person is one whose judgments and emotions are properly aligned to produce the right actions (*Nicomachean Ethics* 1107a1–8). And as I mentioned in chapter 1, Aristotle gave his lectures only to those who were already able to put their judgments into action—whose emotions were mature. (However, he also held that one could *learn* to have the right emotions by repetition—doing what is right until one's feelings lined up with one's judgment; *NE* 1103b1–22.) For Aristotle, a person who had reason without proper feelings was merely clever or, we might say, skillful (*NE* 1144a25–28). But to be fully virtuous, a person had to have the proper temperament. Both Plato and Aristotle were concerned with moral education—temperament—as well as intellect. Socrates assumed that intellect, or reason, was all-powerful, and so there was no need for him to attend to the other aspects of the person. But that approach led to his trial and ultimately to his conviction and execution. (And, indeed, it cannot be said that there is any interlocutor in the early Socratic dialogues who is clearly improved by his encounter with Socrates.[22]) Aristotle put his critique of Socrates this way, without naming names:

> Now if arguments were in themselves enough to make men good, they would justly . . . have won very great rewards . . . ; but as things are, . . . they are not able to encourage the many to nobility and goodness. . . . What argument would remould such people? It is hard, if not impossible, to remove by argument the traits that have long since been incorporated in the character.[23]

And in parallel we find Wittgenstein saying things such as:

> Difficulty of philosophy not the intellectual difficulty of the sciences, but the difficulty of a change of attitude [*Umstellung*, conversion?]. Resistances of the will must be overcome. . . . Philosophy requires a resignation, but one of feeling and not of intellect. And maybe that is what makes it so difficult for many.[24]

> If it is said on occasion that (someone's) philosophy is a matter of temperament, there is some truth in this. A preference for certain comparisons [*Gleichnisse*] is something we call a matter of temperament & far more disagreement rests on this than appears at first sight.[25]

> I don't try to make you *believe* something you *don't* believe, but to make you *do* something you won't do.[26]

> Schopenhauer once said, "If you try to convince someone and get to a certain resistance, you then know you are up against the will, not the understanding." You are up against something else here. We have prejudices of thought.[27]

And this, I think, brings Wittgenstein closer to Plato. As Wittgenstein came to realize increasingly, and particularly by 1931, a person's temperament was at least as important as his skill in addressing philosophical (and, let us recall, personal spiritual) problems.

Plato's so-called Middle Dialogues had mythical stories in them. Wittgenstein's friend Oets Bouwsma reported a conversation that they had in 1950: "Wittgenstein reads Plato—the only philosopher he reads. But he likes the allegories, the myths" (61). Perhaps in the myths Wittgenstein saw the (CV 62/71; April, 1947) "quite different artillery" that he sought, but never found, in his own work (CV 24/28; 1933 or 1934): "I believe I summed up where I stand in relation to philosophy when I said: really one should write philosophy only as one writes a poem [*dichten*]. That, it seems to me, must reveal how far my thinking belongs to the present, the future, or the past. For I was acknowledging myself, with these words, to be someone who cannot quite do what he would like to be able to do."

In "the ancient quarrel between philosophy and poetry" (*Republic* 607B), we can see Wittgenstein wishing to side against Socrates but, I would say, also with Plato—who found ways of making philosophy poetic. Yet at certain times Wittgenstein expresses the feeling that he is unable to participate in the quarrel except on Socrates's terms.

Let us survey some of Wittgenstein's aims for his philosophy, to remind ourselves what it is he is trying to accomplish. While this is not meant to be an exhaustive list, it covers his main aims.

Aim A When considering instances of a concept, Wittgenstein said as early as the *Blue Book*, "We are inclined to think that there must be something in common" to all the instances (BB, 17). "Don't say: 'They *must* have something in common, or they would not be called [by that name]'—but *look and see* whether there is anything common to all" (PI §66). That is, don't insist on finding something common. A usable concept does not need to have a set of necessary and sufficient conditions—an essence. Wittgenstein sometimes gives the impression that he takes the position that concepts have no essence. But I think he is better understood as holding that they *needn't* have an essence. The point is that if you look, you *may not* find an essence, not that if you look you *will fail* to find an essence. The aim is to relieve the temptation to insist that all concepts have essences.[28]

One might approach this by showing that some particular concept in fact has no essence. That would then constitute an exception to the principle that all concepts have essences (a principle Socrates seems to accept), so that could be the point behind Wittgenstein's extended discussion of "game" in PI §66. But I don't see him as committed to proving *that* as an exception, or any particular concept as an exception. He is instead trying to show the kinds of considerations that point away from there being an essence. Wittgenstein went on to suggest that what held the instances of a concept together was "a complicated network of similarities overlapping and criss-crossing: similarities in the large and in the small." He characterized these similarities as "family resemblances" (PI §67), and held that they were sufficient to give the concept all the unity that it needed. So we could say that Wittgenstein's aim is to get people to stop *insisting* that concepts have an essence and to be *satisfied* with the sort of similarities among instances that he calls family resemblances.

Aim B When considering a set of similar phenomena, don't insist on finding a theory about them. Wittgenstein says that it "is our craving for generality" that "makes it difficult for us to take this line" (BB, 17). He calls this our "contemptuous attitude towards the particular case" (BB, 18). Wittgenstein identifies the source of this craving for generality as "our preoccupation with the method of science" (BB, 18). Wittgenstein has great respect for science, as indicated by his own extensive training in engineering and aeronautics. He certainly believes there are theories to be found and valued in science. But the problem arises when that attitude is carried over into all realms of life—for example:

> Philosophers constantly see the methods of science before their eyes, and are irresistibly tempted to ask and answer questions in the way science does. This tendency is the real source of metaphysics, and leads the philosopher into complete darkness. (BB, 18)

The issues here are similar to those concerning the search for an essence. Indeed, Wittgenstein discusses these together in the *Blue Book*. One can undermine the search for a theory by trying to show exceptions to any theory that is offered. But sometimes doing that is mistaken for arguing for a theory in the opposite direction—as though offering an exception constitutes advocating a theory of a different sort. So it is that when Wittgenstein argued against mentalism, he was then accused of advocating behaviorism. A voice in the *Investigations* accuses, "Aren't you nevertheless a behaviourist in disguise?" (PI §307). In fact, Wittgenstein did not believe in "isms" in philosophy. In this connection, he once said that he had considered using as the motto for his book (what was eventually published as the *Philosophical Investigations*) a line from Shakespeare:

> Hegel seems to me to be always wanting to say that things which look different are really the same. Whereas my interest is in showing that things which look the same are really different. I was thinking of using as a motto for my book a quotation from *King Lear*: "I'll teach you differences."[29]

But the matter of seeing or missing differences is not purely intellectual. In a lecture in 1938 he explains:

> I very often draw your attention to certain differences. . . . What I'm doing is also persuasion. If someone says "There is not a difference", and I say: "There is a difference" I am persuading, I am saying "I don't want you to look at it like that."[30]

For Wittgenstein, the *desire* to generalize and theorize raises the dangers of idealizing and oversimplifying. This is thus a balancing act. Science idealizes to a certain extent, but we have decided the costs of idealization are worth the benefits of theories in science. Wittgenstein does not see comparable benefits in other realms, including philosophy, and so he resists theories and wants us to resist the *temptation* to theorize as well.

Aim C A general principle that Wittgenstein adheres to is that explanations come to an end somewhere. He states it in so many words several times, including the opening paragraph of the *Investigations*. And he makes parallel claims that reasons, justifications, grounds, doubts, definitions, tests, and interpretations all come to an end.[31] He doesn't really see these claims as any kind of theories, because he sees them as truisms, or rules of grammar—and philosophy seeks to remind us of truisms: "Philosophy only states what everyone admits" (PI §599).[32]

But what goes beyond the truisms is that Wittgenstein sees us as tempted to push the desire for these explanations, and so forth, too far. In his view, they come to an end sooner than we think or are inclined to admit, so his aim is to counter our temptation to always push further. That temptation may have served us well in science, but he thinks it does us a disservice elsewhere. If Wittgenstein can relieve us of this sort of temptation, then it will allow us to rest content with concepts that are not defined (by an essence) or phenomena that are not explained (by a theory). But this will happen only if we can actually stop the search, the demand, for more. As he wrote in a notebook from 1933–1934:

> This is connected, I believe, with our wrongly expecting an explanation, whereas the solution of the difficulty is a description, if we give it the right place in our considerations. If we dwell upon it, and do not try to get beyond it.
>
> The difficulty here is: to stop.[33]

Wittgenstein makes the point, perhaps too strongly, in this way: "All *explanation* must disappear, and description alone must take its place" (PI §109). Perhaps his point could better be made by saying that at some point explanation must end and description take its place. This general aim, to get us to stop our *demand* for further . . . , is a component of the previous two aims.

Aim D When considering some phenomenon, don't try to understand it or consider it out of its context. One of Wittgenstein's students in the 1940s, Wasfi Hijab, reported that Wittgenstein "always emphasized the importance of context for understanding things—when we ignore the context, what remains is flawed."[34] Wittgenstein felt that philosophers were particularly prone to take concepts that have a place in ordinary language games and discuss and analyze them as though they retain a meaning outside those games. We can discuss in a law court what it means to act freely or not, but a philosopher wants to know if we ever are truly free. We can discuss whether we know or only believe that Saddam Hussein has weapons of mass destruction, but a philosopher wants to know whether we ever truly know anything. Words like *really* and *truly*, or capital letters, or emphatic pronunciation are signs that a word is being considered outside its context. Wittgenstein says that the philosophical "confusions that occupy us arise when language is, as it were, idling, not when it is doing work" (PI §132). And he continues the metaphor: "For philosophical problems arise when language *goes on holiday*" (PI §38). Instead: "What we do is bring words back from their metaphysical to their everyday use" (PI §116).

Context is especially important in trying to understand notions such as meaning or rule following. The tendency to treat such phenomena as independent of their context contributes to the feeling that what is characteristic of the phenomena must be found "in" the phenomena rather than in the role of the phenomena in relation to other things. This can lead us to suppose that understanding something is to be identified as the feelings we have when we take ourselves to understand something. Or that there is a kind of aura that accompanies the phenomena into any context. It also leads to the idea that concepts such as "simple" have a meaning that is independent of our interests in using the concept, such that we could look for what is absolutely simple, as he did in the *Tractatus*. In all these kinds of cases, Wittgenstein's aim is to get us to *attend to* rather than *ignore* the context.

Aim E When considering some rule, in mathematics or in the application of concepts, look for its basis in our human regularity, not in some sort of metaphysical reality.

This puts Wittgenstein most clearly in conflict with Plato, insofar as the Form of something, say the Beautiful, underlies the applicability of the concept, in that particular instances of beauty "participate" in the Form of the Beautiful (*Phaedo* 100b–d):

> I assume the existence of a Beautiful, itself by itself. . . . . . .If there is anything beautiful besides the Beautiful itself, it is beautiful for no other reason than that it participates in that Beautiful. . . . . . .Nothing else makes it beautiful other than the presence of, or the participation in, or however you may describe its relationship to that Beautiful we mentioned, for I will not insist on the precise nature of the relationship, but that all beautiful things are beautiful by the Beautiful.

Plato presents us with a powerful picture. A Form seems to be, in fact, a metaphysical embodiment and satisfaction of the Socratic (insistence on the) search for a definition. While Socrates rarely manages to articulate a satisfactory definition of anything, he remains convinced it is possible. And Plato affirms or assures this in metaphysical terms—the Form, so to speak, embodies what Socrates seeks. It may be that it is in fact beyond our capacity to put into words, but what we aim for or gesture at is "there" in some sense (*Republic* 509b–c): "although the Good is not being, but something yet beyond being, superior to it in rank and power." Glaucon then interjects: "By Apollo, what daemonic hyperbole!" (with a pun: superior power . . . , daemonic power). And Socrates confesses: "It is your own fault, you forced me to tell my beliefs about it." Here we see Plato himself starting to make fun of the idea, so in some similar fashion, Wittgenstein wants to loosen the hold that this picture, this way of looking at things, has on us.

But there are more recent examples of the same approach. Wittgenstein remarked about his colleague C. D. Broad: "Poor Broad thinks of philosophy as the physics of the abstract."[35]

Wittgenstein sees this picture playing itself out especially in mathematics. In this case, the "infinite" extent of mathematics exceeds our finite abilities and thus leads to a picture of mathematics that only God can fully know (PI §426):

> A picture is conjured up which seems to fix the sense unambiguously. The actual use, compared with that traced out by the picture, seems like something muddied. Here again, what is going on is the same as in set theory: the form of expression seems to have been tailored for a god, who knows what we cannot know; he sees all of those infinite series. . . . For us, however, these forms of expression are like vestments, which we may put on, but cannot do much with, since we lack the effective power that would give them point and purpose.

And (RFM, 408):

> What harm is done e.g. by saying that God knows *all* irrational numbers? Or: that they are already all there, even though we only know certain of them? Why are these pictures not harmless?

In all of these cases, Wittgenstein's aim is not to get us to believe a certain proposition, but to act in a certain way. He notes that our actions are a function of our inclinations and temptations, and so these are what he seeks to address.

Aim F When considering the substantives, or nouns, in our language, don't assume their grammar is always the grammar of physical objects, which provides for numerical identity beyond qualitative indiscernibility. In a lecture in 1936, Wittgenstein warned:

> We are tempted to use the grammar which we use for a word designating a physical object—we are tempted to use this grammar for words that designate impressions. In our primitive language most substantives relate to some physical object or another. When then we begin to talk of impressions, we have a temptation to use the same kind of grammar. . . . Our craving is to make the *grammar* of the sense datum similar to the grammar of the physical body.[36]

Or, as he puts it in a later lecture, "It seems to people unavoidable to hypostatize a feeling."[37] Just as language can have other functions than description, so too, nouns can designate without importing the grammar of physical objects. We need to broaden our view of the possibilities, instead of gravitating toward the familiar.

Wittgenstein has a more general concern about substantives, that they not be assumed to refer to entities of any kind. As he says in the opening lines of the Blue Book (BB, 1), "(We are up against one of the great sources of philosophical bewilderment: a substantive makes us look for a thing that corresponds to it.)" In this case, it might be a list of rules: "You wouldn't be so tempted to ask the question whether [the meaning is a list of rules], unless you supposed that when you have a substantive 'the meaning' you have to look out for something at which you can point & say 'this' is the meaning."[38] Wittgenstein sees Platonism about mathematics as falling into this kind of error—he suspects it is a sort of "alchemy": "Is it already mathematical alchemy, that mathematical propositions are regarded as statements about mathematical objects,—and mathematics as the exploration of these objects?" (RFM, 274).

Aim G And,. finally, of course, there is: "What is your aim in philosophy?—Show the fly the way out of the fly-bottle" (PI §309). Wittgenstein has certain methodological purposes, primarily associated with relieving a sort of fixation that we fall into when dealing with philosophical problems.

Wittgenstein came to look for an approach to philosophy that would go beyond the intellect and address the temptations and resistances of will. He sometimes sees this further move as a matter of poetry. It is not a substitute for his other methods, but a supplement—aiming at something else. In the next chapter, we survey his thoughts about, and his encounters with, this "poetry."

5 Wittgenstein and Poetry

While Wittgenstein was rather poorly read in the history of philosophy, his reading in literature, especially German-language literature, is impressive. He was raised in a highly cultured family in which literature was taken seriously. McGuinness reports, "Reading of books . . . —by Tolstoy, Kierkegaard, Dostoevsky and Gottfried Keller—was part of the culture of his generation of the family. They tended to model and guide their lives by literature such as this. It was perhaps their nearest approach to religion."[1]

When Wittgenstein was detained in a prisoner-of-war camp for several months after the First World War, he and his fellow prisoners spent endless hours reading aloud and discussing literature. His friend Ludwig Hänsel described the rich cultural life at the camp: "There was chamber music and gymnastics, soccer clubs and exhibitions of paintings. . . . Talks for example about satanism (weak) and Anderson's fairy tales (amusing). In general, a great number of talks and lectures. Everyone found his audience. The course of lectures about German literature the greatest and most appreciative one. . . . And there were plenty of books."[2] Hänsel commented on the depth of his reading at that time: "Wittgenstein has thoroughly appropriated what he read with pleasure. Knows a lot by heart and is self-taught. Reliably recognizes the best stuff, dogmatic resistance against all half-truths and falsehoods."[3] This fund of knowledge and depth of understanding served him all his life. Near the end of his life, in 1950, Wittgenstein's friend Bouwsma affirmed that Wittgenstein "when he reads, what he reads is in bright gold and shining and it is for so long imprinted and ready in his mind."[4]

Wittgenstein brought his love of literature to his teaching in elementary school in rural Austria in the 1920s. Only months into his first teaching assignment in Trattenbach, he wrote to his friend and now supervisor, Ludwig Hänsel, to order books for his students. He ordered books from a

Children's Library series, and by ordering one hundred copies altogether he was able to get a discount:

> 16 copies "30 German Legends from Grimm" [this is not the same as Grimms' Kinder- und Hausmärchen]
> 16 copies "Gulliver's Voyage to Lilliput" [by Jonathan Swift]
> 16 copies "Munchhausen's Travels on Land" [based on the adventures of Baron von Münchhausen]
> 16 copies "Selection from the Treasures" [by Johan Peter Hebel]
> 16 copies "The Caliph Stork" & "The Little Muck" [by Wilhelm Hauff]
> 16 copies "Fables from Lessing, Gellert, & Hebel" [that is, Gotthold Ephraim Lessing, Christian Fürchtegott Gellert and Johan Peter Hebel]
> 4 copies "2 Legends from Tolstoy" [namely, "Three Questions" & "What Men Live By"]

He promised to repay Hänsel the 500 crowns by postal order.[5]

Some insight into Wittgenstein's attraction to literature was provided by his old friend Rudolf Koder, a fellow teacher from his days in Puchberg, who said that "he read literature for two reasons: because he admired stylistic eloquence as found in the Mörike of 'Mozart auf der Reise nach Prag' and because he considered it philosophically profound as was the case with Busch's 'Eduards Traum.'"[6]

Beginning in 1927, Wittgenstein had occasional meetings with members of the Vienna Circle, especially Moritz Schlick, Friedrich Waismann, and sometimes others, such as Rudolf Carnap and Herbert Feigl. Wittgenstein was reluctant to have such meetings but eventually consented to some. The circle met on Thursday evenings at 6:00 p.m. in the gloomy mathematics seminar room on the ground floor of the University of Vienna science building complex on Boltzmanngasse. Circle members were interested to learn more about the *Tractatus*, which they had previously studied carefully—having read large portions of it aloud, discussing it "sentence by sentence," but, according to Feigl, "only on relatively rare occasions could we get [Wittgenstein] to clarify one or another of the puzzling or obscure passages in his work. . . . On occasion, he would read poetry to us (e.g., that of Rabindranath Tagore)."[7] When relating this latter fact Brian McGuinness adds "usually sitting with his back to the audience."[8]

In 1933 or 1934 Wittgenstein confessed in a notebook:

> I believe I summed up where I stand in relation to philosophy when I said: really one should write philosophy only as one *writes a poem* [*dichten*]. That, it seems to me, must reveal how far my thinking belongs to the present, the future, or the

> past. For I was acknowledging myself, with these words, to be someone who cannot quite do what he would like to be able to do.[9]

Ever since this passage was published in von Wright's edition of *Vermischte Bemerkungen* in 1977, scholars and students of Wittgenstein have wondered what it meant or could mean. The first problem this passage raises is how to translate *dichten*. Marjorie Perloff calls it "all but untranslatable, because there is no precise English equivalent to the German verb *dichten*—a verb that means to create poetry but also, in a wider sense, to produce something fictional, as in Goethe's *Dichtung und Wahrheit*, where fiction is opposed to truth." After discussing a number of proposed translations, Perloff prefers one by David Schalkwyk—"philosophy should be written only as one would *write poetry*"—and a more colloquial one by David Antin—"one should really only do philosophy as poetry."[10]

But apart from issues of translation, the passage is perplexing because, as Schalkwyk explained, "The problem arises both from the lack of a sustained context for the remark and the absence of any systematic use of the notion of the poetic or the verb '*dichten*' in Wittgenstein's writing."[11] In fact, however, there is considerably more context for this comment, which follows. But even so, we lack a larger narrative that makes sense of *why* he says what he does *when* he does. In this chapter, I provide a sense of what Wittgenstein meant by, and why he thought that, philosophy should be written as one would write poetry and how his views on this evolved over time.

There is actually a fair bit of additional evidence that can be brought to bear on this matter. Some of it Schalkwyk marshaled; some has not been noticed; some of it has come to light only recently. What follows is a chronological account of poetry (*Dichtung*) as it arises in Wittgenstein's life and work.

In Wittgenstein's 1927–1928 meetings with members of the Vienna Circle he sees reading poetry aloud as an alternative, even a preferred alternative, to discussing philosophy. Presumably he thinks that it shows what cannot be said. Apparently the *Tractatus* already had gone too far in putting these things into words, so now he will refrain from adding more words (of explanation).[12] Reading poetry aloud, with his back turned, seems a perfect performance of TLP 6.53: "The correct method in philosophy would really be the following: to say nothing except what can be said . . . and then, whenever someone wanted to say something metaphysical, to demonstrate [*nachzuweisen*] to him that he had failed. . . ." "Demonstrate," ten years on, does not mean *prove* but *point out*. "Although it would not be satisfying to the other person—he would not have the feeling we were teaching him philosophy—*this* method would be the only strictly correct one." This reminds one of the Zen master Duksan "teaching" (rather: training) his students to stop asking questions by slapping them with a *keisaku*.

In January 1929 Wittgenstein returns to Cambridge to do further research in philosophy. At Keynes's urging, he is welcomed back to the secret discussion group known as the Apostles into which he had been inducted in 1912. Keynes arranges a dinner on his second day back in Cambridge, and at several meetings in 1929 he makes the acquaintance of newer members, who were also associated with the Bloomsbury Group, including Julian Bell. But this reconnection did not last long due to severe differences of character, style, and value.[13]

Wittgenstein makes the acquaintance of the literary critic F. R. Leavis at an "at-home" sponsored by the elderly logician W. E. Johnson. On one occasion, which Leavis describes as "soon after [Wittgenstein's] return to Cambridge," Wittgenstein asks Leavis if he knows "a man called Empson." Leavis praises some poems of William Empson that he has just reviewed, including "Legal Fiction," which he reads aloud to Wittgenstein, who impresses Leavis with his impromptu articulation of its poetic analogical structure.[14] While Wittgenstein apparently had no previous acquaintance with Empson's poetry, he was widely read in German and Austrian poets.

On November 17, 1929, Wittgenstein delivers a lecture titled "Ethics" to the Heretics Society, a student group at Cambridge.[15] On January 20, 1930, he begins teaching at Cambridge—offering a lecture on Mondays and a discussion class later in the week.

In February 1930, Julian Bell publishes "An Epistle on the Subject of the Ethical and Aesthetic Beliefs of Herr Ludwig Wittgenstein (Doctor of Philosophy)"—a poetic critique of Wittgenstein, addressed to Richard Braithwaite, published in the student literary magazine the *Venture*.[16] Bell (1908–1937) was a history and English undergraduate student at King's College, Cambridge. He would have known Wittgenstein from meetings of the Apostles, and he may have attended the lecture on ethics. John Maynard Keynes described Bell as "a great lumbering lion-like creature, with thick tawny curls, a ridiculous nose and eyes . . . a big babyish joyful aesthete."[17] Bell's footnote to the poem's republication in 1932 indicates that it refers to Wittgenstein's views "on art and morals advocated by him three years ago"—that is, in 1929.[18] Bell's life ended prematurely when he was killed in the Spanish Civil War, where he served as an ambulance driver.

While Bell's critique of Wittgenstein casts interesting light on my thesis that Wittgenstein was still an esotericist in 1929, as discussed in chapter 1, what is interesting in this context is Bell's recommendation that poetry would be more effective in persuading Wittgenstein's audience:

> Reason dismist, how can he get his way?
> He may command, but we need not obey.
> His only method then is to persuade;
> He should have come to us to learn his trade.
> Persuasions, verse's great prerogative,
> By which the poets love, and sometimes live.
> Values all that philosophers escape
> The poets catch, and give them form and shape.
> His words t'express his meanings were too weak,
> But what if Racine, Milton chose to speak?
> In ten neat syllables forever lies
> All heroes feel, all knowledge of the wise:
> Where Dryden's couplets march with ringing stride
> There is no value missed or left outside.[19]

It is quite clear that Wittgenstein did not heed this advice at this time, if he even read it, but this offers an indication that the "ancient quarrel between poetry and philosophy" was on the minds of his listeners.[20] Bell may overstate the effectiveness of poetry, but he raises the issue and makes the case.

That Wittgenstein was not prepared to heed or even hear this advice at this time is clear from an incident at the February 7, 1930, meeting of the Cambridge Moral Sciences Club. At this meeting, attended by some thirty members with G. E. Moore in the chair, Richard Braithwaite gave a talk titled "Time." Apparently at one point, he "quoted poetry—Francis Thompson and Ronsard—and I am told," the student Arthur MacIver wrote, "that Wittgenstein mopped his brow in anguish, for he cannot abide the quoting of poetry in philosophical contexts." Wittgenstein's vivid reaction had to be reported to MacIver because "personally I was seated on the floor just under him and could not see his face."[21] Apparently the thirty attendees had more than filled the chairs squeezed into Braithwaite's rooms. Wittgenstein's negative reaction here fully accords with his scorn for those "Julian Bells."

In November 1930, as Wittgenstein was reflecting on his reading of Renan's *History of the People of Israel*, he praises the "*unpoetic* [*Undichterische*] mentality" of the Israelites, "which heads straight for what is concrete," and calls it "characteristic of my philosophy."[22]

In previous chapters, I have conjectured that around the early part of 1931, Wittgenstein began to have a special concern with the noncognitive issue of how to get other people to accept his views. In my view, this concern arose from his interactions with students in class (chapter 2), and then began to show itself in his writings (chapter 3). If poetry, or *Dichtung*, is especially well suited to influence people's attitudes, as Julian Bell proclaimed, and if Wittgenstein eventually *thought* that it was well suited to accomplish this, then that would account for his eventual interest in poetry as a mode of doing philosophy.

I. A. Richards is best known to philosophers for his association with C. K. Ogden, the publisher of Wittgenstein's *Tractatus*. The two of them coauthored *The Meaning of Meaning* in 1923. But Richards's connection to Wittgenstein actually predates the *Tractatus*. As a Cambridge undergraduate, Richards read "Moral Sciences" at Magdalene College and attended lectures by G. E. Moore in 1912 that Wittgenstein also attended.[23] In the book collaboration with Ogden, the first appendix, "On Grammar," was written by Richards and contained the first published discussion of the picture theory of the *Tractatus*. Richards did not encounter Wittgenstein again until he attended some of Wittgenstein's classes in 1930, Michaelmas 1931, and Michaelmas 1932.[24]

Richards apparently did not start writing poetry until the early 1950s, and in March 1960 he composed and published the poem "The Strayed Poet: Ludwig Wittgenstein."[25] The poem is based on the *Tractatus* and especially Richards's experience of Wittgenstein's lectures.[26] In a letter from Richards to his wife, he wrote, "I've begun a big poem on Ludwig Wittgenstein—in which I can put my own views on all the fundamental points over which he made such a mystery and a mess." On March 11, 1960, he reports to her: "I enclose the latest poem. 'The Strayed Poet'. May seem a little savage? But the wreckage that savage man has made of philosophy is something to wonder at. It may seem a little obscure in places—not though to those who have been in touch with *Tractatus* and with the disciples' attitudes to all others!"[27] In addition to writing this *as* a poem, Richards calls Wittgenstein a (strayed) "poet."[28]

Discussing the poem's publication in a letter of May 19, 1960, Richards writes: "It is likely to cause a little rumpus in some PHILOSOPHIC CIRCLES—as you know. . . . It would be fun if it could start a set of raids by poetry on philosophy! (Though, I suppose, they have almost always been going on. However, NOT, of late, in the most controversial areas.)"[29] So Richards also proposes to resurrect this ancient quarrel.

In August 1931, preceding the beginning of classes at Cambridge that Michaelmas term, Wittgenstein writes to his boss, G. E. Moore, "I've been very busy since I left Cambridge and have done a fair amount of work. Now I want you to do me a favour: I don't intend to give any formal lectures this term as I think I must reserve all my strength for my own work."[30] He did offer discussion classes, but this gave him more time to focus on what I think was a transition in his thinking about how to approach his work and engage his readers.

On November 7, 1931, Wittgenstein reflects in his diary on Kierkegaard's strategy of writing: "There is something teasing about Kierkegaard's writing. . . . There is also no doubt that one who teases me forces me to deal with his concern & if that concern is important, this is good."[31] Wittgenstein is concerned here with Kierkegaard's use of pseudonymous authorship. This gave Kierkegaard the ability to set out a view without endorsing it himself.[32]

Kierkegaard often refers to himself as a poet (*digter*, in Danish), and even a dialectical poet.[33] The Danish *digter* and its cognates *digtning* and *digte* have the same breadth of meaning that the German *Dichter*, *Dichtung*, and *dichten*, respectively, have. Kierkegaard's pseudonymous authorship is not unlike the way in which Plato uses the dialogue format as a tool to raise and investigate issues.[34] In fact, Socrates himself seems to have used this same sort of device through his claims of ignorance and his ironic speaking.[35] It is this poetic approach that allows Kierkegaard to engage the interest and passion of the reader.

We know Wittgenstein was deeply impressed by Kierkegaard's work. He learned Danish in order to be able to read Kierkegaard in the original, and he called him "by far the most profound figure of the last century."[36] But he is not quite so impressed by this aspect of his work (continuing the diary passage from above): "And yet there is something in me that condemns this teasing." Wittgenstein wonders if he suffers from some "ressentiment" here—resentment mixed with envy.[37] And he continues, "[Kierkegaard's] work already doesn't taste like the work of a poet [*Werk eines Dichters*]. He imitates the poet with as it were incredible mastery, but without being a poet & that he isn't one after all becomes noticeable in the imitation." Wittgenstein is unsure here of the source of his own feelings. Presumably he takes Kierkegaard to be fundamentally a philosopher and theologian, not a writer. He doesn't say what this "incredible mastery" of imitation is missing. But perhaps he suspects that Kierkegaard is still a better writer than he himself is.

Kierkegaard laid out the purpose for this pose in his "Point of View for My Work as an Author." He is interested in finding ways to address readers that take account of the reader's psychological state:

> There is a great difference . . . between these two situations: one who is ignorant and must be given some knowledge, and therefore he is like the empty vessel that must be filled or like the blank sheet of paper that must be written upon—and one who is under a delusion that must first be taken away. Likewise, there is also a difference between writing on a blank piece of paper and bringing out by means of chemicals some writing that is hidden under other writing. Now on the assumption that someone is under a delusion and consequently the first step, properly understood, is to remove the delusion—if I do not begin by deceiving, I begin with direct communication. But direct communication presupposes that the recipient's ability to perceive is entirely in order, but here that is simply not the case—indeed, here a delusion is an obstacle. That means a corrosive must first be used, but this corrosive is the negative, but the negative in connection with communicating is precisely to deceive. What then does it mean "to deceive"? It means that one does not begin *directly* with what one wishes to communicate but begins by taking the other's delusion at face value.[38]

This is just what Wittgenstein saw as his task as well, as I have discussed in chapters 3 and 4. When he edited remarks in MS 110 into typescript form—TS 211—gathering material together that pertained to Frazer, Wittgenstein moved these comments to the front:

> One must start out with error and convert it into truth.
>
> That is, one must reveal the source of error, otherwise hearing the truth won't do any good. The truth cannot force its way in when something else is occupying its place.
>
> To convince someone of the truth, it is not enough to state it, but rather one must find the *path* from error to truth.[39]

In fact, the "fair amount of work" that Wittgenstein reported doing while in Vienna that summer included reorganizing and dictating this very material.

But Kierkegaard's approach bothers Wittgenstein, being a sort of trick: "The idea that someone uses a trick to get me to do something is unpleasant. It is certain that it takes great courage (to use this trick) & that I would not—not remotely—have this courage; but it's a question whether if I had it, it would be right to use it. I *think* that aside from courage it would also take a lack of love of one's fellow human being."[40] There seem to be two separate concerns here: whether Wittgenstein would be able to do what Kierkegaard does and whether it would be right to do so if he could.

Wittgenstein sees his own situation as somewhat parallel to what he sees as Kierkegaard's situation. Kierkegaard is not really a poet, but he tries to use poetry—in this case, pseudonymous writing—as a tool "to get me to do something"—which is exactly what Wittgenstein himself wants to accomplish. Wittgenstein wrote in his notebook around this time, "I don't try to make you *believe* something you *don't* believe, but to make you *do* something you won't do."[41] At this point Wittgenstein is very skeptical about this use of poetry because he sees it as a kind of manipulation. Apart from any ability or inability to use this tool, he doesn't think he has either the courage or the right to use it.

Instead, what Wittgenstein proposes to use at this point is the now-famous notion of a perspicuous representation (*übersichtlichen Darstellung*).[42] But it remains to be seen how effective this can be in achieving Wittgenstein's goal. It at least has the advantage, in Wittgenstein's mind, that it involves no deception of the sort he detects in Kierkegaard.

In fall 1932, Nicholas Bachtin comes to Cambridge to do a PhD. Bachtin (1896–1950), younger brother of the Russian literary critic Mikhail Bakhtin, was a classicist and linguist with wide-ranging interests who became a close friend of Wittgenstein. His dissertation would be on the origins of the Centaur-Lapith myth. Nicholas had a great love and knowledge of poetry, and it may be that his friendship with Wittgenstein was instrumental in providing Wittgenstein with a more positive conception of poetry. Bachtin remained in Cambridge until 1935, and then held academic posts at Southampton and later Birmingham. Wittgenstein frequently visited Bachtin and his wife in Birmingham. What little we know about Bachtin and his relationship with Wittgenstein comes from a memoir by Fania Pascal, who refers to Bachtin as "an intimate friend of Wittgenstein's." She quotes Bachtin's wife as saying, "Wittgenstein loved Bachtin," and tells of "the interminable discussions that went on between the two men."[43] Bachtin had a great interest in poetry, and from his posthumously published papers it is possible to get some idea of how Wittgenstein might have thought about poetry, or at least how he heard Bachtin thinking about poetry.[44]

One of Bachtin's colleagues recalls, "It was most of all poetry that excited Bachtin, 'the musical illuminating word,' as he called it."[45] Wittgenstein's own search for what he called the *erlösende wort* is well known.[46] A friend of both Bachtin and Wittgenstein, the Marxist classicist George D. Thomson dedicated a book to Bachtin as follows: "He was by nature a poet, but, compelled by circumstances to forego the writing of poetry . . . [47]

In one of his papers, titled "Pushkin," Bachtin discusses a poem by Alexander Pushkin about his late classmate Anton Delvig (the four lines "are from a poem written in 1831 for the anniversary banquet . . ."): "Poetry like that rings in one's memory, follows one through life; it has a nourishing and sustaining power such as no precept of wisdom or metaphysical truth can ever have; it brings with it the intense feeling of significance and joy. . . . those latent potencies of expressive language on whose working Pushkin's poetry is mainly dependent."[48] Here Bachtin emphasizes the noncognitive aspects of Pushkin's poetry. In another essay, Bachtin returns to this idea: "As such, poetry is capable of a direct, quasi-magical action on reality which it is called upon to transform."[49]

Bachtin does not consider Tolstoy's work to be (what he calls) poetry.[50] But it certainly falls within the German concept of *Dichtung*, and it has just the effect Wittgenstein seeks. In his essay "Tolstoy's *War and Peace*," Bachtin explains what he takes to be the Russian approach to art: "The attitude is best summed up in a familiar Russian formula which is so simple and so self-evident that it may seem almost ingenuous: 'Art must teach us how to live.'" He continues by insisting, "There is no other work [save for *War and Peace*] to which the formula that 'Art teaches us how to live' seems to apply more directly or more obviously. And it teaches us how to live not by means of ideas or moral precepts but by affecting our reactions, by sharpening our vision and extending our direct experience far beyond its natural limits."[51] Wittgenstein would have been interested in its ability to teach us "by affecting our reactions." Recall McGuinness's characterization (quoted above) of the role of literature in Wittgenstein's family: "Reading of books . . . —by Tolstoy, Kierkegaard, Dostoevsky and Gottfried Keller—was part of the culture of his generation of the family. They tended to model and guide their lives by literature such as this."

Wittgenstein opens the chapter titled "Philosophy" in the 1933 Big Typescript with this heading: "Difficulty of philosophy not the intellectual difficulty of the sciences, but the difficulty of a change of attitude. Resistances of the will must be overcome." And then he makes reference to Tolstoy in this vein:

> Tolstoy: . . . What makes a subject difficult to understand—if it is significant, important—is not that some special instruction about abstruse things is necessary to understand it. Rather it is the contrast between the understanding of the subject and what most people want to see. Because of this the very things that are most obvious can become the most difficult to understand. What has to be overcome is not a difficulty of the intellect, but of the will.[52]

Here Wittgenstein is alluding to Tolstoy's views in "What Is Art?" He prefaces the comment with: "The meaning (meaningfulness) of a subject lies in its being generally understandable." This is one of Tolstoy's main points in that essay: "The assertion that art can be good art and yet be incomprehensible to a large number of people is so wrong. . . . Great works of art are great only because they are accessible and comprehensible to everyone."[53]

The reason Tolstoy holds this view is that for him, the purpose of art is to move us by conveying a feeling from the artist to the spectator or reader or listener: "If the work of art has the aim of infecting people with the feeling experienced by the artist, how then can we speak of incomprehension?"[54] If it fails in this purpose, it is not art (or not good art).[55] Wittgenstein is applying this approach to philosophy. The difficulty is one of the will—(effective) philosophy must engage the will and move us, just as with (effective) art. Can we say, effective art and philosophy are affective?

Rush Rhees was a doctoral student who came to Cambridge in fall 1933 to study with G. E. Moore. He eventually began to attend Wittgenstein's lectures in earnest in the 1935 Michaelmas term and went on to become a close friend of Wittgenstein—later being designated one of Wittgenstein's literary executors in his will. But it turns out that Rhees also attended some of Wittgenstein's lectures right away in the 1933 Michaelmas term. Rhees never mentioned this earlier encounter in his published memoirs, but a recently discovered letter (written in German) testifies to it. In a letter to a former teacher at the University of Innsbruck, Alfred Kastil, on November 5, 1933,[56] he explains that he had attended a couple (*ein Paar Mal*) of Wittgenstein's lectures but did not intend to continue. After characterizing Wittgenstein's style, he comments on his method:

> He constantly talks in *Gleichnissen* (which are only partly real examples), and says himself that he always thinks in *Gleichnissen*. If something is not clear, then he does not seek to give an explanation in simple sentences, but he looks for a new *Gleichniss*. This method combines, however, with his philosophical position according to which the answer to the most important philosophical questions is not given by propositions and theories, but can be "*shown*" only through *Gleichnisse* or "symbolic forms."[57]

This letter is interesting for more than one reason. As far as I know, there are no students' notes from Wittgenstein's regular lectures on philosophy during this academic year, so this provides at least (and at last) a glimpse of them.[58] But more interesting, it shows Wittgenstein's particular concern with how his ideas were conveyed.

The German term *Gleichnis* occurs in various forms in much of Wittgenstein's writing.[59] However, its presence is obscured for English readers by the fact that it gets translated in various ways—likeness, simile, comparison, and parable.[60] All of these are plausible translations and appropriate in one context or another, yet they differ from each other. Probably "comparison" is often the most natural.

In dictations Wittgenstein made in English to his student Francis Skinner in the so-called Pink Book, we find, "Examples and similes are always useful. If I could give you enough of them, that would be all that would be necessary. Usually we think of similes as second-best things, but in philosophy they are the best thing of all."[61] The Pink Book has not been convincingly dated, though it is likely around 1933–1934. Presumably Wittgenstein is here mentioning similes in English, where he would have said *Gleichnisse* in German. Much later, Wittgenstein's last student, Wasfi Hijab, recalled that "Wittgenstein sometimes spoke in metaphors and parables." Introducing a particular story, Wittgenstein said, "I will call this a 'parable,' the parable of the wall."[62] So Wittgenstein (like his translators) also used various English words to characterize his approach.

Jesus is well known for telling parables in the gospel accounts. Luther's German translation of the Bible renders these consistently as *Gleichnisse*.[63] And Wittgenstein adopts this German word for them. In a notebook he wrote, "The *Gleichnisse* of the N. T. leave room for as much depth of interpretation as you like. They are bottomless." This was incorporated into the 1998 edition of *Culture and Value*, where, unfortunately, Winch rendered it as "the comparisons of the N. T. . . ."![64] When Jesus introduces his parables, he says things like, "The kingdom of Heaven is likened unto [King James Version]/ may be compared to [Jerusalem Bible]" (Matthew 13:24, 18:23). Wittgenstein is well known for presenting imaginary scenarios in his later work. They have the fictitious character of *Dichtung* and can be seen as parables.

Kierkegaard wrote hundreds of parables, incorporating them into his pseudonymous and nonpseudonymous works.[65] They constitute an important part of his attempt to deceive through indirect communication and thereby bring readers "into what is true."[66] In the introduction to a collection of Kierkegaard's parables, the editor writes, "Kierkegaard's parables aim not merely at a change of mind but a change of will. Kierkegaard does not tell his parables with the expectation that his hearers will experience a casual illumination or fascination, but rather that they might say to themselves, 'Aha! I know how it is and it makes a difference in the way I understand myself and make fundamental choices!'"[67] This is what Wittgenstein is seeking, and so he sees Kierkegaard as a fellow traveler.

Sometime in 1933 or 1934, during the same year of classes that Rhees just reported on, Wittgenstein writes the following lines, separated in a notebook (MS 146) as indicated:

> p. 32: "(The presentation of philosophy can only be composed as a poem [*nur gedichtet warden*].)"
>
> . . .
>
> p. 50/=25v: "I believe I summed up where I stand in relation to philosophy when I said: really one should write philosophy only as one *writes a poem* [*eigentlich nur dichten*]. That, it seems to me, must reveal how far my thinking belongs to the present, the future, or the past. For I was acknowledging myself, with these words, to be someone who cannot quite do what he would like to be able to do."[68]
>
> . . .
>
> p. 55: "Ease of mind occurs in philosophy when the redeeming word is found."

It is unclear what Wittgenstein is referring to when he writes, "I believe I summed up where I stand in relation to philosophy when I said . . ." This could well refer to the statement eighteen pages earlier in the notebook, which I have just quoted. But then he did write "when I *said* [*sagte*]," so it may refer to lectures or conversations. Yet no such lines have been found in lecture notes either. The subject may have come up in conversations with Bachtin.

When Wittgenstein writes that he is "someone who cannot quite do what he would like to be able to do," he is indicating a change of mind from his earlier reflections on Kierkegaard. He still does not think he can do philosophy as poetry in this way, but he now would "like to." Apparently he has lost his qualms about this.

At around the same time, in MS 115, Wittgenstein takes remarks from MS 146 and other sources and compiles them into a further draft, where he has chosen to place the three remarks from MS 146 just quoted above into a consecutive passage (p. 30):

> (The presentation of philosophy can only be composed as a poem.)
>
> (Really one should write philosophy only as one *writes a poem* [*dichten*]. That, it seems to me, must reveal how far my thinking belongs to the present, the future, or the past. For I was acknowledging myself, with these words, to be someone who cannot quite do what he would like to be able to do.)
>
> Ease of mind occurs in philosophy when the redeeming word is found.

Since Wittgenstein places the lines from pages 32 and 50 next to each other and deletes the phrase, "I believe I summed up where I stand in relation to philosophy when I said . . . ," this gives a strong indication that it was that very line that he was referring back to. But his repair is not extensive enough, since he has in left in place, "For I was acknowledging myself, with these words," which is awkward without the earlier phrase.

By bringing the last line, about the redeeming word, together with the line about doing philosophy as poetry, we again see Wittgenstein connecting how philosophy is done with its noncognitive effect.

It is well known that Wittgenstein was obsessed with Dostoevsky's *Brothers Karamazov*. In 1949, Wittgenstein's friend O. K. Bouwsma commented that "he [Wittgenstein] must have read every sentence there fifty times."[69] Now that we can see the nature of Wittgenstein's interest in poetry, it is noteworthy that Dostoevsky has Ivan call his famous story of the Grand Inquisitor a "poem" [*поэма*, which seems to be roughly equivalent in breadth to *Gedicht* in German]; in fact, Ivan calls it a poem seven times in the course of introducing and telling it—for example: "My poem is called 'The Grand Inquisitor'; it's a senseless thing, but I want to tell it to you."[70]

Some four years pass during which Wittgenstein continues to teach in Cambridge for two years, visits Russia to investigate the possibility of moving there, spends over a year living alone in Norway, and then returns to Cambridge. On April 23, 1938, in MS 120, he writes: "If, rather than a more correct way of thinking, I want to teach a new movement of thought [*Gedankenbewegung*], my purpose is a 're-valuation of values,' and with this I come to Nietzsche as well as to the opinion [*meiner Ansicht*] that the philosopher should be a poet [*Dichter*]."[71] "Revaluation of all values!" is the closing line of Nietzsche's "The Antichrist."[72] Wittgenstein's remark here brings together various themes of interest.

By distancing himself from seeking "a more correct way of thinking," Wittgenstein seems to be suggesting that mere cognitive correctness is not his goal (or his primary goal). Rather, he characterizes his goal as conveying "a new movement of thought" that constitutes a "revaluation of values." His concern is with changing noncognitive uptake—what one cares about—and this requires a poetic approach. This does not seem to be any kind of endorsement of Nietzsche's own revalued values but of Nietzsche's concern with that sort of thing, and with his attempt to approach it in a nonstandard literary fashion.[73]

The phrase *Gedanken bewegung* has a notable history in Wittgenstein's thinking, leaving its mark several times over the years.[74] It embodies something like a perspective, for which he sees a contrast between, on the one hand, an artist's or his own current work, and, on the other, that of scientists and even that of his own earlier work. This kind of difference creates a difficulty of understanding, which can be discerned in the history of the mind, mental concepts, and the situation of those so separated. And he here shows a concern to change this movement of thought—but it will be not by conveying new facts or thoughts but by changing how one thinks. He thinks that for this job, a "philosopher should be a poet."[75]

Sometime in the period February to April 1940, Wittgenstein writes in a notebook: "I am a second-rate poet [*Dichter*]. If I am also as a one-eyed king among the blind. Yet a second-rate poet would do better to give up poetry [*das Dichten aufzugeben*]. Even if he stands out among his fellow men."[76] This continues the pessimism of 1933–1934 that Wittgenstein "cannot quite do what he would like to be able to do." And perhaps it renews the qualms of 1931 that it would not "be right" for a second-rate poet to do this.

Recently notes by Rush Rhees of a number of his conversations with Wittgenstein have been published. While Rhees does not date this particular conversation, it seems to fall sometime in the span of 1945 to 1946:

> I remember one time when Wittgenstein was mentioning Nietzsche's remark: "We—i.e. philosophers—want to be learnt by heart."[77] Wittgenstein was emphasizing the difference between a book on philosophy and a theoretical or scientific work. He was completing the Part I of the *Investigations*.[78] In connexion with this "We want to be learned by heart", he said that he could understand why certain ancient philosophers had tried to write what they had to say as poems.[79] (Once or twice later he referred to his manuscripts of the *Investigations* as "my poems.")

Rhees concludes his recollection: "I made some silly bantering remark such as: 'Well, why don't you do that?' 'Yes,' said Wittgenstein. 'Now let's imagine what that would be like. Suppose I wrote it all in a poem. And then people would write about this, in *Mind*. . . . !'"[80] Here we have an ambiguity between writing the *Investigations* as a poem, presumably in the stylistic sense of rhythm and rhyme, and writing it as *Dichtung*. It would seem that he considers himself to be attempting the latter ("my poems") while rejecting the former ("in a poem"). This suggests that Wittgenstein has been trying, and sees himself as trying, to meet the challenge he set out in 1933–1934.

Iris Murdoch studied philosophy at Cambridge beginning in 1947 and was friendly with several of Wittgenstein's former students. While she did not know Rhees, she did know Wittgenstein's students Wasfi Hijab, Kanti Shah, and Georg Kreisel. In a February 11, 1948, letter, she wrote: "I was much struck by a remark of [Wittgenstein's] quoted to me lately, about the book he is writing now. He said: 'This stuff is no good. If this was *philosophy* one could learn it by heart.'"[81]

Presumably a poetic approach helps one learn philosophy "by heart," not because it rhymes but because it imprints the lessons on one's heart, so to speak. The lessons constitute a change of heart, as we say. And learning the philosophy by heart means that it has changed one's movement of thought. It has led not just to a change of beliefs but to a change of dispositions.

Around the same time (October 31, 1946), Wittgenstein laments in one of his notebooks, "Oh, why does it seem to me as if I were writing a poem [*schrieb ich ein Gedicht*] when I am writing philosophy?"[82] This confirms his attempt to meet the challenge in the way he described to Rhees and supports the conjectured dating of that conversation.

In the interval before his last term of teaching Wittgenstein writes (April 5, 1947):

> Just as I cannot write verse [*Verse*], so too I can only write prose *up to a certain point*, & no further. There is a quite definite limit to my prose, & I can no more overstep *it*, than I would be able to write a poem [*ein Gedicht zu schreiben*]. *This* is how my equipment is constituted; it is the only equipment available to me.[83]

Here Wittgenstein again seems to be equating writing a poem with writing in verse. Presumably that is not what he imagined in his 1933–1934 challenge. While we must be careful to distinguish between verse in the narrow sense and poetry in the broader sense, it is possible that Wittgenstein is becoming more pessimistic (not that he was ever really optimistic) about his ability to write "poetry" well enough to accomplish what he hopes.

The pessimistic turn in Wittgenstein's thinking is confirmed not two weeks later (April 13 or 14, 1947) by two remarks he writes in his notebook: "Quite different artillery is needed here from anything I am in a position to muster." And "(It is as though I wanted to change men's and women's fashions by talking.)"[84]

I believe that this marks an admission of defeat in Wittgenstein's attempts to teach and to write in a way that will accomplish his goal of changing people's movement of thought. It comes just before his very last term of teaching at Cambridge. And it comes at a point when I imagine he may have begun to give up on his attempt to address the noncognitive elements of philosophy in his writing. I think the "different artillery" he has in mind is primarily the ability to write philosophy as poetry or other means than prose that addresses only the cognitive aspect of philosophical problems.

In May 1947, Wittgenstein gives his final course lectures at Cambridge. He later said his reasons for retiring from teaching were that he wished to finish his book and that his teaching was unsuccessful.[85] After a sabbatical in the Michaelmas term, he resigns at the end of the year.

On December 16, 1948, in his notebook, Wittgenstein contemplates his dilemma: "Are you a bad philosopher then, if what you write is hard to understand. If you were better, then you would make it easy to understand what is difficult—But who says that is possible?! [Tolstoy]."[86] Here again he returns to Tolstoy's view about art—that good art is understandable. What Wittgenstein means by understanding, as in the earlier context, has to do with uptake and the will, not just with intellectual comprehension. The matter of being "hard to understand" concerns whether one is successful in addressing the noncognitive aspects of philosophy. Here he affirms the goal but again expresses pessimism about meeting it.

Piero Sraffa was a long-time conversation partner with Wittgenstein. They met shortly after Wittgenstein's return to Cambridge in 1929, and Wittgenstein credited him, in the Preface to the *Philosophical Investigations*, with stimulation that led to "the most consequential ideas in this book." While they met regularly for about ten years, their relationship gradually deteriorated after that, at least so far as their intellectual discussions went. In summer 1949, Wittgenstein visits his friend and student Norman Malcolm in Ithaca, New York, for three months. While he is there, he writes to Sraffa, summing up his view of their relationship, which he took to have a more general moral:

> I have *very slowly* in my life come to the conviction that some people *cannot make themselves understood to each other*, or at least only in a very narrowly circumscribed field. . . . In order to understand why it's impossible, or almost impossible, for certain people to understand each other, one has to think *not* of the few occasions on which they meet, but of the differences of their *whole lives*; and there can be nothing more different than your interests and mine, and your movements of thought and mine.[87]

Whereas in 1938 Wittgenstein was trying to "teach a new movement of thought," he now no longer sees how that would be possible.

Finally, in 1950, Wittgenstein writes the following in a notebook: "I think that in order to enjoy a poet [*Dichter*] you have to *like* the culture to which he belongs as well. If you are indifferent to this, or repelled by it, your admiration cools off."[88] I don't know that Wittgenstein meant this line to apply to himself as a writer or to philosophy as a subject to be addressed. But in my book *Wittgenstein in Exile*, I proposed that most contemporary philosophers are indifferent to Wittgenstein or have at best a cool admiration for him because they do not like the nineteenth-century culture with which he identified himself and the associated inclination to stop explanation. I ended the book with that quotation.

So, that is a time line of Wittgenstein's comments on and dealings with poetry from the 1920s onward. Based on this, I believe that we can construct a narrative that makes sense of *why* he says *what* he does *when* he does about philosophy and poetry.

At the time of the *Tractatus* and the meetings with members of the Vienna Circle, Wittgenstein sees poetry as something that can fill the silence commended at TLP 7: as something that can show what cannot be said. This is clear in Wittgenstein's correspondence with Engelmann about the poem by Johann Ludwig Uhland, "Count Eberhard's Hawthorn," where he writes: "The poem by Uhland is really magnificent. And this is how it is: if only you do not try to utter what is unutterable then *nothing* gets lost. But the unutterable will be—unutterably—*contained* in what has been uttered!"[89] While the transition away from the views of the *Tractatus* from the late 1920s to the early 1930s is not perfectly clear or easily summarized, Wittgenstein continues to maintain a definite separation of philosophy from poetry. His anguish over "the quoting of poetry in philosophical contexts" in early 1930 fits this separation.

But as a result of his teaching, beginning in January 1930, Wittgenstein came to see, roughly by spring 1931, that it was important to address the difficulties that his students had accepting his views. Thus, he came to see the need to address what I am calling the noncognitive aspects of philosophy. His appreciation of this need is clear from passages from 1931 to 1933, where he claims that philosophy is as much a matter of the will as the intellect, so he tries to find ways to address the will. This is shown in his concern for things like our "temptations" and "inclinations." He begins to address these in his classes and then in his writings. But he struggles to find a way to address them successfully. Poetry (or *Dichtung*) seems to be one possibility—a possibility he took seriously from about 1931 until the late 1940s. He struggles with this possible form of doing philosophy both because of his inability and his qualms about its legitimacy. But as he develops his own dialogic style of writing, which I believe originates in his lectures and which has some resonance with Plato's dialogic style, and as he creates and reflects on imaginary scenarios, he sees these as a sort of *Dichtung*—poetry in a broad sense. Thus, he talks about his passages as "my poems" and himself as a "second-rate poet." This is Wittgenstein's newly forged artillery.

In the next chapter, we turn to some specific examples of how Wittgenstein tries to do philosophy as poetry.

6 Wittgenstein's Poems

In the early 1930s, Wittgenstein lamented his inability to write poetically. Yet not only did he write poems; later he even thought of himself as writing poems.

We know of two poems by Wittgenstein, both apparently written for Marie Fillunger, a family friend and a highly regarded singer of his mother's generation, and both expressing thanks for her knitting socks for him! One, written in 1925 on the occasion of Fillunger's seventy-fifth birthday, entitled "*Gesang an Filu* [Song for Filu]," praises her singing and her knitting woolen socks; the other, written perhaps a year later, when Wittgenstein was a gardener, again alludes to socks. Both are written in a standard rhythmic rhyming form.[1] Fillunger was frequently a guest at the Wittgenstein household and occasionally sang *Lieder* to his mother's piano accompaniment. Why she and her socks provoked Wittgenstein to poetic expression is not clear.

More interesting, though, is how Wittgenstein came to think about his philosophical work. Rush Rhees, as noted in the previous chapter, commented on Wittgenstein's lectures in the 1933 Michaelmas term as follows:

> He constantly talks in *Gleichnissen* [in similes, parables?] (which are only partly real examples), and says himself that he always thinks in similes. If something is not clear, then he does not seek to give an explanation in simple sentences, but he looks for a new simile. This method combines, however, with his philosophical position according to which the answer to the most important philosophical questions is not given by propositions and theories, but can be "*shown*" only through similes or "symbolic forms."[2]

This letter shows Wittgenstein's concern with *how* his ideas were conveyed and presumably received.

Wittgenstein is well known for presenting imaginary scenarios in his later work. They have the fictitious character of *Dichtung*. "Simile" might be the best translation for *Gleichnis*, except that Rhees says that they are "only partly real examples," which does not sound quite appropriate for similes. Perhaps the main difference between similes and parables is one of length. Kierkegaard wrote hundreds of vignettes, incorporating them into his pseudonymous and nonpseudonymous works.[3] They constitute an important part of his attempt to deceive through indirect communication and thereby bring readers "into what is true." Sometimes Wittgenstein called them simply "examples." Isaiah Berlin recollected, "I felt I was in the presence of a very demanding genius: . . . the examples were wonderful—'Half a mo,' half a mo,' I will think of an example.'"[4]

Recently, Rush Rhees's notes of a number of his conversations with Wittgenstein were published. While Rhees does not date this particular conversation, it seems to fall sometime in the span of 1945–1946: "I remember one time when Wittgenstein was mentioning Nietzsche's remark: 'We—i.e. philosophers—want to be learnt by heart.'[5] Wittgenstein was emphasizing the difference between a book on philosophy and a theoretical or scientific work. He was completing the Part I of the *Investigations*.[6] In connexion with this 'We want to be learned by heart', he said that he could understand why certain ancient philosophers had tried to write what they had to say as poems.[7] (Once or twice later he referred to his manuscripts of the *Investigations* as 'my poems.')"[8] At what is likely to be around the same time (October 31, 1946), Wittgenstein wonders in one of his notebooks, "Oh, why does it seem to me as if I were writing a poem [*schrieb ich ein Gedicht*] when I am writing philosophy?"[9] So Wittgenstein eventually comes to see himself as writing poetry, at least in the German sense of *Dichtung*.

Wasfi Hijab was one of Wittgenstein's students from 1945 to 1947. Wittgenstein was officially the director of his dissertation, which was planned on the relationship between science and religion. In addition to attending Wittgenstein's classes, Hijab and Elizabeth Anscombe met twice weekly with Wittgenstein to discuss philosophy of religion. These meetings "were typically spent walking around the Trinity fellows' garden . . . deep in discussion. Wittgenstein occasionally told rich, colorful stories. Hijab called these insightful stories 'parables.'" In a taped interview from 2002, Hijab said, "Wittgenstein sometimes spoke in metaphors and parables," and in introducing one of these stories about a wall, Wittgenstein "said, 'I will call this a "parable," the parable of the wall.'"[10] We will examine this "parable" later in the chapter.

In this chapter, I present some of Wittgenstein's imaginary scenarios and compare them with parables and stories from other sources. These are not the better-known scenarios from the *Philosophical Investigations*, such as the grocer counting out five red apples or the builder ordering slabs (§§1, 2). I hope to show that these kinds of vignettes, which Wittgenstein thought of as parables and poems, might have had a noncognitive purpose—one that is familiar to writers and relatively unfamiliar to standard philosophers. These are vignettes that are quite memorable in Wittgenstein's work or have the potential to be memorable—the sort of thing that one might well "learn by heart." In juxtaposing these vignettes with parables from other writers, I am not suggesting that Wittgenstein was taking an idea or an approach from another source, though this is possible in some cases. Rather, I want to see how what Wittgenstein is trying to do is comparable to what some writers do—*dichten*. I think that is what he meant when he said that philosophy ought to be done as poetry. But it is also important to remember that Wittgenstein did not feel that he was ultimately successful in accomplishing this. Nevertheless, we have evidence that he kept trying into the 1940s.

Nuno Venturinha has recently noted, "It is highly significant that so many scholars write on Wittgenstein but no one has adopted his heterodox literary style, still less the poetic discourse he suggests."[11] What follows is my attempt to explore how Wittgenstein might have made use of such poetic discourse.

Here are some of Wittgenstein's poems that I discuss. They range from memorable one-sentence aphorisms to longer parables:

Wittgenstein's Poems

1. Parable of the Seeds
2. The Lion
3. The Woodsellers
4. 5 O'Clock on the Sun
5. "Bububu"
6. The 2-Minute Man
7. "We Are Only Doing Philosophy"

8. The Fly Bottle
9. Parable of the Wall
10. Can an Animal Hope?
11. Rembrandt
12. Games
13. "An Expression Has Meaning Only in the Stream of Life"
14. Beetle in the Box
15. "Tell Them I've Had a Wonderful Life"

Parable of the Seeds

Almost right from the start in the *Philosophical Investigations*, Wittgenstein presents a scenario in which a shopkeeper selects five red apples. In answer to the question *how* he is able to operate with the words *red* and *five*, we are told, "Explanations come to an end somewhere" (PI §1). In the later notes collected as *On Certainty* (§34), he reiterates: "But these explanations must after all come to an end." This is a truism—Wittgenstein might have called it a rule of grammar—but it is a truism that, oddly enough, is easy to lose sight of. It's the kind of thing we need to be reminded of (PI §127): "The work of the philosopher consists in assembling reminders for a particular purpose." What is that purpose? Well, for instance, we tend to push too far in our drive to understand. Yet not everything can get explained (Z §315): "'Why do you demand explanations? If they are given you, you will once more be facing a terminus. They cannot get you any further than you are at present.'" Indeed, "Explanations come to an end somewhere."

And the truism holds not just for explanations, but for reasons (PI §326 and BB, 143): "the chain of reasons has an end"; justifications (OC §192 and PI §485): "justification comes to an end"; grounds (OC §204 and §110): "giving grounds . . . comes to an end"; doubting (PPF §32 and PO, 377): "Doubting has an end"; testing (OC §164); substantiation (OC §563) and interpretation (RFM, 342): "Interpretation comes to an end." In each case the drive for further . . . explanations, reasons, justifications, grounds, doubts, tests, interpretations . . . leads us ultimately in either a circle or an infinite regress. That is the truism.

Being truisms, these claims are apt for inclusion in Wittgenstein's philosophical remarks. He holds (PI §599), "Philosophy only states what everyone admits." And as a preface to his 1941 discussions with Robert Thouless (PPO, 382), "Wittgenstein started by saying that all statements he would make would be obviously true. If I could challenge any of them he would have to give way. Might seem trivial and unimportant because so obviously true. But going over things already known to and accepted by me, he would make me see things in a new way."

If we accept these truisms, then we will come to realize that it is untenable to feel that there *must* be a further . . . explanation, reason, justification, ground, interpretation in every situation. And so we can relax, content that, say, some words cannot, or may not, be given essentialist definitions. But Wittgenstein's use of these truisms is generally more ambitious than this, for he usually wants to insist that justification, say, ends not just *somewhere*, but *sooner than we expected*. It ends . . . here (PI §217): "If I have exhausted the justifications I have reached bedrock, and my spade is turned. Then I am inclined to say: 'This is simply what I do.'"

For Wittgenstein, it is important not only *that* we stop but *where* we stop. In a lecture on April 28, 1947, one student reported that Wittgenstein said, "It is important in philosophy to know when to stop—when not to ask a question." Another student reports this as, "One of the great difficulties in philosophy is to know where to stop."[12]

This challenge, to know when/where to stop, can be found most infamously in Wittgenstein's parable of the seeds (which is very different from Jesus's parable of the seeds, discussed later in another context). The parable does not appear in the *Philosophical Investigations* but is well known from *Zettel* (sourced and cited here from RPP1; selected by Wittgenstein from MS 134; April 3–4, 1947):

> §903. No supposition seems to me more natural than that there is no process in the brain correlated with associating or with thinking; so that it would be impossible to read off thought-processes from brain-processes. I mean this: if I talk or write there is, I assume, a system of impulses going out from my brain and correlated with my spoken or written thoughts. But why should the *system* continue further in the direction of the centre? Why should this order not proceed, so to speak, out of chaos?

And then comes the parable:

> The case would be like [*ähnlich*] the following—certain kinds of plants multiply by seed, so that a seed always produces a plant of the same kind as that from which it was produced—but *nothing* in the seed corresponds to the plant which

comes from it; so that it is impossible to infer the properties or structure of the plant from those of the seed that it comes out of—this can only be done from the *history* of the seed. So an organism might come into being even out of something quite amorphous, as it were causelessly; and there is no reason why this should not really hold for our thoughts, and hence for our talking and writing. (cf. Z §608)

§904. It is thus perfectly possible that certain psychological phenomena *cannot* be investigated physiologically, because physiologically nothing corresponds to them. (=Z §609)

§905. I saw this man years ago; now I have seen him again, I recognize him, I remember his name. And why does there have to be a cause of this remembering in my nervous system? Why must something or other, whatever it may be, be stored-up there *in any form*? Why *must* a trace have been left behind? Why should there not be a psychological regularity to which *no* physiological regularity corresponds? If this upsets our concepts of causality, then it is high time they were upset. (=Z §610)

. . .

§909. Why should not the initial and terminal states of a system be connected by a natural law, which does not cover the intermediary state? (Only don't think of *influence* [*Wirkung*]!) (=Z §613)

. . .

§918. . . . But must there be a physiological explanation here? Why don't we just leave explaining alone? . . . (=Z §614)

How can we be brought to stop the search for an explanation—to "leave explaining alone"? This thought experiment seems to address two of Wittgenstein's aims, as listed in chapter 4: aim C, to stop looking for a further explanation, and aim D, to attend to the context—in this case, the history of the seeds.

The parable first appeared in a notebook in 1937 and then was discussed in lectures in 1938 and again in lectures in 1947. I have discussed these passages extensively in several publications, but here I begin by commenting on their nature as a parable.[13] One of the points I have made about this story is that it has changed in notable respects in various retellings. The version laid out in 1937 and discussed in lectures in 1938 is more interesting, in my view, and plausible than the better-known version quoted here. And the versions discussed in lectures in 1947 are similarly more interesting and plausible. Another point to make is that when the story appears at two different times in lectures in 1938, it has a different point each time. These are characteristics of parables—that there may be no canonical version of them and that they can be used in different ways at different times.[14] As Wittgenstein wrote in his preface to the *Philosophical Investigations*, "The same, or almost the same points were always being approached afresh from different directions."

Biblical parables have these characteristics. Certain parables of Jesus are told in more than one gospel with notable differences. The differences can be put down to unreliable transmission of the parables from telling to written records, or they can show that Jesus told the parables differently at different times.[15] And Jesus (or the gospel writers) can use roughly the same parable to make different points in different contexts. The parable of the talents/pounds (Matthew 25:14–30 and Luke 19:11–27) illustrates both of these points.[16] So Wittgenstein's parable of the seeds, in its various incarnations, functions as other parables do.

Wittgenstein wonders "Why don't we just leave explaining alone?" And he asserts several times in multiple contexts: "Explanations come to an end somewhere." But it is one thing to assert and accept this truism and another thing actually to bring the search to a halt: "The difficulty here is: to stop" (Z §314).[17] What would it take to get us to stop insisting on an explanation in this sort of case? In other words, the challenge is not simply to get us to realize the intellectual truth—or remind us of the truism—but to change our behavior. Recall Wittgenstein's assertion: "I don't try to make you *believe* something you *don't* believe, but to make you *do* something you won't do."[18] Viz., stop—here and now.

Wittgenstein's treatment of Frazer's remarks (discussed in chapter 3) fits in here. Wittgenstein wants to relieve people like Frazer of the expectation of an explanation of religious practices and bring them to be satisfied with a synoptic description of them. While Wittgenstein asserts that "the satisfaction being sought through the explanation follows of itself" from a perspicuous representation, we can wonder whether it does and whether there are more effective means.

Are there examples of poems or parables—stories—that might accomplish the sort of thing Wittgenstein was after? That would get one to be satisfied with something short of explanation? Or bring explanation to an end?

One (in)famous question that raises these kinds of concerns is: "What was God doing before he created the world?" Apparently, this question was raised by the ancient Manichaeans, provoking a response by St. Augustine. In his *Confessions*, Augustine writes:

> This is my reply to anyone who asks, "What was God doing before He made heaven and earth?" My reply is not that which someone is said to have given as a joke to evade the force of the question. He said: "He was preparing hells for people who inquire into profundities." It is one thing to laugh, another to see the point at issue, and this reply I reject. I would have preferred him to answer "I am ignorant of what I do not know" rather than reply so as to ridicule someone who has asked a deep question and to win approval for an answer which is a mistake.[19]

Wittgenstein would have been well aware of this passage and this issue, as he had a high regard for Augustine's *Confessions*.[20]

While Augustine takes the high road, Martin Luther does not. In an account of some of his conversations, we read: "When one asked, where God was before Heaven was created, St. Augustine answered: He was in himself. When another asked me [i.e., Luther] the same question, I said: He was building Hell for such idle, presumptuous, fluttering and inquisitive spirits as you."[21] This reply has taken on an apocryphal life of its own. According to one story, Luther was conversing with his students over a meal, as he often did, when one of them asked a question: *What was God doing before he created the world?* To this Luther is said to have replied, *God sits under a tree and cuts branches and rods, to beat up people who ask useless questions to which he has not provided the answers!* According to another story, when Luther was lecturing to seminarians one day on the creation of the world in the Book of Genesis, some seminarian asked, "Doctor Luther, what was God doing before he created the world? What would he have done with himself for all those years?" There was snickering among the other students. "What was God doing before he created the world?" Luther roared. "He was gathering sticks to make switches to beat the devil out of stupid people like you who ask such stupid questions!" In this telling, the reply seems not to be a "joke" (as St. Augustine had labeled it) but more like a threat.

It is this apocryphal version of the Luther story that Kierkegaard later adopts. At the opening of Kierkegaard's play *The Battle between the Old and the New Soap Cellars*, he writes that (in published form) it will begin: "With a frontispiece showing Luther sitting in a hazel tree cutting switches for people who ask useless questions. Some of them are seen to be lying on the ground; others will be found scattered around in the book. The inexperienced will perhaps mistake them for dashes."[22]

Here we find two sorts of responses to a problematic question—the reply by Augustine, which takes the question seriously: "I am ignorant of what I do not know" (or as related by Luther: "He was in himself."), and the reply from Luther (and endorsed by Kierkegaard), which attempts to deflect the questioner and reject the question.[23] These are attempts to get you to "do something you won't do"—namely, stop asking.

Wittgenstein himself considers these same two kinds of responses in a different context. In his Cambridge course lecture on December 2, 1946, he considers a case where a sleepwalker performs some activity and someone asks whether the sleepwalker is thinking when he does that. One might say, "We don't know," as though he either is or is not thinking, and there is some hope that we would eventually know. But, Wittgenstein adds, "There would be nothing wrong if in this case we taught a man to answer 'Shut up!'" since in this case the question is not well defined.[24] Here we see Wittgenstein trying "to make you *do* something you won't do": stop asking!

The threatening response (from Luther and from Wittgenstein) is similar to God's response to Job in the well-known story from the Hebrew testament. I have discussed this much more fully in my book *Wittgenstein in Exile*, but will only emphasize the parallel here. Despite his suffering, Job insists he has done nothing wrong and requests an explanation from God. God responds from out of the whirlwind, essentially offering a sublime display that overawes Job and his friends: *Who are you to ask these questions? I'm in charge here.* He in turn asks Job a series of questions not meant to be answered. In sum: "Enough!" To which Job replies: "What can I say?" and continues, "I know that you are all-powerful. . . . I retract what I have said." A commentator writes: "Job is no longer asking 'why?' . . . There is now for him a place where the problem is not solved, but it is beginning to dissolve. . . . It does not disturb him any longer at the point where it first disturbed him. He is willing to leave it." God has gotten Job to stop asking, and perhaps the telling of the story has gotten the reader to stop asking.[25]

Consider a different deflection of explanation in one of Tolstoy's *Twenty-Three Tales*, "Two Old Men": Two old men journey to the Holy Land, but one gets sidetracked caring for a needy family. The one who completes the journey feels unfulfilled and wonders at the spiritual journey of the other. The other replies, "That's God's business, neighbor, God's business." Then the one wonders about the assistance rendered to the needy family, and the other again replies, "That's God's business, neighbor, God's business." Finally,

"Efim sighed, and did not speak to Elisha of the people in the hut, nor of how he had seen him in Jerusalem." His desire for an explanation has been quelled or at any rate silenced.[26] It is well known how impressed Wittgenstein was with Tolstoy's stories. He even marked "Two Old Men" as one of his four favorites.[27]

More than saying that God knows the answer and we don't, Elisha suggests that it isn't our business even to inquire after these matters. And the story seems to quell, or at least it seems intended to quell, the desire to inquire. In contrast, the Luther story tries to repel the desire to inquire.

The notion of quelling a need to ask questions also lies behind Dostoevsky's treatment of Ivan's challenge to Alyosha in *The Brothers Karamazov*. I have discussed this more extensively in my book *Wittgenstein in Exile*, but the parallel to Tolstoy's story is instructive. Ivan marshals examples of children suffering outrages in order to reject God's world in which such things happen. Ivan rejects all possible rational explanations—he is driven by the need to understand, but he has no resources to do so. Having made the strongest possible case on Ivan's behalf, Dostoevsky then responds by offering book 6 of the novel, "The Russian Monk"—a telling of the story of the life of the character Father Zosima. It is a response aimed at readers by appealing to their emotions in a way designed to calm the urge to ask "*Why?*" By using Church Slavonic and other forms of language reminiscent of the religious experience of Russian Orthodox services, Dostoevsky hopes to offer "an oblique answer . . . so to speak in artistic form."[28] Wittgenstein's love and mastery of Dostoevsky's *Brothers Karamazov* is well known.

Instead of diverting attention from a problem, one might simply ignore it. Bertrand Russell famously articulated a paradox that threatened to undermine the logical foundation of mathematics that Frege sought to construct. While Frege never did find a satisfactory way of revising his theory to address the problem, Russell himself created and then complicated a theory of types. The mathematician Philip Jourdain was especially interested in this problem and wrote a humorous account of how mathematicians had responded to Russell's paradox:

> Nearly all mathematicians agreed that the way to solve these paradoxes was simply not to mention them; but there was some divergence of opinion as to how they were to be unmentioned. It was clearly unsatisfactory merely not to mention them. Thus Poincaré was apparently of [the] opinion that the best way of avoiding such awkward subjects was to mention that they were not to be mentioned.[29]

This is basically the strategy of saying "don't ask." Jourdain then quotes a passage from Russell:

> But "one may as well, in talking to a man with a long nose, say: 'When speaking of noses, I except such as are inordinately long,' which would not be a very successful effort to avoid a painful topic."[30]

Jourdain goes on to describe a German mathematician of the time, Arthur Schoenflies, who basically defined the problems as "philosophical" and of no concern to the "mathematical process":

> The majority of mathematicians have followed Schoenflies rather than Poincaré, and have thus adopted tactics rather like those of the March Hare and the Gryphon, who promptly changed the subject when Alice raised awkward questions.

Jourdain then quotes the passages from *Alice's Adventures in Wonderland* with responses to questions from Alice: "'Suppose we change the subject,' the March Hare interrupted, yawning. 'I'm getting tired of this.'" And "'That's enough about lessons,' the Gryphon interrupted in a very decided tone.'"[31] In both cases the query is brought, perhaps unsatisfyingly, to an end.

Another approach to diverting an inquiry uses humor directly. Augustine suggests that the "building Hell" response was meant as a joke, but Drury relates a story that more clearly has the character of a joke:

> At one time I told Wittgenstein of an incident that seemed to interest and please him. It was when I was having my oral exam in physiology. The examiner said to me: "Sir Arthur Keith once remarked to me that the reason why the spleen drained into the portal system was of the greatest importance; but he never told me what that importance was, now can you tell me?" I had to confess that I couldn't see any anatomical or physiological significance in this fact. The examiner then went on to say: "Do you think there *must* be a significance, an explanation? As I see it there are two sorts of people: one man sees a bird sitting on a telegraph wire and says to himself `Why is that bird sitting just there?', the other man replies `Damn it all, the bird has to sit somewhere.'"[32]

What is interesting about all these stories is that they do not just claim or argue that inquiry should stop; they in some sense try to bring it to a halt. This is what Wittgenstein wants to be able to do, by "poetic" means.

Franz Kafka expresses the state that Wittgenstein aims for at the end of his story, "The Test," about a servant waiting for work in a tavern:

> "Why do you want to run away? Sit down and have a drink! I'll pay." So I sat down. He asked me several things, but I couldn't answer, indeed I didn't even understand his questions. So I said: "Perhaps you are sorry now that you invited

> me, so I'd better go," and I was about to get up. But he stretched his hand out over the table and pressed me down. "Stay," he said, "that was only a test. He who does not answer the questions has passed the test."[33]

Wittgenstein never succeeded in composing a poem or parable that would bring a halt to an ill-advised search for explanation or justification. Of course, there could not be anything that would do this comprehensively; more likely he would need to counter the urge on an ad hoc basis. What works here may well not work there. (See Wittgenstein's comments about the fly bottle.) But we can now see what kind of thing Wittgenstein needed and sought, and how some of these stories might serve that purpose—by doing philosophy as poetry.

The Lion

PI, part ii, p. 223 (= PPF §327 in the fourth edition): "If a lion could talk [*sprechen*], we could not [*könnten . . . nicht*] understand him."[34]

This is more like an aphorism than a parable, but both fall into the range of *Dichtung*. This line arose rather late in Wittgenstein's thinking, first appearing in 1947 or 1948 with only slight elaboration (MS 167, p. 12v): "If the lion could talk, we could not understand him. He becomes a mystery to us by a certain behavior, enigmatic."

I believe this aphorism presents us with a paradox: if we can't understand the lion, then we are in no position to suppose that it is talking. Lions are not, after all, the sorts of things known to talk. And if we *could not* understand him, then it seems that we would never be in a position to suppose he is talking. If I were in Manila, I might well say: "If the vendor talks to me, I wouldn't (be able to) understand her." After all, vendors, and people generally, in Manila are the sort who can and do talk. Yet even though I wouldn't (now be able to) understand her, I could. I could if I studied the language. When it comes to a lion, where there is no tradition of lions talking, it seems our only way of supposing the lion to be talking is by way of understanding.[35] Attributing talking seems to presuppose some capacity for understanding. Denying understanding undercuts attributing talking. As Wittgenstein is recorded as saying in the Yellow Book (1933), "Before [a sentence] is understood it is ink on paper. One might say it has meaning only for an understanding being. If there were no one to understand the signs we would not call the signs language."[36]

The paradoxical nature of this claim can be brought out by reflecting on what came to be called Moore's paradox: "It is raining, but I don't believe it is raining." Moore called it "absurd or nonsensical to say such things," even though it could certainly be true both that it is raining and that I don't believe it is raining."[37] In a letter to Moore, Wittgenstein affirmed that it is an "'absurdity' which is in fact something *similar* to a contradiction."[38] And in conversation with Malcolm, Wittgenstein said that Moore's discovery of this kind of nonsense "greatly impressed him."[39] The absurdity arises from the fact that there is no perspective from which the conjuncts can be jointly asserted. Moore acknowledges (208) that one can certainly say, "It *was* raining, but I didn't believe it was raining," or, "It is raining, but *he* doesn't believe it is raining." Or one can even say, "Suppose it is raining, but I don't believe it is raining." But when I utter the sentence, "It is raining," I imply that I believe it's raining (210). The absurdity comes from the first-person, present assertion.

Wittgenstein's aphorism seems to be a kind of nonsense. But perhaps he is trying to evoke the idea of a different form of life. It seems to be possible that there are other beings that have a language, and hence "talk," even though we cannot understand it (the language) or them.[40] Certainly we could imagine a more primitive form of life about which we might assert: "We can talk, but they (cats?) couldn't understand us." So couldn't we simply reverse this and have the cats assert: "The humans can talk, but we couldn't understand them"? And we are simply imagining a case where, say, the lions stand to us as we stand to the cats. To consider this possibility, it seems we must step out of our perspective, or our form of life, and take a perspective that transcends forms of life (or comprehends all forms of life) to be able to identify two (ours and the lion's) that are incommensurable—that is, neither can understand the other, or at least ours can't understand the other. But as Wittgenstein would be sure to remind us, any investigation will have to proceed from within some (our) form of life. The question is, Can we, from within our form of life, recognize and acknowledge another, incommensurable, form of life?

This question seems designed for treatment by *Dichtung*. Shouldn't we be able to compose a poem, tell a story, in which this happens? A good example along these lines is Stanisław Lem's novel *His Master's Voice*. Astronomers detect a complex repeating "signal." The mathematician-narrator, Peter Hogarth, is part of a secret group asked to decode the signal, to determine whether it means something, and if so, what—in other words, to determine if there is a "sender" who is talking, and if so, to understand what is being said.

Hogarth notes that "a stream of information—human speech, for example—does not always tell us that it is information and not a chaos of sounds" (51). Nevertheless, he operates from the assumption that "the so-called message from outer space . . . is, in all likelihood, a series of signals sent intentionally and with the aid of an artificial-technological device, by a being or beings that belong to some undetermined extraterrestrial civilization" (98). The narrator's view of this possibility is grounded in precisely the reverse human-cat scenario: "If we turn the procedure around in time and send to an Egyptian of the era of Amenhotep a letter written today, he will not understand it, not only because he does not know our language, but also because he has neither the words nor the concepts to set alongside ours" (98).

There turn out to be some rather small ways in which the group makes some progress in interpreting parts of the signal. Hogarth claimed to show that what they received was "the sort of thing to which could be attributed . . . the qualities of an 'object.' . . . I proved that the letter was the description of a phenomenon" (115–116). Other scientists used bits of the signal to compose a substance they called "frog eggs," which had certain surprising and potentially dangerous nuclear characteristics. And the signal seemed to have a vague capacity for promoting organized life (124). But it was never clear whether these phenomena were "meant" by the signal, or whether the "signal" was just noise that served as a sort of random ink blot or Rorschach test (42) through which the scientists invented these outcomes.

Initially the narrator takes the repetition of the signal to be crucial; otherwise, "the received signal will give no indication that it is anything other than a normal (natural) phenomenon" (100). But that by itself does not ultimately suffice to sustain that idea that it is a "message"—that anyone is talking. In the absence of any plausible, sustainable interpretation or understanding of the signal, "it turned out that perhaps the thing was not a letter but a meaningless scrawl" (250). The very failure to understand is what keeps the narrator from maintaining his original certainty: ". . . Could not the whole thing have been only a series of coincidences? Absolutely" (257).

One of the main features of *His Master's Voice* is that there is no opportunity to interact with the source of the signal. This important premise is changed in "Story of Your Life," by Ted Chiang, the basis for the 2016 film

"Arrival." A linguist, Dr. Louise Banks, is enlisted to try to communicate with alien visitors to Earth. In fact, at first Banks is asked to translate alien utterances simply from a recording. She immediately insists this is not possible (94): ". . . if you want to learn the aliens' language, . . . someone . . . will have to talk with an alien. Recordings alone aren't sufficient."

She recounts her interactions with the alien heptapods, and interspersed with this she recounts events in her relationship with her daughter, who dies tragically at age twenty-five. Banks focuses on the alien written language, which she labels Heptapod B. It is "semasiographic" (108), which means it conveys meaning without reference to speech, and is two-dimensional and so nonlinear.[41] Based on examples from physics, she supposes that "the heptapods' idea of what's simple doesn't match ours . . ." (118): "Humans had developed a sequential mode of awareness, while heptapods had developed a simultaneous mode of awareness. We experienced events in an order, and perceived their relationship as cause and effect. They experienced events all at once, and perceived a purpose underlying them all. A minimizing, maximizing purpose" (134).[42] Banks comes to partially inhabit this alien mode of consciousness: "Heptapod B was changing the way I thought" (126). And she seems to use this as a way of coming to terms with her daughter's life and death. This to me is the most moving part of the story. After becoming proficient in Heptapod B, she admits that she still doesn't "experience reality the way a heptapod does. My mind was cast in the mold of human, sequential languages, and no amount of immersion in an alien language can completely reshape it. My worldview is an amalgam of human and heptapod" (140). She concludes that "the heptapods' behavior was presumably explicable from a sequential point of view, but we never found that explanation" (144).

As readers of the short story, we witness one form of life engaging with a possibly different form of life. Before the story begins, we clearly share a form of life with the narrator, Dr. Banks. As the story progresses, Dr. Banks is changed by her engagement with the heptapods. This allows her to understand the heptapods to a certain extent, and the story allows us to still understand Dr. Banks to a certain extent at the end. But she suggests that this understanding is not fully transitive when she says that "we never found that [sequential] explanation." My thought is that insofar as we make an alternative form of life intelligible, we have brought it close enough in contact with our own as to create doubt whether it is indeed an *alternate* form of life. There is no way we could show there are *not* alternate forms of life, but attempts to show there *are* would seem to falter in this way.[43]

Dr. Banks reflects on what it means to the heptapods to interact sequentially with us. She suggests that whereas we view the interaction as freely and gradually conveying information, they may view it as a performative enactment of a fixed chronology. As a way of helping make sense of that view, Banks recalls an occasion when her young daughter wanted her to finish reading a story to her even though she knew exactly how it ended (138). In fact, this experience is not rare. We enjoy listening to music or watching a film we have experienced many times before and know by heart, rereading a book, or acting out a play. These all constitute points of contact and avenues of understanding, even if partial, with the heptapod form of life. Indeed, Banks recounts occasions in her life with her daughter in this same performative fashion and "would have liked to experience more of the heptapod world view, to feel the way they feel" (144). This offers her consolation as a way of conceiving her daughter's life and death.

If we could take a lion to be talking, we could come to understand it in some important respects. This seems to be played out in Chiang's story. If we can't understand it in any meaningful way, we can't very well take it to be talking. This seems to be illustrated by Lem's novel. These stories undermine the original aphorism. So, while this aphorism appears in several manuscripts and typescripts over the 1947–1948 period, I don't think Wittgenstein had fully worked it through.[44] If he had tried to formulate his thought in poetic form, he might have seen that.

The Woodsellers

This can be found in *Remarks of the Foundations of Mathematics* (excerpts from pp. 93–95 in part I of the revised edition):

> §143. . . . People pile up logs and sell them, the piles are measured with a ruler, the measurements of length, breadth and height multiplied together, and what comes out is the number of pence [*Groschen*] which have to be asked and given. They do not know "why" it happens like this; they simply do it like this: that is how it is done.—Do these people not calculate?
>
> . . .
>
> §148. Those people—we should say—sell timber by cubic measure—but are they right in doing so? Wouldn't it be more correct to sell it by weight—or by the time

it took to fell the timber—or by the labour of felling measured by the age and strength of the woodsman? And why should they not hand it over for a price which is independent of all this: each buyer pays the same however much he takes (they have found it possible to live like that). And is there anything to be said against simply giving the wood away?

§149. Very well; but what if they piled the timber in heaps of arbitrary, varying height and then sold it at a price proportionate to the area covered by the piles? [LFM, p. 202: "Wouldn't this be queer? Would you say that these people were asking the wrong price?"]

And what if they even justified this with the words: "Of course, if you buy more timber, you must pay more"?[45]

§150. How could I show them that—as I should say—you don't really buy more wood if you buy a pile covering a bigger area?—I should, for instance, take a pile which was small by their ideas and, by laying the logs around, change it into a "big" one. This *might* convince them—but perhaps they would say: "Yes, now it's a *lot* of wood and costs more"—and that would be the end of the matter. [LFM, p. 202: "We might call this a kind of logical madness."]—We should presumably say in this case: they simply do not mean the same by "a lot of wood" and "a little wood" as we do; and they have a quite different system of payment from us. [LFM, p. 204: "They do this. They get along alright. What more do you want?"]

§151. (A society acting in this way would perhaps remind us of the Wise Men of Gotham.)[46]

§152. Frege says in the preface to the *Grundgesetze der Arithmetik*: ". . . here we have a hitherto unknown kind of insanity [*Verrücktheit*]"—but he never said what this 'insanity' would really be like.[47]

These passages first appear in MS 117 (pp. 45–49), which seems to have been drafted in late 1937 or 1938, and Wittgenstein returns to this vignette in a lecture from the 1939 Easter term.[48] (I inserted some relevant passages from these lecture notes above.) While there is no evidence of a link, it is noteworthy that Wittgenstein spent several months in 1936 and 1937 living alone in a very rural region of Norway, where he doubtless had dealings with woodcutters.[49]

Wittgenstein makes parenthetical mention of "the Wise Men of Gotham," which is in fact a traditional legend associated with the village of Gotham in Nottinghamshire, England. The villagers did not want King John to visit and thereby disrupt their lives, so they feigned imbecility when the royal messengers arrived. The king's messengers "found some of the inhabitants engaged in endeavoring to drown an eel in a pool of water; some were employed in dragging carts upon a large barn, to shade the wood from the sun; others were tumbling their cheeses down a hill, that they might find their way to Nottingham for sale; and some were employed in hedging in a cuckoo which had perched upon an old bush which stood where the present one now stands. In short, they were all employed in some foolish way or other, which convinced the king's servants that it was a village of fools, whence arose the old adage, 'the wise men of Gotham' or 'the fools of Gotham.'"[50]

The people of Gotham in this legend are trying to look crazy ("the fools of Gotham"), but we can see there are plausible reasons ("wise men of Gotham") for their seemingly irrational behavior. So too, the woodcutters might appear irrational for selling their wood by the square foot, yet Wittgenstein offers alternate accounts of how one might set a price. While Frege supposed that the laws of thought of people like the woodcutters could be shown to be wrong, Wittgenstein offers alternate accounts of their pattern of thought that we could possibly accept.

I also see this parable and its discussion as an illustration of the point concerning rule following: that a rule does not in itself determine what its (correct) applications will be, and that there can be various plausible ways that a rule or a concept can be extended. The primary example of this in the *Philosophical Investigations* is the pupil (at §185) who continues the series +2 beyond 1,000 with 1004, 1008, 1012, and so on. But I have to confess that the counting example never grabbed me. So too, the concept of "selling" has clear application in a range of standard cases. Does it also apply to what the woodmen do? Are they going on as we would? Perhaps the woodseller parable has more appeal than the case of counting by 2's. We can see this parable as an attempt to address Wittgenstein's aim D: Don't ignore the context; and aim E: Look for rules in human regularities and not in metaphysics.

A well-known parable that has the same feeling as the woodseller parable is the biblical parable of the workers in the vineyard (Matthew 20:1–16):

> For the kingdom of heaven is like a landowner who went out early in the morning to hire laborers for his vineyard. After agreeing with the laborers for the usual daily wage, he sent them into his vineyard. When he went out about nine o'clock, he saw others standing idle in the marketplace; and he said to them, "You also go into the vineyard, and I will pay you whatever is right." So they went. When he went out again about noon and about three o'clock, he did the

> same. And about five o'clock he went out and found others standing around; and he said to them, "Why are you standing here idle all day?" They said to him, "Because no one has hired us." He said to them, "You also go into the vineyard." When evening came, the owner of the vineyard said to his manager, "Call the laborers and give them their pay, beginning with the last and then going to the first." When those hired about five o'clock came, each of them received the usual daily wage. Now when the first came, they thought they would receive more; but each of them also received the usual daily wage. And when they received it, they grumbled against the landowner, saying, "These last worked only one hour, and you have made them equal to us who have borne the burden of the day and the scorching heat." But he replied to one of them, "Friend, I am doing you no wrong; did you not agree with me for the usual daily wage? Take what belongs to you and go; I choose to give to this last the same as I give to you. Am I not allowed to do what I choose with what belongs to me? Or are you envious because I am generous?" So the last will be first, and the first will be last.

Here the early workers have a notion of fairness in compensation, perhaps "pay proportionate to amount of work," that is not borne out. The landowner seems to have another notion of fairness in compensation, perhaps "a living wage." The early workers might accuse the landowner of being crazy, but that is not the only plausible way to view the situation.

A rabbinic parable starts from a similar premise that one who works less time is paid the same. The workers complain:

> "We have been working hard all day, and this one who only labored two hours receives as much salary as we do."
>
> "It is," answered the king, "because he has done more in two hours than you in the entire day."[51]

Here we are offered a rationale, somewhat like "the labour of felling measured by the age and strength of the woodsman." In any case, the rabbinic parable remains within the framework of what is fair or what is deserved.

Jesus's parable, however, chooses not to offer a rationale of that sort. Instead, the landowner in Jesus's parable changes the frame of reference. Instead of focusing on the labor of the workers, Jesus focuses on the generosity of the landowner. He tries to get the listeners to see the situation differently—as a matter of grace rather than of desert or fairness. Recall Wittgenstein's comment on the woodcutters: "Is there anything to be said against simply giving the wood away?"[52] Could we see the woodcutters as being generous?—Take as much as you can, as long as it all fits in this area! (Old game show giveaways of piling high a single shopping basket within a set amount of time.) Could the woodcutters' approach ever be an advantage to them? Perhaps if the piles kept falling down—if wood couldn't be stacked?

Could we see this situation as parallel to one in which the question was, "How much precision is appropriate?" Different people or groups go in for different levels of precision. There's no right answer, though there are pragmatic factors and different temperaments. "Stand roughly there." Or: "Oh, let's call it a ton."

Is there a right way to sell wood? Wrong ways? Why not by footprint rather than by volume?

Wittgenstein is trying to undermine the seemingly natural supposition that there is a right way to go on that is built into the rule (or concept) itself. Instead he wants to get us to see that any notion of the "right way" comes from our widespread inclination to apply the rule, not from the rule itself (LFM, 182–184; April 26, 1939). The first step in doing this is to show that there might be inclinations to apply the rule in other ways. Wittgenstein really does little to make the "+2" continuation of 1000, 1004, 1008, and so on seem plausible: "I thought that was how I *had* to do it . . ." (§185). Really? One problem here is that the dissenter is just an individual. The alternative gets more psychological plausibility if there is a dissenting *group* that shares an inclination, such as the woodcutters.[53]

In the *Investigations*, Wittgenstein immediately goes on to use pointing as a further illustration, imagining someone who reacts to a gesture of pointing by looking from the tip of the finger toward the wrist. This again feels rather lifeless. But recall that if you try to point to something for a cat, it will only look at your fingertip. Is it wrong? There is a failure here of a certain sort. If humans did this, we'd say they didn't understand.

With the woodsellers Wittgenstein finally considers a conflict between communities, and not just a matter of a deviant individual. "This is what WE do" (cf. PI §217).

Later Wittgenstein talks about a signpost (§198). We can theoretically imagine someone following an arrow in the opposite direction, but again it feels lifeless. Yet consider how arrows do in fact function on highway signs—arrows pointing left or right are clear enough; they are meant to take the sign as defining a two-dimensional plane (oriented in three-dimensional space) and indicating a direction within that plane (and space). But generally arrows pointing up (or down) are not meant to indicate a direction within the plane of the sign. An "up" or "down" arrow generally means to point outside the two-dimensional plane—to continue in the direction from the reader/viewer to the arrow, that is, to continue orthogonal to the plane of the sign—"ahead."[54] So, there is a variety of inclinations one can bring to the rule.

The challenge to get people to see the "right" continuation as a matter of sociology and not as a matter of logic is a genuine one, since we, the readers or listeners, presumably share the inclinations that make a certain continuation (1000, 1002, 1004 . . .) the most natural and therefore (seem) right. How can we get people who already have an entrenched inclination see that it is *only* an inclination (or only *one* inclination)? Not, presumably, by repeating an intellectual argument. (Consider the "ugly American tourist" who, upon being not understood by a non-English speaker, repeats the question again, only louder.)

In trying to dislodge our sense that there is a right way to go on that is built into the logic of things, rather than a right way to go on based on the sociology of the practice, there could be two different strategies: try to get us to see the new way of going on as indeed fitting with values that we already have, but were perhaps not appreciated sufficiently, or try to get us to accept that there are other ways of going on—not within our values but which we can tolerate and acknowledge. Jesus's parable about the workers in the vineyard has sometimes been called the parable of the "generous employer" and sometimes the parable of the "eccentric employer."[55] Those two labels indicate these two different possible strategies.

But in either case, it is useful to tell a story, a parable, a poem, or a joke—a narrative, in which we are carried away in our imagination from our actual inclination and find ourselves accepting another inclination, in spite of ourselves, so to speak. Once we step out of ourselves to take some other inclination seriously, we can see the further point that rightness consists in, and is relative to, a widespread inclination. But seeing this, getting it, is not merely an intellectual apprehension; it has a noncognitive element.

In RFM §150, Wittgenstein briefly mentions another direction one might take: "We should presumably say in this case: they simply do not mean the same by 'a lot of wood' and 'a little wood' as we do." Stephen Toulmin, a student of Wittgenstein in 1946–1947, characterizes Wittgenstein's new style: "Whereas in the *Tractatus* he had resorted to myth, he now used parables or fables." He then recounts an oral parable from Wittgenstein along the same lines as the Woodsellers:

> Suppose an anthropologist finds the members of a tribe, whose language he does not yet understand, cutting up bolts of longitudinally striped cloth and exchanging them for small cubes of wood, uttering as they hand over the cubes the sounds "eena," "meena," "mina," "mo," and so on, always in the same regular sequence. And suppose he discovers that this exchange proceeds always up to the same point, regardless of whether the cloth is (as we should say) single-width or folded double. What should the anthropologist then conclude? Is he to infer that the tribe values cloth only by its length as measured along the stripes; or that the merchants who sell the cloth single-width are rogues; or that the tribe's arithmetic has a different structure from ours; or that "eena," "meena," "mina," "mo" are not their words for "1," "2," "3," and "4" after all; or that this is not really a commercial exchange, but some kind of ritual . . . ? Or might we have no effective way of deciding among these alternatives?[56]

It appears that the Woodseller parable that Wittgenstein developed in the late 1930s has now, by 1946, evolved to emphasize a different point—one only hinted at previously.

The question whether an arrangement is a mere human convention or a reflection of an underlying metaphysical reality has vexed reflective people since ancient times in the debate over (the Greek concepts) *nomos* (custom) and *phusis* (nature). Perhaps the most persistent example of the conflict comes in ethics. Archelaus is supposed to have said, "The noble and the base exist by *nomos*, not by *phusis*," setting off a debate that pitted Socrates, Plato, and Aristotle against Archelaus and later the sophists.[57] While there is no definitive resolution of the issue in general, Wittgenstein thinks there is an unfortunate inclination to ground phenomena in metaphysical reality (*phusis*) rather than in human convention (*nomos*). Aim E directs us to look to human regularity rather than metaphysical reality.

An exaggerated but humorous illustration of this conflict comes from chapter 13 of Ignazio Silone's novel *Bread and Wine*, set in prewar fascist Italy. Some peasants are playing a card game, *sette e mezzo* (seven and a half), in which the king of diamonds is the most important card. For this reason, it has gotten worn in such a way that it is identifiable from the back. A woman proposes that for the purpose of the game, they substitute another card—the 3 of hearts—for the king of diamonds:

> "That's impossible," somebody else said . . . , "Even if we all could agree, it would still be impossible."
>
> "Why?"
>
> "But it's natural," said Mascolo. "The king of diamonds is always the king of diamonds. It could be dirty, or marked, or have a hole in it. But it's still what it is."

> "All we have to do is agree on it," said Danielle. "The game will be better if no one can see who has the king of diamonds in his hand."
>
> "But our agreement would not be enough," said Michele. "There's the law."
>
> "You said the game would go better?" said Matalena. "That may be, but it would be a false game."

Then they decide to ask the "priest," Don Paolo (a revolutionary posing as a priest):

> Someone explained what it was all about, and concluded, "Now tell us who's right."
>
> "This isn't a case of sacred images," said the priest with a laugh. . . .
>
> Don Paolo took the king of diamonds in his hand and asked Michele, "Do you think this has value for itself, or do you think someone gave it a value?"
>
> Michele answered, "It's worth more than the others because it's the king of diamonds."
>
> "Is its value fixed or variable?" said the priest. "Is this card the same in tresche or in briscola or scope? Or is it different?"
>
> "It varies according to the games," said Michele.
>
> "Who thought up the games?" said the priest.
>
> No one answered.
>
> "Don't you think the players thought up the games?" suggested the priest.
>
> Several agreed. There was every reason to believe that the players had thought up the games.
>
> The priest concluded, "If this card varies according to the players' whim, it seems to me you can do with it what you want."
>
> "Bravo! Bravissimo!" several of them yelled.

Then the "priest" uses this admission to make a political point about how governments are arranged by people.

> In the following days the demotion of the king of diamonds was the subject of all kinds of discussions among the peasants of the town.
>
> The village schoolteacher [who supported the government] complained about it personally to the priest.
>
> "In the advanced class," she complained, "I couldn't teach. The boys talked of nothing but that story of the king of diamonds and the three of hearts, without having understood it." . . .
>
> "These people are very ignorant," she said. "If they listen to educated people like ourselves, they almost always understand the opposite of what we say."

And the chapter continues in a similar vein. Here we expose in a humorous fashion the inclination to find a metaphysical basis for a clearly human arrangement. Granted, however, not all cases are so clear-cut.

5 O'Clock on the Sun

PI §350: "You surely know what 'It's 5 o'clock on the sun' means. It means simply that it is just the same time there as it is here when it is 5 o'clock." The passage is itself given in quotation marks, meaning that Wittgenstein is not asserting it but considering it.

This line first appears in MS 116, pp. 141–142, which dates from autumn 1937. This is one of many vignettes in which Wittgenstein draws attention to the importance of context for meaning—what I have called Wittgenstein's aim D: Don't ignore the context.

Chapters 10 to 15 of the 1943 novella, *The Little Prince*, by Antoine de Saint-Exupéry, constitute six vignettes that illustrate in various ways the importance of context by removing the context. In chapter 11, the little prince visits a conceited man who wishes to be admired and who is satisfied with someone going through the motions without any of the background that would make the motions meaningful:

> The second planet was inhabited by a conceited man:
>
> "Ah! Ah! I am about to receive a visit from an admirer!" he exclaimed from afar, when he first saw the little prince coming.
>
> For, to conceited men, all other men are admirers.
>
> "Good morning," said the little prince. "That is a queer hat you are wearing."
>
> "It is a hat for salutes," the conceited man replied. "It is to raise in salute when people acclaim me. Unfortunately, nobody at all ever passes this way."
>
> "Yes?" said the little prince, who did not understand what the conceited man was talking about.
>
> "Clap your hands, one against the other," the conceited man now directed him.
>
> The little prince clapped his hands. The conceited man raised his hat in a modest salute.
>
> "This is more entertaining than the visit to the king," said the little prince to himself. And he began again to clap his hands, one against the other. The conceited man again raised his hat in salute.
>
> After five minutes of this exercise the little prince grew tired of the game's monotony:
>
> "And what should one do to make the hat come down?" he asked.
>
> But the conceited man did not hear him. Conceited people never hear anything but praise.
>
> "Do you really admire me very much?" he demanded of the little prince.
>
> "What does that mean—'admire'?"
>
> "To admire means that you regard me as the handsomest, the best-dressed, the richest, and the most intelligent man on the planet."

> "But you are the only man on your planet!"
> "Do me this kindness. Admire me just the same."
> "I admire you," said the little prince, shrugging his shoulders slightly, "but what is there in that to interest you so much?"
> And the little prince went away.
> "The grown-ups are certainly very odd," he said to himself, as he continued on his journey.

Admiring the conceited man is just like admiring an accomplished musician, only without any of the accomplishments. In chapter 13, there is a businessman who claims to "own" the stars, though his ownership does not involve any of the traditional powers one might have over what is owned. Owning a star is just like owning a scarf, only without the ability to do anything with the star. These vignettes from *The Little Prince* make fun of the idea that certain phenomena might exist without context or out of context. They show a way to turn Wittgenstein's aphorism into a parable. Perhaps the elaboration makes them more persuasive.

"Bububu"

From a slip of paper inserted into the typescript for *PI*, presumably meant to go between §§35 and 36: "Can I say 'bububu' and mean 'If it doesn't rain, I shall go for a walk'?—It is only in a language that I can mean something by something. This shows clearly that the grammar of 'to mean' does not resemble that of the expression 'to imagine' and the like."[58]

When I teach a seminar course on Wittgenstein, I have the students read some passages aloud; this is one of them. But no one has the nerve to read it properly—by running their index finger up and down over their loose lips while making a "B" sound, to imitate a baby. This passage has a point similar to two others in the *Investigations*:

> PI §510: "Try to do the following: *say* 'It's cold here,' and mean 'It's warm here.' Can you do it?—And what are you doing as you do it? And is there only one way of doing it?"

> PI §665: "Imagine someone pointing to his cheek with a grimace of pain and saying 'abracadabra!'—We ask, 'What did you mean?' And he answers, 'I meant toothache.'—You at once think to yourself: how can one '*mean* toothache' by that word? Or, what did to *mean* pain by that word *amount to*? And yet, in a different context, you would have asserted that the mental activity of *meaning* such-and-such was just what was most important in using language."

These two passages arose in close proximity to one another, in MS 116, pp. 131 and 130, dating from autumn 1937. The bububu passage was a later development, probably from 1945, indicated by its literal physical insertion into the typescript for the *Investigations*.

These cases illustrate Wittgenstein's point that the meaning of a word is not simply the mental state or intention of the user; he implies that it depends on its use in an established practice of a language.[59] As aim D suggests, it is only in the context of a language that I can mean something by something. The case of saying "cold" to mean "hot" is somewhat special, since in this case, we can imagine a sarcastic way of saying the word to convey its opposite meaning. But in the other two cases, such means seem lacking.

A vignette from a well-known children's story makes this point clearly: Humpty Dumpty is talking with Alice in Lewis Carroll's *Through the Looking Glass and What Alice Found There* (chapter 6). Humpty Dumpty claims that un-birthday presents are better than birthday presents:

> ". . . There are three hundred and sixty-four days when you might get un-birthday presents—"
>
> "Certainly," said Alice.
>
> "And only *one* for birthday presents, you know. There's glory for you!"
>
> "I don't know what you mean by 'glory'," Alice said.
>
> Humpty Dumpty smiled contemptuously. "'Of course you don't—till I tell you. I meant 'there's a nice knock-down argument for you!'"
>
> "But 'glory' doesn't mean 'a nice knock-down argument,'" Alice objected.
>
> "When *I* use a word," Humpty Dumpty said, in rather a scornful tone, "it means just what I choose it to mean—neither more nor less."
>
> "The question is," said Alice, "whether you *can* make words mean so many different things."
>
> "The question is," said Humpty Dumpty, "which is to be master—that's all."

When Humpty Dumpty explained that by "glory," he meant "a nice knock-down argument," Alice should have asked what he meant by *that*, and the linguistic existentialist would have been set off on an infinite regress.

It is quite likely that Wittgenstein was familiar with the Humpty Dumpty passage. But in any case, the passage gives a striking and memorable illustration of the point Wittgenstein is trying to make. And not only does it make the point, but it does so in a comical fashion that makes fun of the opposite view. It does so in a way that, we might say, displaces the other view. In this respect, it is a good illustration of what Wittgenstein is trying to accomplish.

And although Wittgenstein has not elaborated his cases, as they have been here, they are just the sort of vignettes that could have been elaborated into a memorable, affective, and psychologically effective "poem."

I wrote the following op-ed piece as a brief aporetic dialogue, designed to dislodge the simplistic tendency to suppose meaning is a matter of intent or interpretation:

Pro Football Player: *[Kneels during playing of National Anthem before football game]*

Unhappy Football Fan: I am offended by your disrespecting the U.S. flag, the military and our nation.

P: I am protesting police brutality toward young black men. I intend no disrespect of the flag, the military, our nation or even the police in general. I simply wish to draw attention to this issue.

U: But kneeling during the National Anthem is disrespectful. I interpret it as dishonoring things that are important to me. It is offensive. It doesn't matter what you intend. Can't you find some other way to draw attention to your cause? Couldn't you volunteer in police-community engagement programs?

P: This seems to me the best way to draw attention to this important cause. I intend no disrespect, and it is not my fault that you interpret my action this way.

U: *[Waves Confederate battle flag]*

P: I am offended by your disrespecting black citizens and the U.S. flag

U: I am promoting Southern conservative values of family and tradition. I don't dislike black citizens.

P: But the Confederate battle flag was used by people who enslaved my ancestors and prevented my grandparents from voting.

U: I didn't enslave anyone. I am promoting conservative values. I intend no disrespect of black people.

P: But your flag terrorizes people like me. I interpret your waving that flag as a way of threatening me and my family. It is offensive. It doesn't matter what you intend. Can't you find some other way to promote your values? Couldn't you volunteer in programs that advocate values from your tradition?

U: But waving this flag seems to me to be the best way to draw attention to my values. I intend no disrespect, and it is not my fault that you interpret my action this way.

JK: Clearly the meaning of a symbol or symbolic action is not simply what the person who uses the symbol intends. And equally clearly it is not simply what an observer takes it to mean. A symbol is not innocent just because I don't mean offense, and it is not offensive just because you take offense.

P & U: Then how should we figure out what symbolic actions mean? Apparently, it's not as simple as we first thought.[60]

Presumably readers will identify with one of the two interlocutors, but each interlocutor is brought to reject intent as a source of symbolic meaning and to reject interpretation as a source of symbolic meaning.

The 2-Minute Man

RFM, 336 (part VI, §34):

> Let us imagine a god creating a country instantaneously in the middle of the wilderness, which exists for two minutes and is an exact reproduction of a part of England, with everything that is going on there in two minutes. Just like those in England, the people are pursuing a variety of occupations. Children are in school. Some people are doing mathematics. Now let us contemplate the activity of some human beings during those two minutes. One of these people is doing exactly what a mathematician in England is doing, who is just doing a calculation.—Ought we to say that this two-minute man is calculating? Could we for example not imagine a past and a continuation of these two minutes, which would make us call the processes something quite different?

This passage (from MS 164, pp. 100–101, dated 1941) is similar to another thought experiment that Wittgenstein proposed regarding time (PI §583): "What is a *deep* feeling? Could someone have a feeling of ardent love or hope for one second—*no matter what* preceded or followed this second?—What is happening now has significance—in these surroundings. The surroundings give it its importance." (This derives from MS 129, pp. 111–112, 1944.) Also see PI, part ii, section I, p. 174 = (PPF §3 in the fourth edition):

> "For a second he felt violent pain."—Why does it sound odd to say "For a second he felt deep grief"? Only because it so seldom happens?[61]

All of these examples are designed to illustrate the importance of Wittgenstein's aim D: Don't ignore the context.

Hilary Putnam has introduced "science-fiction examples" involving "Twin Earth" to make the case that meaning is a contextual notion. Putnam's famous examples involve switching the physical environment surrounding a speaker in a way that is analogous to Wittgenstein switching the temporal environment surrounding some phenomenon. Putnam refers to his examples as "my stories" and "our science-fiction story."[62]

Kierkegaard presents what he calls a *Billedet* (picture, or image) that makes striking use of the notion of a momentary time slice, or pause, in the action. "The Freeze of the Mime" (*The Concept of Dread*, 79n, collected in *The Parables of Kierkegaard*, 47):

> There once upon a time were two actors, who . . . came on stage, placed themselves opposite one another, and began a pantomime representation of some passionate conflict. When the pantomimic play was in full swing, and the spectators were following the play with keen expectancy of what was to come after, the actors suddenly came to a stop and remained motionless, as though they were petrified in the pantomimic expression of the instant. This may produce a most comical effect, because the instant becomes accidentally commensurable with the eternal. The effect of sculpture is due to the fact that the eternal expression is expressed eternally; the comic effect, on the other hand, by the fact that the accidental expression was eternalized.

The pause allows us to imagine a different context, or no context, for the action.

Wittgenstein's parable of the seeds could be seen as offering a time slice of the process, during which interval the seeds are indiscernible, while presenting what precedes it as relevant. One might suppose, indeed we do suppose, that the growth process of seeds was *not* context dependent in the way that phenomena of love or hope or calculation are. But Wittgenstein surprisingly imagines the growth process of the seeds as *being* (temporally) context dependent.

"We Are Only Doing Philosophy"

OC §467 (dated April 4, 1951): "I am sitting with a philosopher in the garden; he says again and again 'I know that that's a tree,' pointing to a tree that is near us. Someone else arrives and hears this, and I tell him: 'This fellow isn't insane. We are only doing philosophy.'"

Here, and in several other passages collected in *On Certainty*, Wittgenstein emphasizes that a sentence gets its meaning from being part of an understood language game—for example (OC §423): "Then why don't I simply say with Moore 'I *know* that I am in England'? Saying this is meaningful *in particular circumstances*, which I can imagine. But when I utter the sentence outside these circumstances, as an example to show that I can know truths of this kind with certainty, then it at once strikes me as fishy [*verdächtig*—suspicious].—Ought it to?" And (OC §350): "'I know that that's a tree' is something a philosopher might say to demonstrate to himself or to someone else that he *knows* something that is not a mathematical or logical truth. Similarly, someone who is entertaining the idea that he was no use any more might keep repeating to himself 'I can still do this and this and this.' If such thoughts already possessed him one might not be surprised if he, apparently out of all context, spoke such a sentence out loud. (But here I have already sketched a background, a surrounding, for this remark, that is to say given it a context.)"[63]

The first vignette is remarkably similar to Kierkegaard's story "Bang, the Earth Is Round" (*Concluding Unscientific Postscript*, 174, most of which is collected in *Parables of Kierkegaard*, 50):

> The objective truth as such, is by no means adequate to determine that whoever utters it is sane; on the contrary, it may even betray the fact that he is mad, although what he says may be entirely true, and especially objectively true. I shall here permit myself to tell a story [*Begivenhed*= event, incident], which without any sort of adaptation on my part comes directly from the asylum. A patient in . . . an institution seeks to escape, and actually succeeds in effecting his purpose by leaping out of a window, and prepares to start on the road to freedom, when the thought strikes him (shall I say sanely enough or madly enough?): "When you come to town you will be recognized, and you will at once be brought back here; hence you need to prepare yourself fully to convince everyone by the objective truth of what you say, that all is in order as far as your sanity is concerned." As he walks along and thinks about this, he sees a ball lying on the ground, picks it up, and puts it into the tail pocket of his coat. Every step he takes the ball strikes him, politely speaking, on his hinder parts, and every time it thus strikes him he says: "Bang, the earth is round." He comes to the city, and at once calls on one of his friends; he wants to convince him that he is not crazy, and therefore walks back and forth, saying continually: "Bang, the earth is round!" But is the earth not round? Does the asylum still crave yet another sacrifice for this opinion, as in the time when all men believed it to be flat as a pancake? Or is a man who hopes to prove that he is sane, by uttering a generally accepted and generally respected objective truth, insane? And yet it was clear to the physician that the patient was not yet cured; though it is not to be thought that the cure would consist in getting him to accept the opinion that the earth is flat.

Presumably the physician here doubts the sanity of the escaped patient precisely because the patient does not understand the conditions of relevance and informativeness that guide our language games. That this assertion might lead the doctor to doubt the patient's sanity is repeated in the assurance in the garden that the philosopher is indeed sane.

The Fly Bottle

PI §309: "What is your aim in philosophy?—Show the fly the way out of the fly-bottle." This line—should we call it a crack?—is among Wittgenstein's most memorable. (In chapter 4, I called this aim G.)

A version of this fly-bottle image first appears parenthetically in Wittgenstein's notebooks in 1935–1936: "(The solipsist flutters and flutters in the *Fliegenglocke*, strikes against the walls, flutters further. How can he be brought to rest?)"[64] A *Fliegenglocke* is a fly-proof dish cover shaped like a bell made of glass or wire covering food to keep flies away. A fly caught in a fly bell wouldn't seem to want to leave. More likely, it would want to get in, not out. In this case, Wittgenstein's goal is not to get the fly out but to bring it to rest—presumably so it can get back to the business of eating whatever is being covered (or if it is outside, go elsewhere where food is accessible). In any case, there is no way out for the fly to find. It can escape only if someone lifts the glass. And similarly, it is no fault of the fly that it was trapped; that happened presumably because someone put the glass over while the fly was already there. So, the initial image does not work very well.

The familiar aphorism takes shape in September 1937 (MS 118, pp. 71r–71v, September 8, 1937) while Wittgenstein was living in his cabin in Skjolden: "What is your aim in philosophy?—I show the fly the way out of the fly-bottle [*Fliegenglas*]. This way is, in one sense, impossible to find, and, in another sense, quite easy." The *Fliegenglas* is the more familiar image of the bottle designed to catch flies by luring them in by smell through a hole in the bottom, where they are then trapped by their obsession with flying upward toward the light. Wittgenstein repeats this line and a related one in several places in his manuscripts around that time. In a lecture back at Cambridge from Easter term 1938, Wittgenstein provides a drawing of the bottle for the class and elaborates (*Whewell's Court Lectures*, 7):

> The fly catcher. The fly gets in but can't get out. The stronger the wish to get out, the harder it is for it to get out. (It is fascinated by one way of trying to get out.) If we put the fly in glasses of shapes and shades different to this one, where it will be easier for it to get out, where it was less fascinated by the light, etc., and we trained it to fly out of these, it might fly out of this one also.

This recalls Wittgenstein's image of being stuck in a room with a door that one pushes on, but it only opens inward (CV, 42/48. Who hasn't pushed on a door even when the sign on the door clearly says "Pull"?), or an unnoticed door that is behind one (Malcolm, *Memoir*, 44; and see the "funny story" related at PPO, 384). The latter case was described by Wittgenstein in what is really an oral parable from his lectures. "Wittgenstein once described the situation in philosophy thus":

> It is as if a man is standing in a room facing a wall on which are painted a number of dummy doors. Wanting to get out, he fumblingly tries to open them, vainly trying them all, one after the other, over and over again. But, of course, it is quite useless. And all the time, although he doesn't realize it, there is a real door in the wall behind his back, and all he has to do is turn around and open it. To help him get out of the room all we have to do is to get him to look in a different direction. But it's hard to do this, since, wanting to get out, he resists our attempts to turn him away from where he thinks the exit must be.[65]

Both the fly bottle and the unnoticed door rely on the direction of attention as the key issue. When we suppose the solution to a problem must be found in a certain place, we are unlikely or unable to look in more productive places or directions. (Recall the point in chapter 1 where, in the *Investigations*, Wittgenstein fourteen times addresses what we notice, can get ourselves to think, can be satisfied with, think of, overlook, don't realize, fail to see, or forget.) So Wittgenstein takes his task to be to get us to redirect our attention.

Wittgenstein elaborates the fly-bottle scenario further in comments on a paper by Yorick Smythies on "Understanding" (*Whewell's Court Lectures*, 196; Lent term, 1940):

> Cf. the fly catcher. If you want to let him out, you'd have to surround this by something dark. As long as there is light there, the fly can never do it.
>
> If I am puzzled philosophically, I immediately darken all that which seems to me light, and try frantically to think of something entirely different. The point is, you can't get out as long as you are fascinated. The only thing to do is to go to an example where nothing fascinates me.

The fly is shown the way out by blocking the light that obsesses it, so that only the downward, indirectly lighted direction remains attractive. This shows how much the process is a negative one and also how much the process depends on knowing what happens to obsess the fly and how to redirect the fly's attention. Wittgenstein continues:

First of all, it is not at all clear that this will help every fly.

What happens to work with me doesn't work with him (Prof. Moore)—works with me now, and may not work with me tomorrow.[66]

There are always new ways of looking at the matter.

I constantly find new puzzles (I've thought about this for years, constantly ploughed these fields.)

When looking for a parable that might compare with the fly bottle, it is hard to avoid thinking of Plato's parable of the cave (*Republic*, Book VII, 514a–517a). In German this is standardly known as "*das Höhlengleichnis*."[67]

Assuming the reader is familiar with that parable, I will recount only some highlights:

Next, then, compare the effect of education and that of the lack of it on our nature to an experience [ἀπείκασον, also translated as representation/situation/image] like this . . .

It is a strange image you are describing, and strange prisoners.

They are like us . . .

Plato sees all of us as trapped in the cave, while Wittgenstein thinks it is the philosophers, or the philosophers in us, who are trapped in the bottle. Plato does not address how we got there or why:

Consider, then, what being released from their bonds and cured of their foolishness would naturally be like, if something like this should happen to them. When one was freed and suddenly compelled to stand up, turn his neck around, walk, and look up toward the light, he would be pained by doing all these things and be unable to see the things whose shadows he had seen before, because of the flashing lights. What do you think he would say if we told him that what he had seen before was nonsense, but that now—because he is a bit closer to what is, and is turned toward things that *are* more—he sees more correctly?

Plato does not address how the prisoner is liberated. Wittgenstein himself seems to be the liberator of the fly:

And if someone dragged him by force away from there, along the rough, steep, upward path, and did not let him go until he dragged him into the light of the sun, wouldn't he be pained and angry at being treated this way? And when he came into the light, wouldn't he have his eyes filled with sunlight and be unable to see one of the things now said to be truly real?

. . .

What about when he reminds himself of his first dwelling place, what passed for wisdom there, and his fellow prisoners? Don't you think he would count himself happy and pity the others?

> . . . Yes, he said, I think that he would rather suffer anything than live like that.

(We will come back to this point shortly.)

> Consider this too, then. If this man went back down into the cave and sat down in the same seat . . .
>
> . . . And as for anyone who tried to free the prisoners and lead them upward, if they could somehow get their hands on him, wouldn't they kill him?
>
> Certainly
>
> . . . .

Then there follows a commentary on the parable (517b–518b). This resembles the commentary on the fly-bottle aphorism that Wittgenstein offers in his lectures. There are notable similarities and differences, of course. Plato discusses how the enlightened ones would be gotten to rule:

> It is our task as founders, then, to compel the best natures to learn what was said before to be the most important thing: namely, to see the good; to ascend that ascent. And when they have ascended and looked sufficiently, we must . . . compel them to take care of the others and guard them.

What I focus on first is their functions as parables. It is interesting to note that Wittgenstein's fly-bottle image functions basically as an aphorism, one that he modified only slightly over time. But in lectures and discussions, he elaborated on it, so that orally it took on the dimensions of the parable of the cave. The cave is likely the most famous parable in the history of philosophy. Much of its worth comes from how many dimensions of Plato's philosophy it engages. But the parable of the cave could not be reduced to an aphorism because too much needs to be explained. Amazingly, the fly bottle works its magic in two sentences.

In chapter 5, I noted Wittgenstein's approvingly quoting Nietzsche to the effect that we philosophers want to be learned by heart, and then later disparaging his own work by lamenting that if it was philosophy, one could learn it by heart. We know that Wittgenstein cared about learning things by heart. As Ludwig Hänsel, his friend from prison camp, said about literature, he "knows a lot by heart." Indeed, he seems to have read *Brothers Karamazov* dozens of times and could quote passages from memory. And his Russian teacher, Fania Pascal, recalls that "once he [Wittgenstein] quoted a Pushkin lyric to me" (p. 21).

Despite his pessimism, some passages from Wittgenstein really do manage to rise to this level—and the fly-bottle aphorism is one of them. It is brief, but more important, it is memorable, offering a remarkable comparison and an unexpected image.

While the art of learning things by heart has become something of a lost art, it still remains in religious circles. In my own experience, biblical passages such as the Twenty-Third Psalm, or the Lord's Prayer, or the Apostles' Creed are regularly recited in church services without the need of a script. It is notable that all three of these cases, at least when recited in English, are recited in an archaic English from (the era of) the King James translation of the Bible. While the use of multiple translations of the Bible may be valuable from a semantic point of view, helping to better capture the nuances of meanings in the texts, it makes it less likely that readers will commit passages to memory.

Another passage from Wittgenstein that has risen to the level of memorability is the closing line of the *Tractatus*: "Whereof one cannot speak, thereof one must be silent." That, of course, is in the original Ogden-Ramsey translation. Pears and McGuinness later render it as, "What we cannot speak about we must pass over in silence." The original translation is more memorable: it has a poetic feeling that is not unconnected with its use of the archaic words *whereof* and *thereof*.

Among the parts of *Brothers Karamazov* that most impressed Wittgenstein was book 6, about the Russian monk, Father Zosima. Passages from this book drew on the language of Church Slavonic and echoed rites of the church that would have been familiar to the original Russian readers. Dostoevsky did this so that it would have a certain emotional effect on readers. Wittgenstein learned Russian specifically so that he could read Dostoevsky and Tolstoy in the original.[68] All of this would have contributed to being able to learn passages by heart.

But there is another point worth considering. Earlier I noted that I would return to Plato's claim that the person liberated from the cave "would rather suffer anything than live like that." In the parable Plato tells, this seems convincing, but in fact it is not at all clear. Case studies of people who have either gained sight for the first time or regained sight after a long period of blindness contain virtually no success stories. One might suppose, and blind patients or their family members often do suppose, that gaining sight will be a tremendous asset. In fact, surprisingly, it is not. For those who have come to live and flourish as blind, adding a sense is apparently only disorienting.

Oliver Sacks, the late neuropsychologist, personally studied such a patient, Virgil, and collected historical memoirs from several others, in the paper "To See or Not to See."[69] One thing that becomes clear is that seeing is not simply opening a window (or, rather, opening blinds) onto the world; rather, it is something that we learn to do. And we generally learn to do it at a stage when our brains have and use the capacity for acquiring that ability. When it is not acquired or when it is lost for a long period of time, that capacity gets put to other purposes and is not (easily) available for such use again. As a result, vision has no useful place in the patient's relation to the world. Sacks and others emphasize "the emotional dangers of forcing a new sense on a blind man—how, after an initial exhilaration, a devastating (and even lethal) depression can ensue" (138). Sacks finds no successes to report and concludes his own case study, "Now, at last, Virgil is allowed not to see, allowed to escape from the glaring, confusing world of sight and space, and to return to his own true being, the intimate, concentrated world of the other senses that had been his home for almost fifty years" (152), He is happily back in the cave—for good.

This gives one considerably more sympathy for the residents of the cave. While Plato notes the need for the liberated prisoner to adjust to the glare of the fire and then of the sun (515c–516b), he assumes that the adjustment will happen, and happen fully. And this is what sighted people assume as well. But it turns out to be extremely problematic. And when Plato imagines that the prisoners would try to kill the enlightened person when he returns to the cave (517a), that is not far from how the previously blind person in fact feels toward those (including perhaps his own previously optimistic self) who advocated for the sight-giving surgery.

This, I believe, constitutes an illustration of the qualms that Wittgenstein expressed about Kierkegaard's approach: "The idea that someone uses a trick to get me to do something is unpleasant. It is certain that it takes great courage (to use this trick) & that I would not—not remotely—have this courage; but it's a question whether if I had it, it would be right to use it. I *think* that aside from courage it would also take a lack of love of one's fellow human being."[70] I propose that the trick here is using a good story to foist an untested idea on the reader, and the moral question becomes whether Plato shows "a lack of love of one's fellow human being" thereby. Here is a danger of *Dichtung*: sometimes our imagination misleads us.

While Wittgenstein sought to lead philosophers out of the fly bottle, J. N. Findlay praised Ernest Gellner's controversial critique, *Words and Things*, as "worth reading if only for its account of Wittgenstein driving escaped men back into the cave."[71]

Parable of the Wall

This story is known only through oral tradition; Wittgenstein's student Wasfi Hijab recounted it on several occasions. This is a transcription of Hijab's oral account in 2002:

> [Wittgenstein told] another parable that he also tried to use to explain what he was doing. He said "I will call this a 'parable,' the parable of the wall."
>
> Somebody was living in a village, and in that village there was a very high wall. And, nobody had ever crossed the wall. But, there were faint traces on the wall as if there were gates, but nobody has ever opened any of them. One time somebody [viz. Wittgenstein] noticed that there were many holes on these walls, and also he noticed that there were small, shining, glittering keys, golden keys scattered all about. And he tried to apply some of these keys in the right order to some of these holes. And then he found that he could open the gates very easily. But the keys had to be applied in the right order. And then people went around saying that all the gates had been opened, and this was not true. And some people said that nothing had been opened, and this was also not true. People around him were fascinated by the small, glittering, golden keys. And they started playing with them. And they forgot that the purpose of the keys was to open the gates.

Then the person who recorded Hijab's account adds, "Wittgenstein's reminders are the keys to resolving philosophical confusions. . . . Perhaps the most vivid image in the Parable of the Wall is the people (presumably philosophers) in rapt fascination playing with the keys that Wittgenstein had used to open gates. These people focused entirely on the keys themselves. They forgot what the keys were good for. . . . The moral of the story is that we should be doing more than simply playing with the keys." Then the recorder returns to the source: "Hijab added, 'Of course he [Wittgenstein] was making this remark about some student of his who was writing or publishing and really making use of the keys without really trying to use them properly.'"[72] So we have the parable, and then an interpretation of the parable.[73]

On page 12 of MS 133 (October 24, 1946, during Wittgenstein's last academic year teaching), there is a moving interjection: "Oh, a key can lie there for ever, where the master [locksmith] put it down, and never be put to use to unlock the lock the master made it to open." In MS 138, p. 17a (February 9, 1949), Wittgenstein writes, "Philosophers such as Wisdom, Ayer, et. al. They show you a bunch of keys they have stolen, but they can't open any doors with them."

This parable resembles the fly bottle in the sense that it is a fascination that keeps the villagers in the village—playing with the keys rather than using them, or flying toward the light and ignoring the escape route. (In this way, this parable is associated with achieving aim G.) In both cases, Wittgenstein recommended a strategy for lowering the fascination—attending to ordinary uses of words: "Compare the solution of philosophical problems with the fairy tale gift that seems magical in the enchanted castle and if it is looked at in daylight is nothing but an ordinary bit of iron (or something of the sort)."[74] And recall the strategy of darkening all which seems light by finding an example that no longer fascinates.

Comparing the various failed and successful ways of doing philosophy reminds one of Jesus's parable of the sower, which compares the fates of various failed and successful seeds (Mark 4: 2–9):

> And he taught them many things by parables, and said unto them in his doctrine, Hearken; Behold, there went out a sower to sow: And it came to pass, as he sowed, some fell by the way side, and the fowls of the air came and devoured it up. And some fell on stony ground, where it had not much earth; and immediately it sprang up, because it had no depth of earth: But when the sun was up, it was scorched; and because it had no root, it withered away. And some fell among thorns, and the thorns grew up, and choked it, and it yielded no fruit. And other fell on good ground, and did yield fruit that sprang up and increased; and brought forth, some thirty, and some sixty, and some a hundred. And he said unto them, He that hath ears to hear, let him hear.

What is interesting about this biblical parable is that it is followed by an explanation of its meaning as an allegory (Mark 4:10–20), much as Wittgenstein's parable of the wall is too.

Jesus enumerates various ways (soils) in which the seed can fail to flourish, and Wittgenstein enumerates various ways in which the keys can fail to be used (because they have served their purpose—all the doors are open; because they don't work—none of the doors have been opened; and because they are fascinating as shiny objects and not as keys—they are not used as keys). Jesus acknowledges the one kind of soil in which the seeds flourish, and Wittgenstein acknowledges the one kind of use, in the right order, in which the keys can unlock the doors.[75]

What is Jesus's point in telling the parable? To reassure the listeners/disciples that even though his (Jesus's) ministry is often unsuccessful, it is sometimes successful. Does he indicate/assign blame? He does not suggest being careful about where the seeds are sown. In fact in another parable, he indicates we should not worry about seeds growing among weeds: we should let everything grow and God will sort it out in the end (Matthew 13:24–30). So, in general the parable seems to encourage freely sharing the message and not losing heart. In this sense, the listener is encouraged to identify as or with the sower. But the parable also offers the listener the opportunity to place oneself elsewhere in the story: What kind of soil am I? What must I do to be the "good ground"? Wittgenstein in fact picks up on this very imagery when he writes:

> My originality (if that's the right word) is, I believe, an originality of the soil, not of the seed. (Perhaps I have no seed of my own.) Throw a seed into my soil and it will grow in a different way than it would in any other soil.[76]

Wittgenstein also used an analogous image concerning the atmosphere. He often advised his students to leave academia and get jobs in the working class. In 1931 he advised his student and friend Con Drury, "It is essential that you get away from Cambridge at once. There is no oxygen in Cambridge for you." But as for himself, Wittgenstein insisted: "It doesn't matter for me, as I manufacture my own oxygen."[77] In a remark in a notebook from 1942, he later elaborated, "Put someone in the wrong atmosphere & nothing will function as it should. He will seem unhealthy in every part. Bring him back into his right element, & everything will blossom and look healthy. But if he is not in his right element, what then? Well he just has to make the best of looking like a cripple."[78] The "wrong atmosphere" is like the poor soil.

What is Wittgenstein's point in telling the parable? To identify why his teaching has not had its intended effect—students are too optimistic, or too pessimistic, or too fascinated with showing off the tools rather than solving the problems. In this sense, it does not really offer any reassurance. It seems to be aimed at blaming philosophers for their failures.[79] But here too, the listener is given the opportunity to decide whether to use the keys, or just play with them; to wonder which doors have been opened, or remain to be opened; to ask, How is this parable enacted in my life?

Does the parable have a noncognitive effect? It seems to do so by drawing listeners into the story and engaging their emotions. Perhaps we see things differently, or have tools to see things differently, as a result of hearing the story. If we think of Wittgenstein's "poems" as keys in this parable, then we might say that in this chapter, I have been looking at how those keys work, whether there are other keys we might try to use, and how we can use keys to open some doors.

Can an Animal Hope?

PI, part II, section I, p. 174 (= PPF §1 in the fourth edition): "One can imagine an animal angry, frightened, unhappy, happy, startled. But hopeful? And why not? A dog believes his master is at the door. But can he believe his master will come the day after tomorrow?—And *what* can he not do here?—How do I do it?—How am I supposed to answer this? Can only those hope who can talk? Only those who have mastered the use of a language. That is to say, the phenomena of hope are modes of this complicated form of life."

This passage appears earlier (MS 137, p. 114b; December 1, 1948): "It is easy to imagine an animal angry, timid, sad, happy, terrified. But hoping? Hope is a quiet, joyful expectation. (Such an analysis is somewhat repugnant.)" And then it continues as above. In a still earlier notebook (MS 131, p. 128; August 28, 1946), Wittgenstein considers a different example: "Can I then speak of a behavior of anger, for example, and of another of hope? (It's easy to imagine an orangutan angry—but hoping, and why is that?)"[80]

Some concepts exist only as part of a larger network of concepts. The possession of this network of concepts constitutes a mode of being in the world that Wittgenstein calls here a form of life. Some concepts are more separable from the network than others. Thus, animals can be characterized in some ways, or can experience some things, but not others. But how can we know this, or make this case, for certain concepts as opposed to others? This seems to call more for a story than an assertion or an argument.

Dostoevsky was one of Wittgenstein's favorite writers, *The Brothers Karamazov* was his greatest novel. Given his intense his intense engagement with the book, the following story must have been familiar to Wittgenstein. It raises the point that for certain emotions—in this case, pride—there needs to be a certain level of conceptual, indeed linguistic, sophistication:

This Lizaveta was a dwarfish creature, "not five foot within a wee bit," as many of the pious old women said pathetically about her, after her death. Her broad, healthy, red face had a look of blank idiocy and the fixed stare in her eyes was unpleasant, in spite of their meek expression. She wandered about, summer and winter alike, barefooted, wearing nothing but a hempen smock. Her coarse, almost black hair curled like lamb's wool, and formed a sort of huge cap on her head. It was always crusted with mud, and had leaves, bits of stick, and shavings clinging to it, as she always slept on the ground and in the dirt. Her father, a homeless, sickly drunkard, called Ilya, had lost everything and lived many years as a workman with some well-to-do tradespeople. Her mother had long been dead. Spiteful and diseased, Ilya used to beat Lizaveta inhumanly whenever she returned to him. But she rarely did so, for everyone in the town was ready to look after her as being an idiot, and so specially dear to God. Ilya's employers, and many others in the town, especially of the tradespeople, tried to clothe her better, and always rigged her out with high boots and sheepskin coat for the winter. But, although she allowed them to dress her up without resisting, she usually went away, preferably to the cathedral porch, and taking off all that had been given her—kerchief, sheepskin, skirt or boots—she left them there and walked away barefoot in her smock as before. It happened on one occasion that a new governor of the province, making a tour of inspection in our town, saw Lizaveta, and was wounded in his tenderest susceptibilities. And though he was told she was an idiot, he pronounced that for a young woman of twenty to wander about in nothing but a smock was a breach of the proprieties, and must not occur again. But the governor went his way, and Lizaveta was left as she was. At last her father died, which made her even more acceptable in the eyes of the religious persons of the town, as an orphan. In fact, everyone seemed to like her; even the boys did not tease her, and the boys of our town, especially the schoolboys, are a mischievous set. She would walk into strange houses, and no one drove her away. Everyone was kind to her and gave her something. If she were given a copper, she would take it, and at once drop it in the alms-jug of the church or prison. If she were given a roll or bun in the market, she would hand it to the first child she met. Sometimes she would stop one of the richest ladies in the town and give it to her, and the lady would be pleased to take it. She herself never tasted anything but black bread and water. If she went into an expensive shop, where there were costly goods or money lying about, no one kept watch on her, for they knew that if she saw thousands of roubles overlooked by them, she would not have touched a farthing. She scarcely ever went to church. She slept either in the church porch or climbed over a hurdle (there are many hurdles instead of fences to this day in our town) into a kitchen garden. She used at least once a week to turn up "at home," that is at the house of her father's former employers, and in the winter went there every night, and slept either in the passage or the cow-house. People were amazed that she could stand such a life, but she was accustomed to it, and, although she was so tiny, she was of a robust constitution. Some of the townspeople declared

> that she did all this only from pride, but that is hardly credible. She could hardly speak, and only from time to time uttered an inarticulate grunt. How could she have been proud?[81]

Pride seems to hold a position in a conceptual network not unlike the position of hope, so the two cases are relatively similar. Of course, Lizaveta is not an animal, but her intellectual limitations put her on a level different from ordinary people and raise the same kind of questions about the range of concepts that can be attributed to her. It is interesting that the author-narrator appends this bit of conceptual commentary at the end, much as Wittgenstein does in his assertion. But it is well motivated by the account that precedes it. And the account—the story—makes it memorable and persuasive in a way that the assertion by itself is not.

There is a rather vague and confusing account by Bouwsma of a conversation he and several other philosophers had with Wittgenstein when he was visiting Cornell in 1949. They are discussing pride and how it might be exhibited:

> How did I exhibit "pride"? By reading from *The Brothers Karamazov*. W. seemed to approve of this but he made some objection which I did not understand. He said somebody else might write a different book, apparently exhibiting pride in a different light. The point seemed to be that what is relevant is patterns of life which are enmeshed with all sorts of other things, and so this makes the matter much more complex than at first it seemed. . . . Pride is specified in a context of other interests and other human beings. . . . Pride is like an infection, a fever. It isn't located like a sore thumb.[82]

It seems possible—even likely—they were discussing this very passage, making this same point.

Rembrandt

TLP 6.41: "The sense of the world must lie outside the world. In the world everything is as it is, and everything happens as it does happen: in it no value exists—and if it did exist, it would have no value. If there is any value that does have value, it must lie outside the whole sphere of what happens and is the case. For all that happens and is the case is accidental. What makes it non-accidental cannot lie within the world, since if it did it would itself be accidental. It must lie outside the world."

I include a passage from the *Tractatus*. This might seem out of place, especially since I argued in chapter 1 that Wittgenstein was esoteric, not evangelical, at that time. And not being evangelical, he would not have cared greatly about how to convey his point to readers. Of course, there is a large literature about how we should take the propositions of the *Tractatus*, and I do not care to enter into that debate here. But Wittgenstein's esoteric attitude did not prevent him from trying to figure out how to convey his thoughts to those on the *inside*. We know, for example, that in his correspondence with Engelmann, they discussed a poem that Engelmann had sent on April 4, 1917—"Count Eberhard's Hawthorne" (see chapter 4). In a return letter, less than a week later, Wittgenstein praises the poem and notes how it shows what cannot be said. As I indicated in chapter 1, Engelmann was among those that Wittgenstein would have counted as his inner circle at that time and later.

Another member, I conjectured, of that inner circle was his sister Hermine. Ludwig had a close and intellectual relationship with Hermine, which can be traced in the family correspondence.[83] In addition to their correspondence, she kept notes of her thoughts, often ones provoked by her conversations with Ludwig. The conversations tended to be about literature, religion, and philosophy. In these notes, she often recounts things that Ludwig said to her. In February 1917, she recorded the following:

> Ludwig gave me the following comparison [*Vergleich*] in a conversation about Christianity. One could imagine a painting by Rembrandt hung in a room from time immemorial. It was admired and appreciated by the previous owners accordingly, but the present owners have lost all sense [*Sinn*] of it. A stranger, just a simple man, asks the people what that thing is they have hanging on the wall, according to tradition it should be something infinitely valuable & precious, he volunteers himself to undertake a chemical investigation of the thing. It turns out that it is made of ordinary canvas which was coated with oil and some other substance, from which the people conclude that those were badly mistaken who had spoken of the high value [*Wert*] of the object. In a still later time the understanding emerged again and now it seemed incomprehensible that there could have been a time in which Rembrandt could have been evaluated [*bewerten*] according to a chemical investigation.[84]

Here we have a tale that Ludwig seems to have made up and shows that the value of a painting (it is "infinitely valuable" and of "high value") cannot be found in the world—through a "chemical investigation of the thing"—but nevertheless it does have value. The conclusion in the *Tractatus* is that value lies outside the world.

In his course lectures in May 1933, Wittgenstein talked about goodness and beauty. He generally makes the case that goodness (and beauty) are family resemblance concepts.[85] One of the views he *opposes* is that beauty might be some kind of ingredient—an extra quality: "a quality like *kalon* [fine, beautiful] is an ingredient in beautiful things: & could be caught in a bottle by itself."[86] This is the view that the chemist seems to take in his investigation of the Rembrandt painting: He fails to find anything (an expensive ingredient?) beyond the canvas and the oil paints and concludes that the painting lacks value. (Here we have an example of aim F: resisting hypostatization, that value must be a thing.) The view that Wittgenstein considers more seriously here, as I have argued, is that beauty (or goodness) consists in the arrangement of other characteristics, of the sort that the chemist found.[87] Of course, an arrangement is not an entity or an object—so it is not *in* the world, as that notion is understood in the *Tractatus*—but it also is not a nonnatural quality, as G. E. Moore understood that notion.

In December 1933 or early the next year, a little thought experiment occurred to Wittgenstein: "Suppose someone were to say: 'Imagine this butterfly exactly as it is, but ugly instead of beautiful'!?" (first in MS 115, p. 20; then in a context: *Philosophical Grammar*, p. 175, §127; and then as a clipping without context: Z §199). He later adds a comment to it (TS 229, p. 116/TS 230, p. 45): "(The question arises: what is required of us? This would need an explanation.)" Presumably this cannot be done—for it to change from beautiful to ugly is for it to change in some other characteristics, presumably its colors and/or the arrangement of its colors. The thought experiment illustrates this dependency.

Wittgenstein struggles with the connection between value, as in the content of a letter, and what embodies the value, the ink and paper, in his diary entry for January 27, 1937:

> From words no belief follows. . . .
>
> —But aren't there various ways of being interested in ink & paper? Am I not interested in ink & paper when I read a letter attentively? For at any rate while doing that I am looking attentively at ink strokes.—"But here these are only means to an end!"—But surely a very *important* means to an end!—Yes of course we can imagine other investigations of ink & paper which would be of no interest to us, which would appear to us completely inessential to our end. But therefore what interests us will be shown by our sort of investigation. Our subject is, so it seems, sublime & therefore, one would think, it should not deal with trivial & in a certain sense shaky [*unsicheren*] objects but with the indestructible.[88]

Wittgenstein returns to the chemist's idea about the value of the Rembrandt painting in lectures in 1938, where he now sees the issue in different terms as the temptation to look for a thing's worth in its physical ingredients:

> Cf. "If we boil Redpath at 200°C. all that is left when the water vapor is gone is some ashes, etc. This is all Redpath really is." Saying this might have a certain charm, but would be misleading to say the least.
>
> The attraction of certain kinds of explanation is overwhelming. At a given time the attraction of a certain kind of explanation is greater than you can conceive. In particular, explanation of the kind "This is really only this."[89]

The chemist has given in to a temptation. But the stories show how the temptation is misguided.

Games

Wittgenstein's discussion of *game* (at PI §66) is well known. He makes the case that there is not an essence—a set of necessary and sufficient conditions—that characterizes the concept. He made similar claims regarding *language, good,* and *religion.*[90] In each case, the claim is plausible. But as I indicated in a previous chapter, his real aim is not that any particular concept lacks an essence, but that in general, perfectly good concepts may lack an essence. The general claim could be established by producing an exception, showing (at least) one perfectly good concept that lacks an essence. (This is Wittgenstein's central example for aim A.)

But there is a problem with showing that a concept lacks an essence—it is a negative existential. And it is hard to see how to establish a negative existential.[91] How can we show that a concept *lacks* an essence? In his discussion Wittgenstein considers various possible conditions and quickly suggests exceptions, or counterexamples, to the conditions. While his discussion is plausible, it never rules out the possibility of other conditions. It simply stands as a sort of inductive argument: all these plausible conditions failed; therefore, it is probable that all conditions will fail. In this way, Wittgenstein's case is reminiscent of Moore's case that Goodness is indefinable. In *Principia Ethica,* Moore considers various plausible candidates and plausibly dismisses them. But there is no proof that none can succeed. Moore's "open-question argument" apparently works against various proposed definitions—but it is hard to say that it will inevitably work.

It is always open to the Socratic opponent—one who insists there *is* an essence—to offer, or at least believe in, another condition. In fact, Bernard Suits has written a whole book on this issue and offers the following definition: "Playing a game is the voluntary attempt to overcome unnecessary obstacles."[92] I don't wish to arbitrate this debate, but the proposal does seem plausible, and it suggests that there may always be another plausible proposal lurking around the corner. Perhaps we can say that the best way to counter our temptation to find a definition is to wear it down—to intimate its futility. Wittgenstein's friend Drury made such a suggestion to Wittgenstein in a conversation in 1930:

> It may be significant that those dialogues in which Socrates is looking for precise definitions end, all of them, without any conclusion. The definition he is looking for isn't reached, but only suggested definitions refuted. This might have been Socrates' ironical way of showing that there was something wrong in looking for one exact meaning of such general terms.[93]

Drury records no reply from Wittgenstein, but in any case, there is nothing poetic about that approach.

Similar problems arise for Wittgenstein's desire to avoid theorizing about philosophical issues or offering philosophical theories (aim B). While one may show exceptions to proposed theories, it doesn't follow that no theory could succeed. The philosophical theory that was uppermost in Wittgenstein's own mind was the theory of language offered in the *Tractatus*. It is precisely this that Wittgenstein considers in PI §65, leading into his discussion of games, where he returns to his investigation of "the *general form of the proposition* and of language." Even if Wittgenstein felt his account in the *Tractatus* was inadequate, there might always be a better theory, yet to be formulated.

Apparently Wittgenstein was brought to give up not only his theory in the *Tractatus*, but the whole search for such a theory, by his discussions with Piero Sraffa. There seems to have been a particular incident that was crucial to this process. Here is part of the story, as told by one of Wittgenstein's friends:

> Wittgenstein and Sraffa, a lecturer in economics at Cambridge, argued together a great deal over the ideas of the *Tractatus*. One day (they were riding, I think, on a train) when Wittgenstein was insisting that a proposition and that which it describes must have the same "logical form", . . . Sraffa made a gesture, familiar to Neapolitans as meaning something like disgust or contempt, of brushing the

> underneath of his chin with an outward sweep of the finger-tips of one hand. And he asked: "What is the logical form of that?" Sraffa's example produced in Wittgenstein the feeling that there was an absurdity in the insistence that a proposition and what it describes must have the same "form". This broke the hold on him of the conception that a proposition must literally be a "picture" of the reality it describes.[94]

The gesture Sraffa used was akin to giving someone the finger. Sraffa's point was that a gesture could convey meaning in the way language does, and yet it does not do so by representing a state of affairs. It does not get meaning by sharing a logical form. Language does not have to be representational. Another friend said Wittgenstein's "discussions with Sraffa made him feel like a tree from which all branches had been cut."[95] And Wittgenstein himself testified to Sraffa's "stimulus" and its impact on his thinking in the Preface to the *Investigations*.

Clearly this gesture (Could we call it a "poetic gesture"?) had a lasting impact that imprinted itself on Wittgenstein. And the anecdote has had a similar effect on students of Wittgenstein. It opened Wittgenstein up to a new way of thinking. It was more than just an exception or counterexample. It changed his way of thinking, his movement of thought.

Once Wittgenstein gave up his theory that language operated by either saying or showing, he was enthralled by the variety of language. In §23 of the *Investigations*, he asks, "How many kinds of sentence are there?" and replies: "There are *countless* [*unzählige*] kinds." He then proceeds to list about nineteen of them. Three years after the *Investigations* was published, an Oxford philosopher, J. L. Austin, gave a talk on BBC radio, in which he made fun of this reply:

> Certainly there are a great many uses of language. . . . I think we should not despair too easily and talk, as people are apt to do, about the infinite uses of language. Philosophers will do this when they have listed as many, let us say, as seventeen; but even if there were something like ten thousand uses of language, surely we could list them all in time. This, after all, is no larger than the number of species of beetle that entomologists have taken the pains to list.[96]

Austin approached language much as an entomologist classifies insects. He was looking for a theory.

While this reaction by Austin to Wittgenstein came well after the latter's death, the two had crossed paths ten years earlier. On October 31, 1946, Austin gave a talk to the Cambridge Moral Sciences Club on "Nondescription." In his notebook the next day, Wittgenstein wrote: "Yesterday 'Moral Science

Club': I myself conceited and stupid as well. The 'atmosphere' *wretched* [*elend*].—Should I go on teaching?" The difference between Austin and Wittgenstein was not merely a difference of beliefs, but a difference of temperament.[97]

In his approach to understanding the unity of a concept, Wittgenstein seems to have taken inspiration from Johann Wolfgang von Goethe (1749–1832), a German polymath whose work extended from plays and poetry to botany and physics.[98] But he used his literary background to create a humanistic approach to science. Goethe did considerable observational research on plants, offering his scientific account in *The Metamorphosis of Plants* (1790), which is considered a forerunner of later work by Darwin. At first sight, it may seem that Goethe is theorizing in a way that Wittgenstein would reject—for example: "the various plant parts developed in sequence are intrinsically identical despite their manifold differences in outward form," which sounds more like Hegel than like Wittgenstein.[99] And Goethe "now propose[s] to explain it" in his essay.[100] But he sees commonalities that he brings out by comparisons:

> The power shown in gradual vegetative growth is closely related to the power suddenly displayed in major reproduction. . . . In saying that vegetative growth is successive reproduction, while flowering and fruiting are simultaneous reproduction, we are also describing how each occurs. . . . We can say that a stamen is a contracted petal or, with equal justification, that a petal is a stamen in a state of expansion; that a sepal is a contracted stem leaf with a certain degree of refinement, or that a stem leaf is a sepal expanded by an influx of cruder juices. We might likewise say of the stem that it is an expanded flower and fruit, just as we assumed that the flower and fruit are a contracted stem.

And he sums up his account:

> We have sought to derive the apparently different organs of the vegetating and flowering plant from one organ; i.e., the leaf normally developed at each node. We have likewise ventured to find in the leaf form a source for the fruits which completely cover the seed.[101]

Goethe is not revealing hidden causal connections but highlighting similarities through observations of suggested juxtapositions. He elaborated his method in the opening sentences of a fragment entitled "Studies for a Physiology of Plants":

> To arrange things in order is a large and difficult undertaking.
>
> To know an orderly way demands exact knowledge of each individual object. Attention to its character; i.e., differences and similarities.[102]

Goethe's method here could be a statement of Wittgenstein's synoptic approach.[103]

Waismann records (or presents) Wittgenstein's view in just this way: "What we are doing here runs parallel to some extent with Goethe's ideas about the metamorphosis of plants":

> From Goethe stems the conception of the "primal plant": yet surely he saw it only in an idea, not something real. But what then is the problem solved by this idea? *The problem of synoptic presentation*. Goethe's aphorism "All the organs of plants are leaves transformed" gives us a schema by which we group the organs of the plants according to their degree of similarity, as it were around a central case. . . . We see the leaf, as it were, in its natural surroundings of forms. . . . And this is exactly what we are doing; we situate a linguistic form in its surroundings, we see the grammar of our language against a background of similar and related games, and that banishes disquiet [*das bannt die Beunruhigung*].[104]

I have raised doubt about whether a synoptic presentation will necessarily be as effective as Wittgenstein here takes it to be, so it is notable that Goethe took this very point to heart: after publishing his rather dry and academic essay in 1790, he published a poem under the same title in 1798! According to an editor: "Years later Goethe composed a poem also titled 'The Metamorphosis of Plants' . . . in an effort to make his scientific efforts and pursuits more palatable and intelligible to his wife and women friends, though with only limited success."[105]

Goethe's poem consists of elegiac couplets, but what makes it interesting as a poem in Wittgenstein's sense is that it provides a sort of narrative that takes a profusion of plants and characteristics of plants and tells a story of the development of a plant in the abstract that accounts for these—not in a causal sense, but in a way that makes sense out of the profusion. He addresses it to one who is precisely confused:

> You are confused, beloved, by the thousandfold mingled multitude of flowers all over the garden. You listen to their many names which are forever, one after another, ringing outlandishly in your ears. All their shapes are similar, yet none is the same as the next; and thus the whole chorus of them suggests a secret law, a sacred riddle. Sweet lady, could I but at once convey to you in a word the happy solution [*glücklich das lösende Wort*]![106]

After his poetic synopsis, he claims, "Turn now your gaze, beloved, to the many-coloured throng, which no longer moves confusingly before your mind's eye." And he concludes by using the growth of a plant as a simile for human striving through friendship to love. We might say that Goethe has provided a synopsis of the world of plants through a series of poetic comparisons.

Apparently Goethe intended to follow this poem with "a philosophical poem on the whole of nature, a modern Lucretius . . . ," starting with a separate poem based on his magnetic experiments.[107] Goethe provides a historical illustration of Wittgenstein's claim: "The purpose of a good expression or a good comparison [*Gleichnisses*] is that it permits an instant synopsis [*augenblickliche Übersicht*]."[108]

"An Expression Has Meaning Only in the Stream of Life"

Norman Malcolm was one of Wittgenstein's students in 1939 and again in 1946–1947, in the course of which they became friends. Wittgenstein visited Malcolm in the United States in summer 1949. Recalling their conversations in 1949, Malcolm noted:

> One remark of his struck me then, as it does now, as being especially noteworthy and as summing up a good deal of his philosophy. It is "*Ein Ausdruck hat nur im Strome des Lebens Bedeutung* [An expression has meaning only in the stream of life]." Wittgenstein believed that this aphorism was written down in one of his manuscripts.[109]

And, indeed, in a manuscript written shortly before, in spring 1949, we find: "*Nur im Fluß des Lebens haben die Worte ihre Bedeutung* [Words have their meaning only in the flow of life]."[110]

This aphorism (as Malcolm calls it, perhaps after Wittgenstein) echoes concerns from the *Investigations* that philosophical problems arise "when language *goes on holiday*" (PI §38) and "when language is, as it were, idling, not when it is doing work" (PI §132). Wittgenstein proposes to "bring words back from their metaphysical to their everyday use" (PI §116).

This makes it sound as though it is language itself that "goes on holiday," though of course it is we, language users, who use language in its natural language games or not. Presumably it would be ideal if people never misused language in such ways. It is interesting that Wittgenstein finds contrasting images to use here—"going on holiday [*feiert*]" sounds pretty good, while "idling [*leerläuft*]" just sounds lazy. But what would it *be* like to be someone for whom words have meaning only in the flow of life?

In fact, Tolstoy gave us a picture of such a person—the character Platon in *War and Peace*. The protagonist, Pierre, meets Platon in a prisoner-of-war camp. Platon is the archetypal good Russian peasant and soldier:

> To all the other prisoners Platon Karataev seemed a most ordinary soldier. They called him "little falcon" or "Platosha," chaffed him good-naturedly, and sent him on errands. But to Pierre he always remained what he had seemed that first night: an unfathomable, rounded, eternal personification of the spirit of simplicity and truth.
>
> Platon Karataev knew nothing by heart except his prayers. When he began to speak he seemed not to know how he would conclude.
>
> Sometimes Pierre, struck by the meaning of his words, would ask him to repeat them, but Platon could never recall what he had said a moment before, just as he never could repeat to Pierre the words of his favorite song: "native" and "birch tree" and "my heart is sick" occurred in it, but when spoken and not sung, no meaning could be got out of it. He did not, and could not, understand the meaning of words apart from their context. Every word and action of his was the manifestation of an activity unknown to him, which was his life. But his life, as he regarded it, had no meaning as a separate thing. It had meaning only as part of a whole of which he was always conscious. His words and actions flowed from him as evenly, inevitably, and spontaneously as fragrance exhales from a flower. He could not understand the value or significance of any word or deed taken separately.[111]

Platon's conversation embodies the conception of language that Wittgenstein offered: "An expression has meaning only in the stream of life." A person such as this could not get into philosophical confusions. But would we want to be Platon, incapable of philosophical confusion, or even philosophical reflection?

Wittgenstein is sometimes called an "antiphilosopher." You can see why he would get that label if his goal were to (get us to) become like Platon. This criticism might be reinforced with the quotation from Wittgenstein's notebook: "Philosophy is a tool which is useful only against philosophers and against the philosopher in us."[112] But is the philosopher in us just an illness?

The comparison of philosophical puzzlement to an illness (PI §255) raises the parallel question of whether or how a person cured of an illness is better off than a person who never contracted it. A cured person may have two advantages—she may have acquired an immunity to the illness or learned how to cure the illness, which can then be an advantage to others as well.[113]

But despite his comparison, I don't think Wittgenstein saw philosophical problems as simply illnesses. He also regarded the temptations that get us into philosophical problems as natural—built into either the language or our psyche. Could a natural condition really be considered an illness? Is aging an illness?

Perhaps someone who doesn't even encounter philosophical problems is not fully aware or fully reflective. While the cure for philosophical temptation is to appreciate the ordinary language games where our words have their homes, this appreciation isn't complete unless it is accompanied by awareness of its challenges and its alternatives. While there is something to admire in Platon, there is also something missing in him.

When Wittgenstein compared himself to a tour guide, he implied that philosophical puzzlement is like being lost: "A philosophical problem has the form: 'I don't know my way about'" (PI §123). Doesn't a lost person need to get somewhere else? Not necessarily, for not knowing your "way about" does not mean you are in the wrong place—just that you are disoriented. Someone who was disoriented and now is oriented may have the advantage of knowing the lay of the land better. How is a tour guide better than a local? Imagine Platon offering these directions to a person who is lost: "Go down this road and then turn left where that old trailer used to be." Not a great tour guide.

Some years after completing *War and Peace*, Tolstoy himself sought to live a life not unlike that of Platon, but with a difference: "I returned to a belief in God, in moral perfection, and to that tradition which had given life a meaning. Only the difference now was that whereas before I had accepted all this unconsciously, I now knew that I could not live without it." But he had now overcome "the temptation of futile theorizing." There is a kind of knowledge of place that comes from having been displaced. Perhaps what we seek is a critical awareness in place of Platon's naive unawareness.[114] If so, then it is not quite true that Wittgenstein was simply "driving escaped men back into the cave."

Beetle in the Box

PI §253: "'Another person can't have my pains.'—*My* pains—what pains are they? What counts as a criterion of identity here? Consider what makes it possible in the case of physical objects to speak of 'two exactly the same':

for example, to say, 'This chair is not the one you saw here yesterday, but it is exactly the same as it.'"[115]

We have a strong temptation to hypostatize mental states—to treat them as things. This would allow us to endow them with identity conditions that would distinguish between numerical identity (as with physical objects, for which we employ spatiotemporal continuity as the criterion) and qualitative indiscernibility. And this then opens our conception of mental states to undetectable possibilities like the inverted spectrum. Wittgenstein tries to reveal the mistake with this conception, for example, in the following:

> "What I perceive is *this*—" and now follows a form of *description*. The word "this" might be explained as follows: Let us imagine a direct transfer of experience.—But now what is our criterion for the experience's really having been transferred? "Well, he just does have what I have."—But how does *he "have"* it?[116]

Robert Thouless reports a conversation with Wittgenstein in 1941:

> To illustrate how language led us to hypostatise objects, [Wittgenstein] told a story of how he had the experience of his soul being outside his body (in a state of extreme fatigue after watching by the bedside of his mother). But one might ask, how can you, Wittgenstein, have such an experience as of your soul being outside your body? The answer is "I had". It is the language forms to which we have been conditioned all our lives which give us the means of such an expression of experience.[117]

The conversations with Thouless seem to have been a sort of preparation for Wittgenstein to compose an address to the British Academy for its Philosophical Lecture in 1942. The notes Wittgenstein wrote in drafting the lecture (never given), include: "Meaning consisting of the word referring to an object. How a kind of object is hypostatised for a technique of use. . . . What I do deny is that we can construe the grammar of 'having pain' by hypostatizing a private object."[118]

Having labeled the error, the deeper challenge is how to counter the temptation to hypostatization itself (see aim F in chapter 4). Wittgenstein suggests (PI §374) that "the best I can propose is that we should yield to the temptation to use this picture, but then investigate how the *application* of the picture goes." The best illustration of this in Wittgenstein's writing is the "beetle in the box" (PI §293). But is there an application that better brings out the absurdity of such hypostatization?

This is the basis for Norton Juster's children's fantasy adventure novel, *The Phantom Tollbooth*. Much of the humor in the book comes precisely from Juster treating abstractions or mental states as things. Expectations becomes a place: "Expectations is the place you must always go to before you get to where you're going" (19). So, too, the Doldrums is a place (22), and Point of View is a location (102). Having lost his way, the "Whether Man" tells Milo: "If you happen to find my way, please return it, as it was lost years ago" (20).

More relevant to the confusions that Wittgenstein is concerned with, noises are presented as liquids (136–143), and other sounds are presented in great detail (155–157):

> "But I've never seen a sound," Milo insisted. . . .
>
> She picked up a padded stick and struck a nearby bass drum six times. Six large woolly, fluffy cotton balls, each about two feet across, rolled silently out onto the floor. . . .
>
> "Do you know what a handclap looks like?"
>
> Milo shook his head.
>
> "Try it," she commanded.
>
> He clapped his hands once and a single sheet of clean white paper fluttered to the floor. . . .
>
> "Isn't that simple? And it's the same for all sounds. If you think about it, you'll soon know what each one looks like. Take laughter, for instance," she said, laughing brightly, and a thousand tiny brightly colored bubbles flew into the air and popped noiselessly. . . .
>
> "How about music?" asked Milo excitedly.
>
> "Right over here—we weave it out on our looms. Symphonies are large beautiful carpets with all the rhythms and melodies woven in."

In fact, Juster had synesthesia as a child, and the condition extended to words and images. In an interview he reported, "One of the things I always did was think literally when I heard words."[119] His story lays bare the humor in this.[120]

"Tell Them I've Had a Wonderful Life"

Wittgenstein died on April 29, 1951. He had suffered from cancer for a few years, eventually taking hormone and x-ray treatments. But he gave them up in February of that year, and his physician, Dr. Edward Bevan, and his wife, Joan, invited Wittgenstein to stay with them during his final months. Many years later, Dr. Bevan wrote, "I have never met anyone who made a greater impression upon me, and I came to respect and love him. He was a great and a good man, above all . . . honest, humble, unafraid and grateful: and I don't think he was unhappy at the end."[121] As his condition worsened on April 28, Wittgenstein was informed that his friends would be coming the next day. His last words said (in English) to Joan Bevan before losing consciousness were, "Tell them I've had a wonderful life."[122]

Was this an accurate description of Wittgenstein's life? Did he mean to say something consoling for his friends? (After all, he did say, "Tell them . . .") Or something true? What did he mean by "wonderful"? (How) can we understand this? We are left to create a narrative, a story, for this line, because Joan Bevan offered no explanation.

Norman Malcolm, one of Wittgenstein's friends, who, however, was not in England at the time, was the first to publish these words in 1958. Actually, he published them as, "Tell them I've had a wonderful life!" Malcolm found them to be a mystery:

> When I think of his profound pessimism, the intensity of his mental and moral suffering, the relentless way in which he drove his intellect, his need for love together with the harshness that repelled love, I am inclined to believe that his life was fiercely unhappy. Yet at the end he himself exclaimed that it had been "wonderful"! To me this seems a mysterious and strangely moving utterance.[123]

Malcolm seems to have created a mystery for himself by adding the exclamation mark in his quotation. Then, in a revised edition of his *Memoir* in 1984, he decided that though Wittgenstein's life seemed unhappy, he must have derived considerable satisfaction from his work and friendships (84). In 1958, Malcolm interpreted "wonderful" as synonymous with "enjoyable." By 1984, however, he saw it as synonymous with "worthwhile." Malcolm struggled to find a way to make Wittgenstein's dying words fit the narrative Malcolm had constructed in his *Memoir*.

Another model for Wittgenstein's sense of the word could be Frank Capra's 1946 film, *It's a Wonderful Life*. Indeed, it is hard to imagine Wittgenstein, a great fan of popular American films, making this statement without being aware of its similarity to the title of this film. Yet it is equally hard to see what this similarity might have been. None of these interpretations seems satisfying.

Derek Jarman's film, *Wittgenstein*, surprisingly does not include this scene, but an anonymous reviewer of the film, on a gay film website, commented, "Wittgenstein struggled with self-alienation throughout his life. He died of cancer in 1951. His final, mocking words were: 'Tell them I've had a wonderful life.'" If Jarman had included this scene, the words could well have been said caustically.[124] The paragraph in which Ray Monk quotes Wittgenstein's words (579) certainly would support the caustic interpretation, surrounding them, as Monk does, with a foul mood and other caustic remarks.

Another scholar, Peter John, has proposed to interpret "wonderful" literally as "full of wonder."[125] Though this stretches its colloquial use in current English, it is clear that the capacity to wonder was important for Wittgenstein. In his 1929 lecture "Ethics," he offered "wonder at the existence of the world" (PO, 41) as an illustration of what had intrinsic value for him. And he feared that this capacity for wonder was endangered by modern conceptions of science and progress: "Man has to awaken to wonder. . . . Science is a way of sending him to sleep again" (CV, 5/7). So it is fascinating to find that "wonderful" did include this literal meaning in Wittgenstein's circles. In Russell's translations of extracts of passages from Leibniz into English, he offered the following concerning the identity of indiscernibles:

> Things which are different must differ in some way, or have in themselves some assignable diversity; and it is wonderful that this most manifest axiom has not been employed by men along with so many others.[126]

Wonderful, as in "to be wondered at," and rendering Leibniz full of wonder.

Wittgenstein strove to have a life of wonder, and this construal of his dying words would, in a sense, crown that life. If we can achieve a view of the world unconstrained by theories and untainted by a misunderstanding of language, we may find ourselves, as Wittgenstein once put it, "walking on a mountain of wonders."[127]

So here we have a number of examples of where Wittgenstein tried to address certain noncognitive issues, such as our temptations, with more or less success. He himself thought he had rather little success. I have tried to find examples of how these same issues might be addressed by other "poetic" means. It is for the reader to judge whether these are more successful, but they are my suggestions about directions in which one might go, or alternatives one might consider, to achieve the sorts of things Wittgenstein was trying to achieve when he said that "one should really only do philosophy as poetry." There may well be other and better poetic illustrations than these, but my purpose will have been served if the reader is provoked to find or invent them.

7 Doing Philosophy as Poetry

Certainly there is much that goes under the label of philosophy that cannot be done as poetry, in the sense of *Dichtung*. But there is another aspect of philosophical reflection: what it would take to act on our deliberations, what it would take to think about an issue in a certain way. What it would take to resist some misguided picture. This too can be thought of as philosophy—but attending to what I would call noncognitive considerations. It is not crucial to draw a clear line between cognitive and noncognitive, but to appreciate that they focus in different directions. Wittgenstein is drawing our attention to this difference when he says, for example:

> "Difficulty of philosophy [is] not the intellectual difficulty of the sciences, but the difficulty of a change of attitude. Resistances of the will must be overcome. . . . Philosophy requires a resignation, but one of feeling and not of intellect. And maybe that is what makes it so difficult for many."[1]

> "I don't try to make you *believe* something you *don't* believe, but to make you *do* something you won't do."[2]

> "Schopenhauer once said, 'If you try to convince someone and get to a certain resistance, you then know you are up against the will, not the understanding.' You are up against something else here. We have prejudices of thought."[3]

> "I'm not teaching you anything; I'm trying to persuade you to do something."[4]

Here Wittgenstein is concerned with addressing noncognitive issues of the will. But he understands this broadly to include not just what you *do* in an obvious sense, but how you look at things, what you take for granted—a broad array of things that we might lump under temperament. He sees these as crucial to philosophy.[5]

The problem is that philosophers are not used to thinking about such things; indeed, they may seem more like psychology than philosophy. They are not addressed by philosophy as it is typically done. They are addressed more by poetry or literature—what German speakers call *Dichtung*.

Plato claimed to see a deep conflict between these things. He spoke even then of the "ancient quarrel between poetry and philosophy" (*Republic* 607b). Yet it is striking that Plato himself seemed to participate on both sides of this quarrel. So, the issue re-raised by Wittgenstein is not whether one side or the other is right or whether there is a deep conflict between the two, but whether there are ways in which poetry can assist philosophy—whether philosophy can use any of the tools of poetry for its own ends—or whether perhaps they have some ends in common.[6]

In the previous chapter, I looked at a number of cases in which Wittgenstein used or could have used poetic means to achieve some of his goals. In this chapter, I look more closely at how that might work and more broadly at how other philosophers have tried to make it work.

I begin by looking at a poet who is also a literary critic and teacher: Thomas Gardner. Gardner has reflected on the poetic process in ways that are helpful for seeing what Wittgenstein hoped for and what poetry might offer to philosophy. I begin with his reflections in a "Reader's Companion" to a collection of his lyric essays, or prose poems, *Poverty Creek Journal*. His reflections have less to do with the rhyme or rhythm of the writing and more to do with the interaction between the writing and the reader:

> Wallace Stevens, in "Of Modern Poetry" (1940), defines a poem as "the mind in the act of finding / What will suffice." This seems to me to be true of any work organized lyrically: poems, certain sorts of essays, certain sorts of fiction. We see in such work a mind moving—noting and considering, listening to what it has just said, leaping forward or turning back. Rather than reporting on what will suffice, speaking from a position of arrival, this kind of writing dramatizes the act of getting there. What we do when we read such work, as Kenneth Burke illustrates . . . , is reenact that movement. We perform the poem, connecting image to image or turn to turn, making of its various parts a coherent inner action: "For a poem is an act, the symbolic act of the poet who made it—an act of such a nature that, in surviving as a structure or an affect, it enables us as readers to re-enact it."
>
> A poem, we might say, gives us instructions for re-enacting its inner movements.[7]

The act of "reporting on what will suffice, speaking from a position of arrival" is what one usually finds in philosophical writing. It is a natural way to set out a philosophical position.[8]

In fact, the largest part of Wittgenstein's *Tractatus* is very much a report that speaks "from a position of arrival." And not only in the *Tractatus* itself, but even several years later, when Wittgenstein was meeting with members of the Vienna Circle, Carnap reported:

> When [Wittgenstein] started to formulate his view on some specific philosophical problem, we often felt the internal struggle that occurred in him at that very moment, a struggle by which he tried to penetrate from darkness to light under an intense and painful strain, which was even visible on his most expressive face. When finally, sometimes after a prolonged arduous effort, his answer came forth, his statement stood before us like a newly created piece of art or a divine revelation. Not that he asserted his views dogmatically. Although some of the formulations of the *Tractatus* sound as if there could not be any possibility of a doubt, he often expressed the feeling that his statements were inadequate. But the impression he made on us was as if the insight came to him as through a divine inspiration, so that he could not help feeling that any sober rational comment or analysis of it would be profane.[9]

So it is not surprising that the Preface of the *Tractatus* begins, "Perhaps this book will be understood only by someone who has himself already had the thoughts that are expressed in it." Wittgenstein offers very little help in the *Tractatus* that would allow a reader to reenact the process of getting to his conclusions.[10]

But Gardner suggests that what characterizes a poem, in his broad sense, is that it "dramatizes the act of getting there." Here we see the importance of Wittgenstein's dialogical style. Whether we see the style as deriving from his experience in the classroom or not, we are offered a sort of path that gives us, the readers, the opportunity to "re-enact that movement." Recall Wittgenstein's "introduction" to his remarks on Frazer, discussed in chapter 3:

> One must start out with error [*Irrtum*] and convert [*überführen*] it into truth.
>
> That is, one must reveal the source of error, otherwise hearing the truth won't do any good. The truth cannot force its way in when something else is occupying its place.
>
> To convince someone of the truth, it is not enough to state it, but rather one must find the *path* [*Weg*] from error to truth.[11]

The poem must not only enable us, but *engage* us, to reenact the movement of thought of the poet.

So, there is work to do from the side of the reader as well. Gardner writes that "the first task for the reader is to identify those pressures the mind before us is engaged with." "In listening," he says, the audience "finds itself so drawn into the emotions enacted before it that it 'becomes one' with them." He continues: "This will be different for each writer, of course, but the task of the invisible audience is the same—to track the drama, to recreate it internally, to find its motion within ourselves."[12]

This is why, as we noted in chapter 4, Wittgenstein emphasized the importance of speaking honestly about what we *want* to say instead of censoring our reactions—not only censoring what we admit to aloud, but what we admit to ourselves. Only in this way can the temptations be revealed and addressed. Wittgenstein wants to know what we think so that he knows what to offer. As he said to Anscombe: "Let me think what medicine you need."

And here is the difference between an esotericist and an evangelist. An esotericist leaves it to the audience, if there is one, to discern the pressures the poet is engaging; the evangelist wants the audience to be able to discern those pressures, and indeed wants to engage pressures that the audience experiences or is susceptible to. And since poets and audiences vary in their pressures, Gardner reminds us that "this will be different for each writer, of course." Similarly, Wittgenstein noted, "What happens to work with me doesn't work with him (Prof. Moore)—works with me now, and may not work with me tomorrow."[13] And recall Wittgenstein's comment from a 1942 notebook: "At present we are combatting a trend. But this trend will die out, superseded by others. And then people will no longer understand our arguments against it; will not see why all that needed saying."[14] So what Wittgenstein says to readers of his time may well differ from what he would say to readers of our time.[15]

Poetry sometimes has a reputation for being esoteric, where symbols or allusions are recognized only by the cognoscenti.[16] But it is also possible for a poem to be engaging without being parochial. Gardner explains:

> This is how reading takes shape. We pass our eyes across a piece of writing and something causes us to slow down and take notice. Maybe it's a beautiful line or a striking image. In time, working out what is being said and thinking through how one image leads to another, we understand what we are staring at.

Wittgenstein emphasizes the importance of slowing down:

> In philosophy the winner of the race is the one who can run most slowly. Or: the one who gets to the winning post last.
>
> Sometimes a sentence can be understood only if it is read at the *right tempo*. My sentences are all to be read *slowly*.
>
> Where others go on ahead, I remain standing.

> Really I want to slow down the speed of reading with continual punctuation marks. For I should like to be read slowly. (As I myself read.)
>
> This is how philosophers should salute each other: "Take your time!"[17]

Gardner continues:

> But then comes the crucial moment at the heart of any great reading—the moment in which we recognize, within ourselves, the mental and emotional action being described. "I recognize the place," we say, "I know it," and proceed to scroll through the twists and turns of our own inner landscape, working our way through it again and then returning to the poem with that landscape alive in our heads, ready to see and respond. We have eyes to see. Details in the poem matter not because they are "symbols" or "motifs" someone has laboriously taught us to tally but because they are elements of a process we know something about, luminous now and alive. Not elements of a code but turns of thought.[18]

Wittgenstein called them *Denkbewegungen*—movements of thought. That is why the evangelist needs to know the audience and be able to reveal the pressures at work, in himself or herself, and in them. And this is why it is important that the real work of philosophy is left to the reader. As Wittgenstein wrote in a notebook in 1948, "Anything the reader can do for himself, leave it to the reader."[19] But of course the reader must be sufficiently prepared and engaged by the writer.

There is no assuring that we will recognize or resonate with the poet's turns of thought, but that is a path that we might follow, a way to overcome what Wittgenstein calls "resistances of the will."

I think Plato's *Phaedo* is an excellent example of philosophy being done as poetry.[20]

The dialogue takes place in the Athenian jail where Socrates awaits his execution. On the last day of his life, Socrates's friends have gathered to talk with him. Socrates had failed to convince the Athenian jury that he was innocent of the charges against him, but he felt that here he had a final chance to at least convince his own friends that his life had not been misspent, even at the cost of death: "Come then, he said, let me try to make my defense to you more convincing than it was to the jury" (63b). "I want to make my argument before you, my judges, as to why I think that a man who has spent his life in philosophy is probably right to be of good cheer in the face of death." (63e). While there is now no doubt that his life will lead to his death, as it has for a number of martyrs down through the ages since his time, Socrates will continue to hold, as he announced in the *Apology*, that "a good man cannot be harmed either in life or in death" (41d).

The danger that seems to worry Socrates the most in this context is that his friends—those who have witnessed and participated in his many philosophical conversations—will abandon philosophy because it leads to death. Socrates proceeds to offer two, rather weak, arguments to prove that the soul is immortal. and a good deal of the discussion centers on those arguments, as well as on two objections raised by his friends and his replies to them. So it is that the primary attention, paid by scholars as well as teachers of philosophy, has focused on the evaluation of those arguments. And Socrates does not come out looking very good in that light.

Before Socrates begins to reply to the objections to his arguments from Simmias and Cebes, however, he first notes and acknowledges the emotional impact these objections have had. After being persuaded by the reasoning of his two arguments *for* immortality, his friends were now impressed by the reasoning of the two objections *against* immortality. How then can we trust reason? Socrates gave a name to this state—misology: the mistrust, or hatred, of *logos*. Socrates warned, "We should not become misologues, as people become misanthropes. There is no greater evil one can suffer than to hate reasonable discourse" (89d). So he will need to counteract this fear or hatred of reason:

> This then is the first thing we should guard against. . . . We should not allow into our minds the conviction that argumentation has nothing sound about it; . . . we must take courage and be eager to attain soundness, you and the others for the sake of your whole life still to come, and I for the sake of death itself. (90e–91a)

Socrates at this very point realizes the quandary he is in, for the issue at stake is an emotional one: What emotions shall we have in regard to reason—hatred or courage? Knowing that reason itself will not suffice to govern our emotions *about* reason, Socrates comes out with what is, to me, a shocking confession (91a):

> I am in danger at this moment of not having a philosophical attitude about this, but like those who are quite uneducated, I am eager to get the better of you in argument.

His primary task, in the short time remaining to him, is to get "those present," and himself, to "be thoroughly convinced that things are so." So he is giving fair warning that he may (or will) abandon reason in favor of other means to success.

This is all the evidence we need to realize that the *Phaedo* is a so-called Middle Dialogue (written in the middle of Plato's career). That is, it is not Plato's rendition of the kinds of conversations Socrates actually had with people (as in the so-called Early Dialogues, written early in his career). It is Plato's response to Socrates's life: while he retains Socrates as the main character of the dialogue, he now puts words in the mouth of Socrates (and other characters) that indicate more how Plato wished to address the issues. This is not to say that the character of Socrates has become a literal mouthpiece for Plato's views—but Plato is using the dialogue to work through his own take on the issues. I think the historical Socrates would never have taken the position that has just been put into his mouth (about "not having a philosophical attitude"). But I think it was Plato's realization of the limitations of Socrates's approach that led him to present Socrates as he does in the *Phaedo*. We also see this same pattern in the *Republic* and the *Symposium*—Plato retains Socrates as the main character, but uses the dialogue to work through what he saw as the limitations of the man Socrates's approach.[21]

Before we move on, it is worth noting why Socrates goes the route of discussing immortality at all. He explains, addressing his interlocutors (*Phaedo* 95b–c):

> The sum of your problem is this: you consider that the soul must be proved to be immortal and indestructible before a philosopher on the point of death, who is confident that he will fare much better in the underworld than if he had led any other kind of life, can avoid being foolish and simple-minded in this confidence.

Here we see Socrates wondering: "Let me think what medicine you need." Socrates's primary purpose is not to prove the immortality of the soul except as a concession to his friends' expectations. His discussion of immortality is, for him, more of a means to the goal of helping his friends avoid misology.[22]

In fact, a careful reader will realize this. To begin with, Socrates had already explained at his trial that he didn't know whether his soul was immortal (*Apology* 40c): ". . . There is good hope that death is a blessing, for it is one of two things: either the dead are nothing and I have no perception of anything, or it is, as we are told, a change and a relocating for the soul from here to another place." But Socrates also leaves red flags in the course of his discussion in the *Phaedo*. For example, after replying to the objection of Cebes with a rather questionable argument (at 106b–d), Socrates concludes, "And so now, if we are agreed that the deathless is indestructible, the soul, being deathless, is indestructible. If not, we need another argument." For better or worse, they all agree.

Yet after Socrates sums up the argument for Cebes and again asks for assent, Simmias remarks (107a–b), "Certainly . . . I myself have no remaining grounds for doubt after what has been said; nevertheless, in view of the importance of our subject and my low opinion of human weakness, I am bound still to have some private misgivings about what we have said." Socrates then immediately endorses his qualms: "You are not only right to say this . . . but our first hypotheses require clearer examination, even though we find them convincing. And *if* you analyze them adequately, you will, *I think*, follow the argument as far as a man can and *if* the conclusion is clear, you will look no further" (107b; italics added). There could hardly be a plainer invitation to the gathered friends, as well as to future readers, to "look further" and "follow the argument as far as" they can at their leisure and decide for themselves. The point is not so much the proof or even truth of immortality but the process and value of reason.[23]

What is at stake is the value of *philosophy*—literally, the love of wisdom, the love of reason. Yet love is partly an emotion, so the challenge Socrates faces is how to instill, or preserve, the love of reason, or fend off misology, in his friends. The paradox is that we cannot use reason to instill an emotion. It turns out that Socrates's project of philosophy is at the mercy of poetry, or whatever we take to influence emotion. And to make things worse, all this is happening in the face of imminent death. It is fear of death that is really at the heart of his friends' worries. So philosophy here faces two emotional challenges—to instill a love of reasoning and to avert a fear of death—and we can't do this simply with reason.

Socrates knows this and alerts us. Early in the dialogue, he says, "I do not mind telling you what I have heard, for it is perhaps most appropriate for one who is about to depart yonder to tell and examine tales about what we believe that journey will be like" (61e). Later Socrates calls his friends' attitude toward death a "childish fear," and Cebes responds: "Assuming that we were afraid, Socrates, try to change our minds, or rather do not assume that we are afraid, but perhaps there is a child in us who has these fears; try to persuade him not to fear death like a bogey" (77e). Socrates replies, "You should . . . sing a charm over him every day until you have charmed away his fears." Socrates realizes that what is needed is not really an argument but something closer to a bedtime story.[24]

In one sense, that bedtime story is about how Socrates and his friends discussed the arguments for and against immortality on the last day of his life (the previous dialogue itself). But in another more literal sense, Socrates in fact goes on to tell a story—a myth about the afterlife (107c–115a). He begins, "We are told . . ." It offers many details about the fate of the good and the bad after death and comfort that "if the soul is immortal, it requires our care not only for the time we call our life, but for the sake of all time." A story like this also occurs near the end of the *Republic*—the Myth of Er (*Republic* 614b–621b). In a conversation with Wittgenstein near the end of his life, Bouwsma relates that "W[ittgenstein] reads Plato—the only philosopher he reads. But he likes best the allegories, the myths. They're fine."[25] I take this to be a nod toward poetry in philosophy.

Perhaps the best bedtime story, however, is the death scene (116a–118a) of the *Phaedo*—maybe not for children but for would-be philosophers. I always read this five-minute scene aloud at the end of class. It is a very moving story that bolsters the love of reason and counters the fear of death in a poetic fashion. It marshals the sort of artillery Wittgenstein sought but claims never to have found.

I have suggested that Wittgenstein's remarks often resemble a dialogue—rather like a Socratic dialogue, though characters are not identified. In Socratic dialogues, Socrates and the original readers knew who the interlocutors were. In fact, this knowledge often adds important dimensions to the dialogue.[26] Socrates's knowledge of his interlocutors allowed him to know what "medicine" they might need. And as Wittgenstein taught, he also sometimes knew what his students needed. But as he wrote, he lacked this sort of specific information about his readers. Thus, while he addresses tendencies that he has encountered, he can't tailor his comments for particular mind-sets. He tries to anticipate a range of standpoints.

Here is my attempt to do philosophy as poetry in the style of Wittgenstein:

> 694. "What is the meaning of life?"
>
> 695. You may say, "Shouldn't we ask a biologist?" No, we aren't asking about the meaning of "life." For that we would ask the biologists, perhaps with some assistance from Socrates. But for our question, no one looks especially to the biologists. We want advice from some sort of wise person—we are looking for some wisdom.

696. "This is one of the deep questions of philosophy. A paradigm of a deep philosophical question."

697. But, is it a question? Or is it a cry for help?

698. Well, suppose we try to answer the question. Someone might suggest, following Russell, that the definite description "the meaning" implies (or at least presupposes) that there is one and only one meaning of life. This makes it seem as though there is some single deep truth, perhaps concerning the unity of all being. "Doesn't this require a mystical insight?"

699. The question "What is the meaning of life?" produces in us a mental cramp. We feel that we can't point to anything in reply, and yet ought to point to something. (We are up against one of the great sources of philosophical bewilderment: a substantive makes us look for a thing that corresponds to it.)[27]

700. The best I can propose is that we should yield to the temptation to use this picture, but then investigate how the *application* of the picture goes.[28]

701. On this picture, we should answer this question by looking for, and finding, one thing which is life's meaning. But both of these temptations seem misguided: There is not some *thing* which is life's meaning, nor does life get meaning in just *one* way.

702. We sometimes think of the meaning of life in terms of some purpose that is ordained for us by a higher power. One asks, "What does God want me to do with my life? What are God's plans for me? What is God's will?"

703. Greek myths often involve mortals in tiffs between the gods. Helen became a gift that Aphrodite bestowed on Paris in return for him awarding her the prize as the most beautiful goddess. Oedipus is the means fated to kill his father Laius, and bring ruin to his family. In each case there is a purpose ordained from above, but how meaningful is that? Recall the way that Job is enrolled in an argument between God and Satan. The Lord brags about Job's faithfulness: "a sound and honest man who fears God and shuns evil." Satan bets God that Job will not remain so if he is allowed to suffer. God says the bet is on. What if we were created for, or simply assigned, the purpose of amusing God? Would that give my life meaning? Meaning can't just be ordained from above.

704. We are not after the meaning of a word. But perhaps there is a parallel, an analogy. Suppose someone says to me, "The meaning of life is like the meaning of language. Different bits of language have different meanings. Different lives have different meanings."

705. Philosophers very often talk about investigating the meaning of words. But let's not forget that a word hasn't got a meaning given to it, as it were, by a power independent of us. A word has the meaning someone has given to it.[29]

706. If meaning cannot be ordained from above, perhaps it can be chosen by me. Kierkegaard believed that faith was an individual decision—a leap of faith. Hamlet said: "There is nothing either good or bad, but thinking makes it so" (Act II, Scene 2).[30] Can't I give my life meaning?

707. Well, can I give *language* meaning? (*Winnie the Pooh*, Chapter 7. "In which Kanga and Baby Roo come to the Forest, and Piglet has a bath"):

> "The best way," said Rabbit, "would be this. The best way would be to steal Baby Roo and hide him, and then when Kanga says, 'Where's Baby Roo?' we say, 'Aha!'"
>
> "Aha!" said Pooh, practising. "Aha! Aha! . . . Of course," he went on, "we could say 'Aha!' even if we hadn't stolen Baby Roo."
>
> "Pooh," said Rabbit kindly, "you haven't any brain."
>
> "I know," said Pooh humbly.
>
> "We say 'Aha!' so that Kanga knows that we know where Baby Roo is. 'Aha!' means 'We'll tell you where Baby Roo is, if you promise to go away from the Forest and never come back.' Now don't talk while I think."
>
> Pooh went into a corner and tried saying "Aha!" in that sort of voice. Sometimes it seemed to him that it did mean what Rabbit said, and sometimes it seemed to him that it didn't. "I suppose it's just practice," he thought. "I wonder if Kanga will have to practise too so as to understand it."

No, apparently I can't just give a word meaning. (Stipulation is something different.)

708. What would it be like to give my life meaning? Could I ordain my own purpose? "I have decided that if I clasped and unclasped my hands and never turned N.N.E. after turning S.S.W. then that gives my life meaning."[31] "Nothing is either meaningful or meaningless, but thinking makes it so." Of course, I could give my life meaning by undertaking an especially valuable project. But what counts as a meaningful project is not just up to me.

709. Or, could I decide that my life did *not* have meaning? Is that just up to me? Tolstoy, after having written *War and Peace* and *Anna Karenina*, decided his life, that life, was meaningless.[32] Is he right? Is he right *by definition*? Was it up to him?

710. If life is meaningless, it is so objectively, because there is nothing worth living for. It can't be meaningless just because I deem it to be.

711. Language has meaning as it is used in and by a community of language users. Lives have meaning as they are lived in a community. Language cannot be given meaning simply by individual intent or choice. A life can't be given (or denied) meaning simply by individual decision or choice.

712. So, the analogy between the meaning of language and the meaning of life seems to hold up so far.

713. If you ask, "What is the meaning of this word?" I can tell you what it means: "'Lacuna' means gap." So, if you ask, "What is the meaning of this life?" can I tell you what it means? "What is the meaning of Gandhi's life?" I can tell you what he did, what he stood for, and what he cared about. But I can't tell you what he meant, or what his life meant. "Gandhi means a lot to me." "What does he mean to you?" Well . . . The grammar of the meaning of life is similar in some ways and different in some ways from the grammar of the meaning of words. When phrases in our ordinary language have prima facie analogous grammars we are inclined to try to interpret them analogously; i.e., we try to make the analogy hold throughout.[33]

714. Nelson Mandela was dignified. You ask: "Well then, what is the dignity of Mandela?" Um . . . The grammar of dignity doesn't work that way. Instead, we can ask: "What made Mandela's life dignified?" "What did his dignity consist in?" And we can answer. But don't hypostatize dignity, or meaning.[34]

715. Studying the grammar of the expression "the meaning of life" will cure you of the temptation to look about you for some object which you might call "the meaning."[35]

716. "What is the meaning of life?" This sounds profound, but has no answer. It is an ill-formed question.[36]

717. Instead, we could ask, "What makes a life meaningful?" This sounds less profound, but it has many interesting answers, answers which are not the province of philosophy. Life can *have* meaning, without there being some*thing* that it *means*. We can ask "Why is Gandhi's life meaningful to you?" or "What makes Gandhi's life meaningful?" and you could answer.

718. Sometimes an expression has to be withdrawn from the language and sent for cleaning,—then it can be put back into circulation.[37]

719. One sunny morning I decide to be helpful and go out into the yard to pull weeds. Soon my wife runs out shouting, "What are you doing?" She has seen that I am pulling up the newly sprouting zinnias she planted last week. She is not asking me a question, she's expressing her exasperation. She wants me to stop. She wants me to see what I'm doing—in a different way.

720. "What is the meaning of life?" "What's it all mean?" "Does anything matter?" Are these really questions? Are they always questions? Aren't they sometimes cries of despair: "I'm at a loss." "Help me make sense of my life." Tolstoy is expressing bewilderment: "I felt lost and fell into despair." "Life had lost its charm for me."[38]

721. "Life is meaningless." This is no opinion—also not a conviction, but an attitude toward things and what is happening.[39] The question of the meaning of life arises when life becomes a problem. What would it take to see life as meaningful?

What would it take to stop agonizing? Ultimately, Tolstoy uneasily settles for living the life of a simple believing peasant, and writing about their lives.[40]

722. "Perhaps a meaningful life is one that is narrated. To narrate a life is to give it meaning—to see it as meaningful."

Here we have two paths through the philosophical territory of life's meaning. One path tries to relieve the reader of the desire to ask, "What is the meaning of life?" and instead be satisfied with the question, "What makes for a meaningful life?" The other path treats the question as a cry for help, for the right "medicine" rather than for answers.

It might be suggested that there is nothing poetic about these remarks. But recall that as Wittgenstein was drafting the final form of his remarks in part I of the *Investigations*, he referred to the remarks as "my poems." And note that I have focused on the comparisons, the *Gleichnisse*, that would lead readers to view the issue in one way or another.[41] Which comparisons tempt us to look for the meaning of life? Which might relieve us of the temptation? If I have not done this very well, there is at least some consolation in the fact that Wittgenstein did not think he had done what he was attempting very well either. But I think this is the sort of thing he was after.

How might we now do philosophy as poetry? Consider the issue of climate change—something quite different from anything Wittgenstein addressed. What would it take to get people to think about the issue in a different way—in a way that is more active and urgent? Evidence of climate change and its effects seems to have limited influence on people. Is there a way to make people aware of the turns of thought that influence their perspective and to make them more open to other turns of thought? This is my attempt, written as an op-ed piece for the newspaper:

To what shall I compare thee?

Mourning over the destruction of Jerusalem, Jeremiah laments: "To what shall I compare thee? Or to what shall I liken thee, O daughter of Jerusalem? . . . that I may comfort thee . . . for as great as the sea is thy destruction: who shall heal thee?" (Lamentations 2:13).[42] Comparisons matter—indeed, often they make all the difference. If we are trying to understand something, especially something new or unfamiliar, it helps to name it, characterize it, compare it to something more familiar.

What are we to make of the many strong storms and hurricanes, floods, wildfires, and hot weather? Shall we name it "normal climate variation"? That does comfort us—not unusual, not permanent, and most of all not under our control.

Shall we name it "global warming"? But then what about the four feet of snow and frigid temperatures in Montana in September? That's no kind of warming—quite the opposite. Shall we name it "global energizing"? That does not sound so comforting. And that name leads us to ask, is it our fault? Or is there anything we can do? "Who shall heal thee?"

To many it appears that these storms and fires are an indication of worse things to come. How should we understand a looming threat? To what shall I compare thee?

Shall we compare it to a frog in a pan of heating water? There is a legend that if you heat the water slowly enough the frog will never try to get out and soon boil to death. But that has been debunked. Once it gets too warm, a frog will vigorously try to escape.

Shall we compare it to parachuting? Apparently, free-fall is a joyous experience. Parachutists want to experience it as long as possible. How long? Until their feet start to hurt (because they are hitting the ground)? No, that's too long. Well, when should we pull the rip cord? Better too soon than a second too late. In the case of parachuting, we can learn from the experiences of others what is "too late."

Shall we compare it to taking out a loan? I am borrowing some of the carbon capacity of future generations to sustain my use now of fossil fuels for travel, electric power and air conditioning. Isn't this rather like my taking out a loan now to go on a fancy vacation, and putting down as collateral my grandsons' future earnings and expecting them to pay off my loan? Who would feel right about doing that? Or perhaps we imagine that future technology will take care of the problem. Shall we compare that to the thought that we will be able to pay off the vacation loan ourselves . . . if only that big raise comes through that I keep hoping for?

Shall we compare it to gambling? Some of us are more willing to accept risks than others. But in the case of climate energizing, the risks that I am willing to run will not primarily fall on me if things turn out badly—they will fall on my children and my grandsons.

But what about an unprecedented threat, one that we all face together?

We teach our children to avoid risky behavior: "Don't have sex and risk pregnancy." "Don't drink and drive." "Don't experiment with drugs, because you don't know where it will lead you." "Don't take unnecessary chances."

Shall we compare our life-style with risky behavior? By consuming fossil fuels and electric power at the rate we are now, we are risking overspending our carbon budget. We don't know for sure how great the risk is, or how bad the looming threat is. But in cases like this, don't we tell our children to "play it safe"?

Suppose I do worry about these things, but what difference does that make? What can I do?[43] Any change I can make is just a drop in the bucket. But really, it's no different from voting. My vote will never make the difference, so why bother? Because that's what we do—we vote. We stand up for our candidate or our cause. And that one drop can be part of a larger ripple. As Margaret Mead is supposed to

> have said: "Never doubt that a small group of thoughtful, committed citizens can change the world; indeed, it's the only thing that ever has."
>
> Who shall heal thee? Why not compare our attitude with one of trust? We know we are running risks, but we trust that God will take care of us. When the trust is in God, we call it faith.
>
> Once there was a pious man whose town experienced a great rainfall. As the flood waters were rising, a neighbor came by in a truck and offered to drive the man, his dog, and some essentials to safety. "No," the man said, "I have faith in God. I will wait for God to save me." As the waters continued to rise, the man looked out his window to see a first-responder in a boat. "Get in," the responder hollered, "there's still room for you and your dog." "No," the man said, "I have faith in God. I will wait for God to save me." As the waters continued to rise, the man had to climb up onto his roof. Finally, a helicopter swooped past and lowered a rope. "No," the man said, "I have faith in God. I will wait for God to save me." The man drowned, and when he faced St. Peter at the pearly gates he implored, "Why didn't God save me?" St. Peter replied, "You fool. He tried to. Why do you think He sent the truck, the boat and the helicopter?"[44]

This piece tries to identify where people are and why they might think the way they do by way of *Gleichnisse*—comparisons. As writer, I do not have the advantage that Socrates has of knowing his interlocutors. Instead, the essay raises questions about the appropriateness of various comparisons and offers alternatives. Although it implies a position arrived at, it enacts various processes for getting there and invites readers to reenact one or more of those processes.

In addressing what might be a common perspective among unconvinced readers—that we can leave it to God to save us—the essay ends with a joke. Wittgenstein's student and friend Norman Malcolm reported that "Wittgenstein once said that a serious and good philosophical work could be written that would consist entirely of jokes (without being facetious)."[45] Perhaps this is an example. It takes a view that puts the responsibility on God and turns it around so that the listener is asked to look for those ways in which God puts the responsibility on us.

This book offers a narrative—a story—about how Wittgenstein evolved from an esoteric to an evangelical stance, initially through his teaching and soon in his writings. It shows Wittgenstein coming to engage with his students and then his readers. After having been an artillery observer in the war, Wittgenstein becomes an artillery observer in his philosophical work—tracking the difficulties and successes in reaching his audience. After having tried to improve the artillery available to use in the war, Wittgenstein tried to improve the artillery he used in philosophy—looking to *Dichtung*. The narrative takes seriously Wittgenstein's attraction to doing philosophy as poetry as a means to reach his listeners and readers in a noncognitive way and examines both his thoughts about the possibility and several examples of his attempts. Accepting that Wittgenstein felt he did not fully succeed in these attempts, the book examines some examples of doing philosophy as poetry from a variety of sources that might be considered more successful. Perhaps this is an avenue that contemporary, even analytic, philosophers should take more seriously.

Notes

Introduction

1. Letter to Russell, probably June 1914: "I am now building myself a small house [*ein kleines Haus*] here miles from anyone" (WC, 74). In fact, Wittgenstein had arranged to have a house built *for* him. It was not completed until 1915, and he later occupied it only for visits in 1921, 1931, 1936–1937, and 1950. It was eventually torn down and the wood used to construct another house elsewhere. It has since (as of June 2019) been reconstructed with the original wood on the original site in Skjolden.

2. Hermine Wittgenstein, "My Brother Ludwig," 3. Original German in Hermine Wittgenstein, *Familienerinnerungen*, 154. Wittgenstein refers to the July 1912 operation that had repaired his hernia in a letter to Russell in June 1913 (WC, 40). And see his letter to Russell written before the war, around Christmas, 1913: ". . . and I keep on hoping that things will come to an eruption once and for all, so that I can turn into a different person" (WC, 63).

3. GT, 13 (August 9, 1914) and 18 (August 18, 1914). On August 15, between these two quoted remarks, Wittgenstein began writing in his private diary in a code in which he simply reversed the letters of the alphabet. He had started using this code as a child. (Wittgenstein's wartime diaries, containing private as well as philosophical remarks, are cataloged as MSS 101–103 by von Wright. The philosophical remarks were published as NB.)

4. GT, 36 (October 29 and 30, 1914), and 37 (October 31, 1914). October 30: "mich allen Gewalten zum Trotze erhalten" is reminiscent of Goethe's line: "Allen Gewalten/Zum Trutz sich erhalten" ("Lila" Act 2).

5. Drury, "Conversations with Wittgenstein," 149.

6. Keynes to Wittgenstein, January 10, 1915, and Wittgenstein to Keynes, January 15, 1915, in WC, 78–79.

7. Drury, "Conversations with Wittgenstein," 148–149. Many years later, Drury wrote to his friend Rush Rhees: "I knew he [Wittgenstein] was right, that if I killed

a man face to face my future life would not be worth anything to me because of this memory" (July 13, 1969, published in John Hayes, "Drury and Wittgenstein: Kindred Souls," 27). Either Wittgenstein could only handle killing at long range, or he did not view his eventual role of spotter as killing.

8. For more on the job, training, and dangers of a spotter in World War I, see James G. Bilder, *Artillery Scout,* 52–57, 86–88. For a more technical account of spotting in the Austro-Hungarian artillery, see Ortner, *The Austro-Hungarian Artillery from 1867–1918*, 608–612.

9. Quoted in Brian McGuinness, *Wittgenstein: A Life,* 242, see also 258, 262–263.

Here is Bilder's action account of artillery spotting on the western front during World War I (*Artillery Scout*, 137), presumably not much different from spotting on the Russian front:

> As the two men neared the front, the chatter from the machine guns was deafening, and they could hear bullets whizzing around them. They hunkered low as they looked for a good spot to view the enemy lines. . . . They scurried up to the halfway point of the hill, knowing that enemy snipers would be watching for just such a move. Al put on the headset from the field phone while Len looked out at the German lines with his binoculars. Before putting them to his eyes, he looked over at the men of the 37th, who were trying to advance against machine gun fire by moving over open ground with fixed bayonets. The Germans were cutting them down like wheat. Len gaped in horror. He reported the muzzle flashes from Montfaucon and from another location on his map well to the German rear. He had nothing with which to sketch the layout of the enemy trenches but reported the position of the area closest to the infantry. Bullets started to ping uncomfortably close to the three of them. "We've done everything we can do here," Len said. "Let's get the hell outta here before they shell us," Al said. The three men moved down off the hill with extreme prejudice. Upon their return, they learned that the three enemy batteries had been taken out. . . . Considering it was killing, there was a strange sense of satisfaction in a job well done.

10. See my *Wittgenstein in Exile*, 7–13.

11. Hermine Wittgenstein, *Familienerinnerungen*, 155. This passage is included in Hermine Wittgenstein's "Mein Bruder Ludwig," 25. But it is *not* included in the English translation, Hermine Wittgenstein's "My Brother Ludwig," in the well-known *Recollections of Wittgenstein*, edited by Rush Rhees, where it would have appeared on p. 3, indicated by the ellipsis. (This is one of many cases, some to be discussed later, in which we can only wonder at Rhees's editorial decisions.)

12. Ludwig Wittgenstein, "Letters to Ludwig von Ficker," 83 (July 14, 1914) and 84 (July 19, 1914), recount his well-known monetary gifts to Austrian artists (*Küntsler*) who were without means. Beginning in 1913, Wittgenstein also gave 200 pounds per year to enable Cambridge logician W. E. Johnson to have more time for research (WC, 41). It is not clear how long this support lasted. And later, in spring 1918, Wittgenstein made some sort of sizable monetary gift to the German logician Gottlob Frege (see Frege's letter to Wittgenstein, April 9, 1918, in "Frege-Wittgenstein Correspondence," 42/43 and 85–88).

13. Schmidt, "Wittgenstein and World War I: Some Additional On-Line Sources," 181–185. My translation into 2016 US dollars is somewhat conjectural. I have used exchange rates between crowns and dollars or German marks for each year and then used inflation rates between the relevant years and the present to translate into current dollars. There was no official exchange rate in 1918, and so I extrapolated from the inflation of previous years.

14. See Ortner, *The Austro-Hungarian Artillery from 1867–1918*, 260–273 (about the M-11) and 546–549 (about the upgraded M-11/16 and M-16).

15. His sister writes: "You see, you can hardly order a mortar in the way you might order something else, as, for example, my brother Paul ordered the fabric for thousands of military coats, and had them sewn. If the state wants to construct a mortar, it will not need any Ludwig Wittgenstein. The donation which remained simply unused was finally transferred into the 'Kaiser Karl Charity Fund' and dissolved into nothing due to the inflation" (Hermine Wittgenstein, *Familienerinnerungen*, 161). This passage does not appear in Rhees's German edition of Hermine's memoir—it should appear on p. 28—and there is not even an ellipsis to indicate its absence. And it does not appear in the well-known English edition, where it would need to have been inserted on p. 6.

16. Nedo, "Ludwig Wittgenstein: Life and Work," 21. In a private e-mail of September 23, 2016, to me, Nedo elaborated: "Wittgenstein told this to Ben Richards who reported it to me sometime in the late seventies or early eighties." For more about this technique, see http://firearmshistory.blogspot.com/2010/05/barrel-making-early-history.html.

17. According to Felix Salzer, a nephew of Wittgenstein, quoted in McGuinness, *Wittgenstein: A Life*, 204.

18. Monk, *Ludwig Wittgenstein: The Duty of Genius*, 169. Paul Engelmann, Wittgenstein's close friend from the war and afterward, referred to "his threadbare uniform": "he continued to wear his service tunic for a considerable time after the war" (*Letters from Ludwig Wittgenstein*, 90). Comments by his friends indicate that he often carried a rucksack with him even into the 1930s.

19. In his diary for February 20, 1937, agonizing about his religious beliefs in relation to his life: "It [his life] must strive toward the absolute. And the only absolute is, to battle through life toward death, like a fighting, a charging soldier." And the next day, reflecting on the courage needed to live a religious life: "The only way I could ever charge the enemy line is when I am shot at from behind" (PPO, 197, 201). See also, "I am uncommonly cowardly, & I behave in life like a coward in battle" (PPO, 81).

20. CV, 62 (1980)/71 (1998). This appears in MS 134, pp. 147–148, dated April 14, 1947. Denis Paul translates the sentence rather freely: "To join battle in this field one must have fighters armed quite differently from any I can raise." (This translation

was in a document on his website, accessed October 22, 2004, titled "MSS 130–138, 1945–1949." It no longer appears to be accessible.)

Chapter 1

1. This worry came very early on but applied just as well to the finished product, in a May 28, 1912, letter from Russell to Lady Ottoline Morrell, in McGuinness, *Wittgenstein: A Life*, 104.

2. I provide a survey of Wittgenstein's teaching at Cambridge in "The Wittgenstein Lectures, Revisited."

Wittgenstein also worked as an elementary school teacher from 1920 to 1926 in rural Austria, but I have not tried to address any relevance this might have had for his philosophical development. For a discussion of that period and its possible relevance to Wittgenstein's philosophy, see Bartley, *Wittgenstein*; Wünsche, *Der Volksschullehrer Ludwig Wittgenstein* (including correspondence between Wittgenstein and Hänsel); and the impressive new edition of Wittgenstein's *Word Book*, with an introduction by Désirée Weber; as well as Wittgenstein's "Preface to the *Dictionary for Elementary Schools*," PO, 12–27.

3. E.g., Krämer, *Plato and the Foundations of Metaphysics*; Findlay, *Plato: The Written and Unwritten Doctrines*; and more recently Melzer, *Philosophy between the Lines: The Lost History of Esoteric Writing*, 58–67. Aristotle seems to refer to unwritten teachings of Plato at *Physics* 209b15.

4. In his *Nicomachean Ethics*, see *exoterica*: NE 1102a27, 1140a3; and cf. *enkuklika* [popular]: 1096a4. Similar allusions can be found in the *Eudemian Ethics* (1217b23, 1218b32) and the *Politics* (1278b31, 1323a22).

5. NE 1095a3–12.

6. NE 1179b27.

7. Melzer, *Philosophy between the Lines*, 33, contrasts the exoteric works with what he calls "acroamatic" works, "designed for hearing only." This conforms to the notion that Plato and Aristotle saved their esoteric doctrines for lectures to select students at the Academy or the Lyceum.

8. Luke 8:9–10; and also Mark 4:33–34: "Using many parables like these, he spoke the word to them, so far as they were capable of understanding it. He would not speak to them [the crowds] except in parables, but he explained everything to his disciples when they were by themselves."

The oddity here comes from the fact that parables did not have a Hebrew tradition of obscurity or secrecy. See Psalm 78:1–4: "My people, listen to my teaching, pay attention to what I say. I will speak to you in *mashal* [parable, poetry; *parabolais* in the Greek Septuagint], unfold the mysteries of the past. What we have heard and know, what our ancestors have told us we shall not conceal from their descendants, but will tell a generation still to come." Matthew seems to have a momentary sense of the *value* of parables to reveal truth to the crowds when he has Jesus say (Matthew 13:13): "The reason I talk to them in parables is that they look without seeing." That is, the parables might help them to see. . . .

Furthermore, the Sermon on the Mount (Matthew 5–6; and also "Sermon on the Plain" Luke 6: 17–37) is a clear example in the synoptic gospels in which Jesus teaches the crowd *without* speaking in parables.

9. Melzer, *Philosophy between the Lines*, 125–284, and passim. These categories are not meant to be mutually exclusive.

The messages of Jesus, at least as presented in the synoptic gospels, might then be thought to fall into the third category of Pedagogical esotericism—the parables are shared with all, but can only be understood by the insiders, who are given a non-parabolic explanation. However, I think the esoteric interpretation of the parables was not part of Jesus's intent, but a later invention of the gospel writers to account for why the crowds ultimately turned against Jesus. Even so, the invention really does not serve its purpose.

Scientific investigation of sexuality began in Europe near the end of the nineteenth century. Two famous publications were Richard von Krafft-Ebing's *Psychopathia Sexualis: eine Klinisch-Forensiche Studie* (1886) and Albert Moll's *Untersuchungen über die Libido Sexualis* (1897). In both cases, the relevant portions of the title, as well as explicit descriptions or discussions of the sex act, were written in Latin. In this way, only the scientific community, and not the general public, would be exposed to this potentially corrupting material. These illustrate the second and third types of esotericism.

Wittgenstein began to write in code (simply reversing the letters of the alphabet) when he was a child, but did so systematically in the more personal portions of his diary while serving in the war (published as GT). This seems to have been done to hide his personal thoughts from the prying eyes of his military comrades. This would perhaps illustrate the first type of esotericism. When Wittgenstein continued this practice (though less systematically) in his diaries in the 1930s (published as "Movements of Thought" in PPO), he seems to have done so more out of habit than with any secretive purpose.

10. Melzer, *Philosophy between the Lines*, 33. And he goes on to suggest that other theoretical works by Aristotle "transcended the popular level also through the abstruseness of their very subject matter."

Melzer's case for Aristotle's esotericism is based on Aristotle's obscurity: "All parties agree that Aristotle uses obscurity to withhold certain higher truths from most readers" (42). While all parties do agree that Aristotle is sometimes obscure, it is quite a leap from that to the view that he was obscure *for a purpose*. I think most philosophers see his obscurity as a consequence of his obsessive desire to classify and of the fact that what we have from him are not finished, polished writings.

Perhaps he just is hard to understand—like Kant. (Does Meltzer wish to argue that Kant was thereby an esotericist?)

Melzer goes on to argue that there are inconsistencies between Aristotle's known (known to us but presumably esoteric at the time) writings and what we know of his exoteric (presumably public) writings, and even within Aristotle's known (to us) writings. As for the inconsistencies within his known writings, Melzer does not seem to consider the possibility that the writings are from different stages of Aristotle's thinking—as though one might accuse Wittgenstein of inconsistency by comparing the *Tractatus* with the *Philosophical Investigations*. And as for a tension between the exoteric writings and the known writings, Melzer marshals evidence that Aristotle endorses ("heralds," "asserts") the immortality of a personal soul in his exoteric works while refusing to do this in his known writings (42–43). This public dissimulation allegedly was done to protect himself (defensive esotericism) from charges of heresy. Yet the most plausible theory about the exoteric works is that they were *dialogues*, on the model of Plato's. Hence, it is just as problematic to ascribe views to Aristotle, about, say, immortality, based on dialogues as it is to ascribe views to Plato based on their appearance in his dialogues. For a discussion of the problems of ascribing beliefs to Plato based on the dialogues, see, e.g., Cobb, "Plato's Treatment of Immortality in the *Phaedo*," and my discussion in chapter 7, this volume. The irony of all this is that Aristotle was apparently charged with impiety late in life anyway (see the account in Natali, *Aristotle: His Life and School*, 60–64).

11. NE 1095a5.

12. CV, 6/8. (In the pagination I employ, the first number refers to the page in the 1980 University of Chicago edition, the second one to the page in the 1998 revised Blackwell edition.) Original German in MS 109, pp. 204–205 (November 6 or 7, 1930); published in WA3, 111. The italicized unbracketed words were underlined in Wittgenstein's original notebook.

13. Spengler's influence on Wittgenstein is discussed extensively in my book *Wittgenstein in Exile*, especially chapters 2 and 6.

14. CV, 10/12–3. Original German in MS 110, p. 18; published in WA3, 157.

15. Engelmann, *Wittgenstein—Engelmann: Briefe, Begegnungen, Erinnerungen*, 90.

16. Engelmann, *Wittgenstein—Engelmann*, reports: "Wittgenstein found Schlick a distinguished and understanding partner in conversation, all the more so because he appreciated Schlick's highly cultured personality—something which Wittgenstein found essential in his intellectual contacts with others" (in *Letters from Ludwig Wittgenstein: With a Memoir*, 118); and Engelmann reports of the architect Loos, "Loos . . . once said to Wittgenstein: 'You are me!'" (127). Regarding his sister Hermine, see her notes on her conversations with Ludwig, published in *"Ludwig Sagt . . ." Die Aufzeichnungen der Hermine Wittgenstein*.

17. Wittgenstein's connection with Sraffa is well-known. Sraffa's diary (De Iaco, "A List of Meetings between Wittgenstein and Sraffa," 87) shows one meeting between Sraffa, Piccoli, and Wittgenstein on June 3, 1929. De Iaco summarizes what is known about Piccoli's connection to Wittgenstein, basing this on research by Alexandra Marjanović, who claims that "Piccoli and Wittgenstein . . . met at least thirty times between November 11, 1929 and November 12, 1932" (Marjanović, "Introduzione alla vita e alle carte di Raffaello Piccoli: un racconto," 27). Examination of Wittgenstein's appointment diary for April through June 1930 shows four appointments in May and June. Thanks to Brian McGuinness for bringing Piccoli to my attention.

18. See von Wright, "Wittgenstein and the 20th Century" and "The Myth of Progress," in *The Tree of Knowledge and Other Essays*, 88, 207–209. Carnap's book, *The Logical Structure of the World*, was originally published in 1928. Herbert Feigl reports of meetings between Carnap and Wittgenstein in 1927 and 1928: "I recall Wittgenstein, on one occasion, precipitating a quarrel with Carnap, which . . . was mainly an expression of diametrically opposed personalities" (Feigl, "The Wiener Kreis in America," 638).

19. CV, 7/10. And see Nietzsche, "The Gay Science," §381, in *The Basic Writings of Nietzsche*, 176–177:

> *On the question of being understandable*.—One does not only wish to be understood when one writes; one wishes just as surely *not* to be understood. It is not by any means necessarily an objection to a book when anybody finds it impossible to understand: perhaps that was part of the author's intention—he did not want to be understood by just "anybody." Every more noble spirit and taste selects its audience when it wishes to communicate itself; and choosing them, it at the same time erects barriers against "the others." All the more subtle laws of any style have their origin at this point: they at the same time keep away, create a distance, forbid "entrance," understanding, as said above—while they open the ears of those whose ears are related to ours.

20. However, the passage just quoted proceeds in part as follows:

> The book must automatically separate those who understand it & those who do not. The foreword too is written *just* for such as understand the book. . . . If you do not want certain people to get into a room, put a lock on it for which they do not have the key. But it is senseless to talk with them about it, unless you want them all the same to admire the room from outside! The decent thing to do is: put a lock on the doors that attracts only those who are able to open it & is not noticed by the rest.

This may give the impression that Wittgenstein wants to exclude certain people. But I am more inclined to think that he simply did not want those excluded to be resentful. The "lock" is really nothing more than its unintelligibility to the "typical western" mindset.

21. Alexander Maslow, *A Study in Wittgenstein's Tractatus*, p. x. I do not think that Wittgenstein's obscurity is intentional (just as I do not think Aristotle's is intentional or purposive), but Frank Ramsey, who met with Wittgenstein for several days in 1923 to discuss the *Tractatus*, reported to his mother: "Some of his sentences are

intentionally ambiguous having an ordinary meaning and a more difficult meaning which he also believes" (September 20, 1923, published in Wittgenstein, *Letters to C. K. Ogden*, 78). I do not insist on denying that Wittgenstein's esotericism in the *Tractatus* is purposeful. My interest is primarily in the period once Wittgenstein returns to Cambridge.

22. Lemoine, *The Anagogic Theory of Wittgenstein's "Tractatus,"* 9. I have argued that awareness of Wittgenstein's wartime experiences is crucial to the understanding of certain paragraphs in the *Tractatus*, in chapter 1 of *Wittgenstein in Exile*. Brian McGuinness goes so far as to say ("In the Shadow of Goethe: Wittgenstein's Intellectual Project," 448), "No one else could have written his *Tractatus Logico-philosophicus*. Above all, no one who had not been through that War could have written it."

23. Engelmann, *Letters from Ludwig Wittgenstein: with a Memoir*, 94.

24. Feigl, "The `Wiener Kreis' in America," 638.

25. McGuinness, "Editor's Preface," in *Wittgenstein and the Vienna Circle*, 15. Personal communication from Feigl seems to be the source of this information: McGuinness, "Relations with and within the Circle," 189.

26. Feigl, "The `Wiener Kreis' in America," 639; also see Menger, *Reminiscences of the Vienna Circle and the Mathematical Colloquium*,"130–131.

27. Carnap, "Wittgenstein and the Vienna Circle," 462. And recall Engelmann's comments on Schlick (118), quoted in note 16.

28. The full account of this sad story has yet to be told. But the outlines can be found, among other places, in Baker, "Preface," in *The Voices of Wittgenstein: The Vienna Circle*, xviii–xxi.

Apparently, the exclusion of Carnap from ongoing discussions with Wittgenstein led to a larger rift in the Vienna Circle, with Otto Neurath and his students also being excluded from even hearing reports from Waismann on the joint book project with Wittgenstein. This rift was enforced by Schlick, but it presumably originated with Wittgenstein. We learn about this in letters between Neurath and his student Heinrich Neider, in which there is clear resentment. Neurath to Neider (June 8, 1934): "Is the speech of the anointed [Schlick] also of the LORD [Wittgenstein]? How is the Waismann work coming? When does the Lord come down upon this mortal project during the holidays? Or, in the meantime, even the Revelation of Jehovah will have appeared, so that he will then find Waismann's work superfluous!" Neider replied: "The LORD will come to Vienna in June. Prophet and disciples wait with anxious tension. Perhaps the new revelation is beyond human comprehension. Who knows?" Understandably, the secrecy all came to seem esoteric. Neurath to Carnap (January 18, 1935): "About the Schlick Circle, only dark reports reach my ear. The oath to keep silent about everything that is whispered from the holy books binds everyone—unless one 'quotes' the most sacred." Neurath to Neider (April 1935): "When did Wittgenstein drop the atomic propositions? And what about the 'last sentences' you are talking about? Is this all from the esoteric work?" (Manninen, "Wittgenstein's Virtual Presence in the Vienna Circle, 1931–1935").

While Wittgenstein carefully chose his hearers in Vienna, it was in the process of producing a joint work with Waismann that would ultimately be shared. As Wittgenstein wrote to Schlick concerning his work with Waismann (*Gesamtbriefwechsel*, July 31, 1935): "When I last saw Waismann I told him he could use something in my MS for his book.—Who knows if I will ever write anything & I wanted someone to understand my manuscripts & use them. Because I don't want all my work of the last 6 years to have been for nothing."

29. For an account of Wittgenstein's troubled relations with the Apostles, see Levy, *Moore: G. E. Moore and the Cambridge Apostles*, 266–270.

30. Bell, "An Epistle on the Subject of the Ethical and Aesthetic Beliefs of Herr Ludwig Wittgenstein (Doctor of Philosophy) to Richard Braithwaite, Esq., M.A. (Fellow of King's College)," 209, 211 (recently reprinted in Flowers and Ground, *Portraits of Wittgenstein*, 2:499, 501). As for Wittgenstein's "laying down the law," Bloomsbury member Duncan Grant reported (in an interview) on Wittgenstein's pronouncements about music and art "that everything Beethoven said was true, and that a still-life by André Derain that Keynes had bought was without merit" (Rosenbaum, "Wittgenstein in Bloomsbury," 155).

31. PO, 28–35.

32. Hodges, *Alan Turing: The Enigma*, 152–153. I queried Hodges about the source of this story, and he supposed he had gotten it from the late Robin Gandy who would have gotten it from Turing, but he could not remember any details.

33. Findlay, *Plato: The Written and Unwritten Doctrines*, 299. In fact, Findlay calls this "a perfect analogue to the Platonic situation" of esotericism. I find Findlay to be a somewhat unreliable source. In his two memoirs of Wittgenstein, "My Encounters with Wittgenstein" and "Introductory," he manages to contradict himself about Wittgenstein's copy of Russell's *Principles of Mathematics* (171, 19, respectively), and about the location of his lectures (173, 20). And he sometimes seems more intent on making points than on offering an accurate portrayal.

34. Redpath, *Ludwig Wittgenstein: A Student's Memoir*, 46; McGuinness, "Waismann: The Wandering Scholar," 13.

35. This is confirmed by the report of Arthur MacIver (McGuinness, "Arthur MacIver's Diary," 229), quoted in chapter 2, this volume.

36. Wittgenstein's letter to von Wright, March 9, 1939, in PO, 459–460. Also Malcolm, *Ludwig Wittgenstein: A Memoir*, 27; and Hijab, "Preface," draft of an unpublished book "Philosophy Revisited: A Personal Exposition of Wittgenstein," sec. 020: Reflecting on his time at Cambridge from 1945 to 1947, "Wittgenstein refused to

permit a visiting friend of mine to audit one of his lectures, although he welcomed him to audit the whole course. This is the way he expressed his objection. He said that what he was doing was like teaching a new technique for playing the piano. In one session, the auditor may hear a racket of discordant notes and fail to grasp their function in teaching the new technique, unless the auditor perseveres over a whole course." However, it does not seem that Wittgenstein had this requirement (to attend the whole term) in the early 1930s.

37. Malcolm, *Ludwig Wittgenstein: A Memoir*, 53–54, 103. (Lazerowitz is not named in the published version of the letter.) Also see Britton ("Portrait of a Philosopher," 491), who "wrote to Wittgenstein asking his permission to attend his . . . discussion class [in 1931–32]" and got it.

38. Gasking and Jackson, "Ludwig Wittgenstein," 1037.

39. See Klagge, "The Wittgenstein Lectures, Revisited," mentioned in note 2.

40. "Movements of Thought: Diaries, 1930–1932 and 1936–1937," in PPO, 52/53 (MS 183, 45; October 8, 1930). Less than two weeks later, again in his diary, Wittgenstein reflected on the difficulty of interacting with people who did not understand him and how we could handle that (PPO, 60–61; MS 183, 52–53; October 19).

41. The fact that Wittgenstein did not consider his lectures to be occasions for sharing his views only with like-minded disciples is shown by Malcolm's report (*Memoir*, 48; from the period of 1946–1947): "What made Wittgenstein furious was . . . also the implication that Wittgenstein kept the nature of his work a secret. He said that he had always regarded his lectures as a form of publication." And Casimir Lewy recalled, "Wittgenstein once said to me that 'to publish' means 'to make public', and that therefore lecturing is a form of publication" (*Meaning and Modality*, xi).

42. "Movements of Thought: Diaries, 1930–1932 and 1936–1937," PPO, 104–107 (MS 183, 97–98; October 13, 1931).

43. CV, 17/25 (MS 112, 223; November 22, 1931).

44. E.g., WLL, 60, 63.

45. Diary entry for January 28, 1932, in "Movements of Thought," PPO, 149.

46. Gasking and Jackson, "Ludwig Wittgenstein," 1037.

47. PR, 85. The revised version of the "Foreword" appears on p. 7.

48. Rothhaupt, "Wittgenstein at Work: Creation, Selection and Composition of 'Remarks,'" 51–63.

49. Rothhaupt's construction of the so-called Kringel-Buch is unpublished.

50. Anscombe, "Introduction," viii–ix; quoted more extensively in Klagge, "The Wittgenstein Lectures, Revisited," 53.

51. In 1946, one of Wittgenstein's pupils from 1938, James Taylor, reflected back on his experience of Wittgenstein's classes (WC, 394; January 22, 1946):

> If the question is just "Did I feel at that time (or at any other time) that I had been cheated?", then the answer is the one I gave when I last saw you after thinking about it, simply "No". (I have at various times discussed your teaching at Cambridge with other former pupils of yours who in some cases did think they had been cheated; in such discussions I have disagreed in all cases with the other person.) However the original question is not far distant from the question "Did you feel at that time that you had been *misled*?" I should have to answer to this that at that time, & in fact now, I did feel & feel that I was misled. But the sense of "misled" is important. I should say that the sense in which I was misled is such a sense as would almost certainly be applicable in the case of very good, i.e. more or less dazzling, instruction. If one receives very valuable instruction indeed, & is dazzled by it, then one is almost certain, I should have thought, to be blinded to the proper appraisal of some things & aspects of things which are not prominent in that instruction. This is certainly what happened in my case. I found that I had very painfully to accustom my eyes to look at other things in a new way. However at no time in this process (which I suppose is still going on) did I think ill of what you had taught me, or tried to teach me, or of your work in general. I have sometimes been more puzzled than I am now to formulate what the worth of your work consists in, but even at these times I did not think badly of it, nor in fact other than well of it. It was in fact true as you have suggested that I found I could myself do practically nothing with your ideas *directly*, & this was of course most disturbing.

(On the matter of feeling "cheated," see also the brief allusion in Bouwsma, *Wittgenstein: Conversations,* 36.) Two things are clear from this: there was quite a mixed reaction among students to Wittgenstein's teaching, and Taylor experienced Wittgenstein's teaching as an attempt to change his way of looking at things.

52. Oddly, Karl Popper accused Wittgenstein of cultivating "esoter[ic]ism" in his infamous 1946 talk to the Cambridge Moral Sciences Club (PPO, 398). What Popper meant by this is clarified somewhat in a letter to Bertrand Russell, who was also at the meeting, written shortly after the meeting (published in Grattan-Guinness, "Russell and Karl Popper," 13–15). In this letter of October 27, Popper wrote:

> . . . Philosophical activity in Wittgenstein's sense . . . is not exoterically arguable. It cannot, and does not, consist of more than clever guesses about various intended meanings. It leads to a series of "He *may* have meant . . .", but it does not lead to any assertion which can be open to argument. This fact completely destroys any link with the rationalist tradition in philosophy and must lead to esotericity.

It is hard to know what Popper has in mind here, given that none of Wittgenstein's later work had been published in 1946. But consider Popper's criticism of Wittgenstein in *The Open Society and Its Enemies* (2:20):

> From this point of view we may criticize a doctrine like that of Wittgenstein's [in the *Tractatus*], who holds that while science investigates matters of fact, it is the business of philosophy to clarify the meanings of terms, thereby purging our language, and eliminating linguistic puzzles. It is characteristic of the views of this school that they do not lead to any chain of argument that could be rationally criticized; the school therefore addresses its subtle analyses exclusively to the small esoteric circle of the initiated.

Popper goes on, in a note to this text (note 52 to chapter 11, p. 299):

> It appears that irrationalism in the sense of a doctrine or creed that does not propound connected and debatable arguments but rather propounds aphorisms and dogmatic statements which must be "understood" or else left alone, will generally become the property of an esoteric circle of the initiated. And, indeed, this prognosis seems to be partly corroborated by some of the publications that come from Wittgenstein's school. (I do not wish to generalize; for example, everything I have seen of F. Waismann's writing [a one-time expositor of Wittgenstein's views] is presented as a chain of rational and exceedingly clear arguments, and entirely free from the attitude of "*take it or leave it.*")

Popper's comments imply that Wittgenstein is not interested in engaging with the thoughts of others who might disagree with him. The fact that he had not published anything may have contributed to that image.

But there was more behind Popper's accusations. While Popper was never a member of the Vienna Circle or associated with it, he had apparently tried to participate in some of the discussions of Wittgenstein—unsuccessfully. A student of Neurath, Heinrich Neider, wrote to Neurath (late January 1935): "Popper and H [Walter Hollitscher] were not considered worthy to enter the closest circle of the prophet" (Manninen, "Wittgenstein's Virtual Presence in the Vienna Circle, 1931–1935"). Manninen comments: "Now we know what Popper lost and what enraged him all his life: a reading of Wittgenstein."

However, apparently what kept Wittgenstein from publishing was the very sense that he had not yet found the best, or an effective, way to engage with those who might disagree with him. As Wittgenstein put it in his 1933 letter to the editor of *Mind*, renouncing Braithwaite's attempted summary of his views (PO, 156–157): "That which is retarding the publication of my work, the difficulty of presenting it in a clear and coherent form, a fortiori prevents me from stating my views within the space of a letter." The fact that he had still not published anything thirteen years after that might have provoked Popper to suspect that he had no intention of sharing his views publicly. But, in fact, as of 1945 anyway, Wittgenstein was still hard at work trying to publish something that would engage with those who did not share his preferred ways of thinking. He was still trying to figure out how to evangelize. And the Preface to the *Investigations*, dated 1945, makes it clear that he wished to publish his work precisely because versions of his ideas "variously misunderstood, more or less mangled or watered down, were in circulation."

One of Wittgenstein's students from the 1945–1947 period, Wasfi Hijab, in an unpublished memoir, characterized the attitude of some of Wittgenstein's students at that time as "simply getting a kick out of beating others (including Wittgenstein himself) to be first in revealing the 'secrets' of the esoteric school of philosophy at Cambridge" ("Philosophy Revisited: A Personal Exposition of Wittgenstein," November 1995, sec. 217). But while this is the perception of one of his students, I don't see this as reflective of Wittgenstein's intent. Wittgenstein was willing and even anxious to share his views . . . once he was satisfied with their formulation.

53. PO, 161. The first two sentences of this passage are derived from MS 153b, 30r, probably 1931. The last three sentences of this passage date to June 20, 1931 and appear in MS 110, 189; published in WA3, 268.

54. WLL, 63.

55. What exactly do I mean by "noncognitive"? I use the term in primarily a contrastive sense—those factors that are not *simply* a matter of belief. The examples I marshaled from PI give a sense of the range of such factors: psychological and emotional states and pressures, as well as volitional states. I suppose my use of the term reflects the contrastive term *noncognitivism* in metaethics. Clearly it is a family-resemblance concept, not one with an essence.

56. Cavell, "The Availability of Wittgenstein's Later Philosophy," 71.

57. Stern, *Wittgenstein's Philosophical Investigations: An Introduction*, 22.

58. Heal, "Wittgenstein and Dialogue," 64–71.

59. Already in the *Blue Book,* we find Wittgenstein inserting other voices into his reflections: "Now you might ask . . ." (BB, 3) and itself in quotation marks: "'But surely the word "I" in the mouth of a man . . .'" (67). The *Blue Book* makes for a nice work to test this idea, since it was dictated, but in something very like, or substituting for, a classroom setting.

60. James Taylor, on his way to taking up a teaching post in Australia after the war, met the tragic fate of dying in a pub brawl (Monk, *Ludwig Wittgenstein: The Duty of Genius*, 402).

61. Britten, "Portrait of a Philosopher," in *Portraits of Wittgenstein*, 2:496.

62. "Appendix II: Wittgenstein's 1938 Preface," 188. Original German preface in *Philosophische Untersuchungen: Kritisch-Genetische Edition*, 209.

63. CV, 62/71, 18/25, and 61/70.

64. Bouwsma, *Wittgenstein: Conversations,* 9, also 36 (August 5, 22, 1949). For more evidence of pessimism about his teaching at this time, see Tranøy, "Wittgenstein in Cambridge," 17, and Malcolm, *Ludwig Wittgenstein: A Memoir,* 53.

65. Drury, "Conversations with Wittgenstein," 160.

66. CV, 66/75 (MS 136, 81a). He certainly did not mean *us* as the "better kind of reader."

67. CV, 77/88 (MS 137, 134b; December 26, 1948). Winch's translation of "*unter vier Augen*" as "tête-à-tête" is not literal.

68. *Letters to C. K. Ogden*, 78.

69. In chapter 8 of my book *Wittgenstein in Exile,* I trace the evolution of Wittgenstein's thought on a certain issue concerning the relationship between physiological

phenomena and mental phenomena and claim that this change in purpose, from evangelical back to esoteric, helps explain what he says at that point. But again, I consider research on this issue to be preliminary.

70. See, for example, Anthony Kenny's "Introduction to the Revised Edition" of his classic book *Wittgenstein*. After lamenting the waning influence of Wittgenstein's ideas in contemporary philosophy, he decides the best antidote is to repeat his explanations of those ideas (xii–xx). I don't mean to criticize this; after all, that's how philosophers operate, only it's not how Wittgenstein wanted to operate.

Recall the caricature of the "ugly American" tourist as one who, upon not being understood in a foreign country, repeats the question in English, only more distinctly and loudly.

71. MS 155, 42r (1931, written in English). I discuss this further and cite additional statements of the view in chapters 4 and 5.

72. CV, 62/71 (MS 134, 143).

Chapter 2

1. Letter of January 18, 1929, from Keynes to his wife Lydia Lopokova (Monk, *Ludwig Wittgenstein: The Duty of Genius*, 255).

2. Reported in Wood, *Bertrand Russell: The Passionate Skeptic, A Biography*, 156.

3. Undated letter from Empson to Julian Trevelyan, incoming secretary of the Heretics: "I have got a promise from Wittgenstein to speak next term but that is absolutely all" (*Selected Letters of William Empson*, 9). (This corrects our mistaken statement in PO, 36, that the invitation came from Ogden.) An advertisement of upcoming events for the Heretics announced: "Anyone who feels sufficiently interested is invited to attend. Later speakers will include Dr Wittgenstein, Arthur Waley, and Professor Piccoli" (*Cambridge Review*, October 18, 1929, 27). Why Wittgenstein accepted Empson's invitation is unclear. But Wittgenstein had already known about Empson's poems, as indicated by his conversation with F. R. Leavis in early 1929 ("Memories of Wittgenstein," 66–67).

4. Announcement for Sunday, November 17, in the Calendar section of the *Cambridge Review* November 15, 1929, viii): "The Heretics: L. Wittgenstein, Esq., on 'Ethics,' in Falcon Yard, 8.30." In the absence of this information, the lecture has come to be titled "A Lecture on Ethics." An earlier announcement indicates the Heretics' lectures were held in the Conservative Club Rooms, located at Falcon Yard, which was off Petty Cury.

5. Arthur MacIver, who attended the lecture, as noted in his diary that evening (McGuinness, "Arthur MacIver's Diary," 220).

6. *Wittgenstein und die Musik*, 28.

7. Anscombe called the lecture "*extremely* 'Tractatussy'" (Anscombe, "The Simplicity of the Tractatus," 177).

8. "A Lecture on Ethics," in PO, 44 (the full text is 37–44). Other, presumably earlier, drafts of the lecture, which differ in some interesting ways from the published typescript, can be found in Wittgenstein, *Lecture on Ethics*.

9. Black, *Max Black: A Memoir*, 57. The interview was conducted in 1987 by S. P. Rosenbaum, the Bloomsbury scholar and son-in-law of Max Black.

Additional details of the occasion are related by another student, Arthur MacIver, who noted at the time that the audience "cannot appreciate religious feeling or argue except sophistically" (McGuinness, "Arthur MacIver's Diary," 220). Julian Trevelyan wrote in *Indigo Days*: "I remember [Wittgenstein] lecturing to the Heretics . . . on Ethics, which he considered a huge nonsense" (18). Piero Sraffa's diary shows that he planned to attend the lecture (De Ioca, "A List of Meetings between Wittgenstein and Sraffa," 87).

10. Arthur MacIver (McGuinness, "Arthur MacIver's Diary," 220):

> Wittgenstein made a magnificent speech—though there was little in it that was not in the "Tractatus"—though it was wasted on the Heretics, who cannot appreciate religious feeling or argue except sophistically.

Then MacIver recounts the aftermath, which indicates others who had attended the talk:

> After the meeting [Maurice] Cornforth thought we could get hold of Wittgenstein and have a discussion with him in the Corner House, but the Corner House was reserved for the committee of the Heretics, who carried Wittgenstein in with them. So a strange company consisting of [Desmond] Lee, Cornforth and myself, a Canadian, an American, some nondescripts and two women from Girton, Miss Klugman, known as Kitty, a very able Jewess who has taken a first in Moral Science and now took charge of our whole party, and her friend Miss Thompson, known as Tom, wandered around Cambridge looking for an open pub, drank coffee at the coffee-stall in Market Hill and only broke up when it became quite apparent that no pubs are open to undergraduates after ten o'clock on Sunday nights in Cambridge.

MacIver later (222) mentions meeting "a physicist" who had been at the Heretics lecture—probably W. H. Watson. In the Preface to his *On Understanding Physics*, Watson says (ix), "During the years 1929–31, I attended Wittgenstein's lectures in Cambridge . . . ," which suggests he was at this lecture, since Wittgenstein's regular lectures didn't begin until 1930.

Julian Bell's poem, "An Epistle on the Subject of the Ethical and Aesthetic Beliefs of Herr Ludwig Wittgenstein (Doctor of Philosophy)," was first published in February 1930 and revised and reprinted in 1932. The 1932 reprinting adds a postscript that it is intended as a satire and "solely as a criticism of certain views on art and morals advocated by [Wittgenstein] three years ago [i.e., in 1929]" (in Flowers and Ground, *Portraits of Wittgenstein*, 2:498–504). The dating and contents suggest that Bell may have attended the lecture on ethics. But he mainly had contact with Wittgenstein through the Apostles in 1929 (see Monk, *Ludwig Wittgenstein: The Duty of Genius*, 255–258). There is no evidence that Bell attended any of Wittgenstein's course lectures.

11. Moore, in PO, 46.

12. Letter from S. K. Bose to John King, April 5, 1978, on deposit at Wren Library, Trinity College, Cambridge; published in Klagge, "The Wittgenstein Lectures, Revisited," 26.

13. Leavis, "Memories of Wittgenstein," 63. It seems that Leavis's acquaintance with Wittgenstein was largely in 1929 and the very early 1930s, based on the anecdotes that he shares.

14. See, for example, W. E. Johnson: "If *you* think that, what must *I* think" (quoted by Leavis, "Memories of Wittgenstein," 62). Also, Desmond Lee, a student in the 1930 classes: . . . "He completely dominated any discussion in which he took part, and these discussions associated with his lectures were largely a monologue. . . . His personal and intellectual force was so strong that it had a numbing effect on those who listened to him" ("Wittgenstein: 1929–1931," 479–480). A similar impression of Wittgenstein is provided by J. N. Findlay, who had attended Wittgenstein's lectures in 1939–40, but saw himself as the rare exception to this generalization ("My Encounters with Wittgenstein," in Flowers and Ground, *Portraits of Wittgenstein*, 673–674, 679–680).

15. J. N. Findlay, "Introductory," in *Wittgenstein: A Critique*, 19. In "My Encounters with Wittgenstein," Findlay elaborates: "He looked like Apollo who had bounded into life out of his own statue, or perhaps like the Norse god Baldur, blue-eyed and fair-haired, with a beauty that had nothing sensual about it, but simply breathed the four Greek cardinal virtues, to which he added a very exquisite kindness and graciousness that bathed one like remote, slightly wintry sunshine. His clothes were faintly artistic, a corduroy coat, slacks, an open shirt, but very well-kept and clean" (677).

16. Moore, in PO, 48–49. Surprisingly, prospective students selected the days and times of the class. The *Cambridge University Reporter* (December 19, 1929, 441) lists a course, "Philosophy," by Dr. L. Wittgenstein, to be offered Lent term, 1930, and continuing to Easter term, with the footnote: "Lecture and conversation class. Times to be arranged to suit the convenience students, who are requested to call upon Dr Wittgenstein in Mr Braithwaite's rooms, King's College, at 5pm on Friday, January 17." Arthur MacIver duly arrived and noted (McGuinness, "Arthur MacIver's Diary," 229): "I was a little late and found a crowd there, who had already almost decided on the times from five to six o'clock on Mondays and from five to seven o'clock on Thursdays, and so, after a little protest from Cornforth on behalf of Irving, it was decided."

17. McGuinness, "Arthur MacIver's Diary," 229–230. Wittgenstein's own report confirms that of MacIver (letter to Koder, in *Wittgenstein und Musik*, 32): "You will be pleased to hear that I was able to hold my lecture yesterday, which I had been

anticipating with some anxiety and that it went better than expected. It was just like back then in Puchberg where I could barely speak in the first hour & then got stronger and stronger." (Koder was the music teacher at the elementary school in Puchberg where Wittgenstein taught from 1922 to 1924.)

18. Moore, "Wittgenstein's Lectures in 1930–1933"; WLL and WLA. While MacIver's diary has survived, his notes have not. Nevertheless, as we see below, he sometimes indicates topics and events from the lectures in the diary.

19. WLM. Concerning Moore's note taking, I. A. Richards reports: "Moore was in an armchair, at [Wittgenstein's] elbow, taking down every syllable. When Wittgenstein would start a sentence ten times, Moore would write it on his pad ten times up to the point where he broke it off" (interview of Richards, "Beginnings and Transitions," 27). (Richards attended classes sporadically over the first three years.)

20. Moore, "Wittgenstein's Lectures in 1930–1933," 52.

21. WLM: May term 1933, lecture 2b, 8:66, 313.

22. The exception: Drury, on May 4, 1931. Otherwise: Harold Ursell, three times on January 23, 1933, once on May 15, 1933, and once on May 26, 1933; Francis Skinner, on January 23, 1933; L. C. Young, on February 17, 1933; Mrs. Helen Knight, twice on May 15, 1933; and I. A. Richards, on May 22, 1933.

23. See the explanation by Moore, "Wittgenstein's Lectures in 1930–1933," 49.

24. McGuinness, "Arthur MacIver's Diary." MacIver's diary also gives many names of attendees during Lent term 1930 that I was not previously aware of: Braithwaite, Cornforth, Irving, Du Val, Black, Guest, Cooley, a Polish woman, a Catalan professor, a "strange man," and Middleton. For a survey of what we know about the attendees and circumstances of Wittgenstein's lectures this term, see my essay "The Wittgenstein Lectures, Revisited." Regarding note taking, MacIver remarked on January 27 (232) "of a course of lectures so planless as this one can make no genuine record."

25. McGuinness, "Arthur MacIver's Diary," 241.

26. Black, *Memoir*, 55–57. Where Black says, "With idiots to work with, what can you expect?" I assume he is quoting Wittgenstein.

I. A. Richards's poem "The Strayed Poet: Ludwig Wittgenstein," may make reference to this very event: "Such the torment felt, the spell-bound listeners watched and waited for the words to come, held and bit their breath while you were dumb. . . . But—should you want a blaze, try prompting! Who is the next will drop a brick?" (Richards, *Internal Colloquies,* 184). Richards attended at least some of Wittgenstein's lectures in the 1930 Lent and Easter terms and, as noted in the next paragraph, knew Black.

Max Black was a mathematics student at Queens' College, Cambridge, who attended Wittgenstein's lectures in Lent and Easter terms in 1930 and graduated in

1930. The interview also reveals an informal friendship with Wittgenstein (53-55), but the "Memorial Minutes" for Black, in Sturgeon and Brown, state that "at Cambridge he knew Moore, Russell and Ramsey, as well as such figures as I.A. Richards, C.K. Ogden and William Empson" (61). They are oddly silent about any connection with Wittgenstein. Of course, Black went on to publish *A Companion to Wittgenstein's Tractatus* in 1964.

27. McGuinness, "Arthur MacIver's Diary," 242. "Du Val" was presumably Patrick Du Val, who was completing his PhD in algebraic geometry in Trinity College. "Guest" was David Hayden Guest, a first-year mathematics student at Trinity. Braithwaite was a University Lecturer in Moral Science at this point who had studied physics and mathematics as an undergraduate. Wittgenstein's appointment diaries from the early 1930s show various appointments with all of these men.

Frank Ramsey died on January 19, the day before the first meeting of this course. On February 14, the *Cambridge Review* published a poetic tribute to Ramsey written by Du Val, "On a Philosopher Dying (F. P. R.)."

28. This is as good a place as any to reply to some claims made by Kimberley Cornish, in Cornish, *The Jew of Linz*. To address only the issues most relevant to Wittgenstein and his students:

Cornish (52) refers to "[Wittgenstein's] students—Bell, Cornforth, Haden-Guest and Cornford." There is no evidence that Julian Bell was one of Wittgenstein's students. As indicated in note 10 above, Bell knew Wittgenstein through the Apostles and may have attended the "Ethics" talk. There is no evidence that John Cornford was a student of Wittgenstein. On p. 68, Cornish writes: "Another of Wittgenstein's students, as we have seen, was John Cornford." But he is only alluding to his own previous assertion. Cornford was a history student, and a memoir of his life makes no mention of Wittgenstein (Sloan, *John Cornford: A Memoir*). See also comments by Wittgenstein concerning Cornford, which imply that he knew him but did not have him in his classes (in Hintikka, "Intellectual Autobiography," 37). Maurice Cornforth and David Haden Guest were indeed both students of Wittgenstein—Cornforth from 1930 to 1932 and Guest in 1930 and 1931–32. (Guest and Black were in Göttingen for the 1930–31 academic year.) Both Cornforth and Guest were extremely independent minded, and their writings are full of criticisms of Wittgenstein's views (mainly in the *Tractatus*). On p. 63, Cornish claims that the Marxist economist Maurice Dodd "attend[ed] Wittgenstein's lectures." Again, there is no evidence I know of for this claim.

McGuinness ("Introduction," WC, 8) writes, "Three of the four Cambridge men killed in [the Spanish Civil] war were pupils of his and the fourth was John Cornford." The other three that McGuinness counts as his students are Julian Bell, David Guest, and Ivor Hickman, but I see no evidence Bell attended his classes.

29. Diary entry for October 31, 1931, in "Movements of Thoughts," PPO, 117. The parenthetical about mathematicians is written and then crossed out by Wittgenstein in the diary. The physics student who at that time seemed to most impress

Wittgenstein was W. H. Watson, who went on to publish *On Understanding Physics* in 1938 and credit Wittgenstein (ix) for his influence.

30. WLM: Lent term 1930, lecture 5, 4:23, 23. Notes of that day's lecture by Desmond Lee (WLL, 10–11) make no mention of the issue over transfinite numbers, though they do mention other topics discussed that day. (Lee, a classicist, likely had no idea what the mathematicians were talking about.)

31. In the following weeks' lectures Wittgenstein briefly returned to the issue, as Black indicated: "Different rules apply to 'infinite' & to any numeral: it doesn't answer the question 'How many?'" (WLM: 4:35—March 3, 1930, 31). "Word 'infinite' not a numeral. It occurs in connection with 'possible'" (WLM: 4:37—March 10, 1930, 33). And, "Does Law of Excluded Middle apply to mathematical propositions? e.g. about infinity" (WLM: 4:69—May 26, 1930, 58). He then returns to these issues more fully in the much later lecture on January 23, 1933 (231–235).

Wittgenstein's extended silences during lectures are confirmed by Wasfi Hijab (who attended lectures from 1945 to 1947): "In the course of a lecture Wittgenstein would often stop for two to three minutes to collect his thoughts. In a two-hour class perhaps fifteen to twenty minutes would be silence" (Klagge, "The Wittgenstein Lectures, Revisited," 54). And also Findlay, "My Encounters with Wittgenstein," 680.

32. In a much later lecture, Moore notes: "Are there 5 successive 7's in development of π? If we find them, that proves there *are*. If we don't find them, doesn't prove there aren't. It's something for which we've provided a test for truth, but *not* for falsehood; & this must be quite different sort of thing from where *both* are provided. . . . 'Infinite' does *not* stand for a number or a quantity" (WLM: May Term 1932, lecture 4, 6b:10, 157).

33. Russell, "The Limits of Empiricism," 143. Russell's phrase is slightly misquoted by Michael Dummett, without a citation, as "a mere medical impossibility" (in Dummett, *Elements of Intuitionism*, 59–60) and thereafter is often repeated as such by Dummett, David Chalmers, and others. It is slightly misquoted, also without a citation, as "medical limitations" by Peter Hacker, in Baker and Hacker, *Wittgenstein: Rules, Grammar and Necessity*, 180 (and again in Hacker, *Wittgenstein, Meaning and Mind*, 183). Wittgenstein alludes to this phrase in PI §208: "The fact that we cannot write down all the digits of π is not a human shortcoming [*Unzulänglichkeit*], as the mathematicians sometimes think."

34. RFM, 267, 269, 272–273.

35. In the Michaelmas term lectures in 1932, these issues return in a related context. Looking back on the *Tractatus* in the class meetings on November 25 and 28, Wittgenstein diagnoses an error in his handling of universal generalization as a logical conjunction of cases. Conflating these two cases is tantamount to treating infinite sets as (very) large finite sets, which he called "a temptation, to which I yielded in *Tractatus*" (WLM: Michaelmas term 1932, lecture 7b, 7:34, 215; cf. Moore,

"Wittgenstein's Lectures in 1930–1933," 89). In his published article summarizing the lectures, Moore ties these comments on the *Tractatus* back to the earlier discussions of infinity and continues by recounting the relevant points made in the March 3, 1930, lecture (Moore, "Wittgenstein's Lectures in 1930–1933," 90).

36. Klagge, "The Wittgenstein Lectures, Revisited," 27. The German original in MS 107, 247; published in WA2, 174.

37. Cornforth, "Recollections of Cambridge Contemporaries," 95–96.

38. Recall Anscombe's account from lectures in 1944 (cited in chapter 1): After offering a natural objection that others in the class were inclined to dismiss, ". . . Wittgenstein checked them by taking it seriously, saying 'Let me think what medicine you need . . .' The 'medicine' was effective, and the story illustrates Wittgenstein's ability to understand the thought that was offered to him in objection" (Anscombe, "Introduction," 1981, viii–ix). This was an ability that Wittgenstein did not have (or did not use) in 1929 and 1930, but did have and use in 1933 and 1944.

39. "Philosophy," in PO, 160/161. The first paragraph is related to comments Wittgenstein entered in MS 153b, 30r, which seem to be from 1931. The second paragraph of this passage was first drafted on June 20, 1931 (MS 110, 189; published in WA3, 268.)

It is interesting that Wittgenstein alludes to the difficulty of holding back an outburst of anger or rage—which is just how Black had characterized Wittgenstein's outburst. Controlling one's outbursts and controlling one's philosophical temptations can be equally difficult. For more on Wittgenstein's anger, see Drury, "Conversations with Wittgenstein," 109 and 219.

40. WLL, 63. Moore's full notes do not mention this. (Moore calls Easter term "May term.")

41. McGuinness, "Arthur MacIver's Diary," 243.

42. Nor is there mention of this in Lee's notes (WLL, 11–12). For the following lecture, however, Moore does note Wittgenstein saying: "It was objected that . . ." to which he then responds (WLM: Lent term 1930, lecture 7, 4:30, March 3, 28). But such interjections are rare in Moore's notes. Lee's notes for the following lecture also begin: "To all this it may be objected. . . . To this objection the answer is. . . . To which it may be further objected. . . ." (12).

43. Klagge, "The Wittgenstein Lectures, Revisited," 41; originally in Redpath, *Ludwig Wittgenstein: A Student's Memoir*, 31.

44. Compare a similar and famous case from Bertrand Russell's lectures and notes. In Russell's 1918 lectures on logical atomism, he refers back to lectures he had given at Harvard in 1914 when "I argued that there were negative facts, and it nearly produced a riot: the class would not hear of there being negative facts at all" (Russell, *The Philosophy of Logical Atomism*, Lecture III. Atomic and Molecular Propositions,

74). Bernard Linsky is preparing a publication of Harry T. Costello's notes of Russell's spring 1914 lectures at Harvard for Philosophy 21: Advanced Logic. The topic was discussed on April 11, 1914, yet Costello's notes for that lecture give no indication of a riot and only allude to the issue. It turns out that Costello was himself "one of the chief rioters" (in "Logic in 1914 and Now," 248–249).

45. For a discussion of subjunctive mood in the *Tractatus*, see Nordmann, *Wittgenstein's* Tractatus, 133ff.

46. A survey of all the courses that Wittgenstein taught, from 1930 to 1947, is provided in Klagge, "The Wittgenstein Lectures, Revisited." This indicates where notes can be found for various lectures.

47. Whether this is a change in how students participated or in how note takers saw their job is hard to say. For notes from the 1939 lectures on the foundations of mathematics, see LFM. Student interventions are also more common in notes for the lectures in 1946 and 1947 (LPP).

48. This is so even though Wittgenstein deviated from form by calling all of these "lecture" classes and not designating any of them as "discussion" classes (Moore, "Wittgenstein's Lectures in 1930–1933," 48 n3).

49. Malcolm, *Ludwig Wittgenstein: A Memoir,* 25.

50. The published notes for these lectures were compiled by Cora Diamond from four sets of students' notes, one of which was from Malcolm. Interestingly, Malcolm's notes (specifically Malcolm, *Math Notes*) only rarely indicate interventions by students (23–24, 47–48), making it seem mostly like a smooth flow of thinking from Wittgenstein, which "he could have done had he been alone."

51. See LFM, 211 (May 3, 1939), 67–68 (February 8, 1939).

Chapter 3

1. MS 105, pp. 2, 1 (published in original German in WA1, 3, 4). The labeling of Wittgenstein's typescripts and manuscripts is due to G. H. von Wright, "The Wittgenstein Papers," which was originally published in 1969 and was updated by von Wright more than once. The latest version was published in 1993 in PO. We added an "Addendum" to this in the same book, 507–510, and a further "2002 Addendum" in PPO, 407–410.

2. Letter from Wittgenstein to Moore, WC, 181. Wittgenstein dictated selections from MSS 105, 106, 107, and part of 108 (published in original German in WA1 and WA2).

3. The resulting dictated typescript was labeled TS 208. Letters from Russell and Littlewood reporting on the TS and on Wittgenstein's work are published in WC, 83, 187. (Russell says he spent "five days in discussion with him"; Littlewood says he spent "6 or 8 sessions of 1 hour to one hour and a half.") Their recommendations

resulted in a grant of £100 (see letter from Wittgenstein to Moore, June 18, 1930, WC, 188, and editor's note on 184). McGuinness, in his editorial footnotes to WC, originally claimed (181–182 in the 2008 hardback edition) that the material that Russell saw was the so-called Moore volume—TS 209. But he changed his account in the 2012 paperback revised edition (182) to claim that Russell saw TS 208. Denis Paul seems to have had it right all along (Paul, *Wittgenstein's Progress*, 17). TS 208 has now been published in Wittgenstein, *Wiener Ausgabe*, vol. 7.

The cut-and-pasted minute book that Wittgenstein gave to Moore was labeled TS 209, and was eventually published as *Philosophical Remarks*, edited by Rush Rhees. The material was fortunately preserved by a typed copy and a microfilmed copy, as Rhees accidentally left the original in a telephone booth in Paddington Station in London (see the letter from Rhees to Anscombe and von Wright, July 26, 1962, published in Erbacher, Jung, and Seibel, "From the Archives—The Logbook of Editing Wittgenstein's *Philosophische Bemerkungen*, 111–112)!

4. Wittgenstein's will reads in part that "R. Rhees Miss G.E.M. Anscombe and Professor G.H. von Wright" may "dispose of as they think best" all his "unpublished writings and also the manuscripts and typescripts thereof," and "shall publish as many of my unpublished writings as they think fit. . . ." The thought that "Wittgenstein's main editor was himself" was emphasized by André Maury in his unpublished paper, "Bemerkungen: Description vs. Reflection," given at the "Von Wright and Wittgenstein in Cambridge: G. H. von Wright Centenary Symposium," Strathaird House, Cambridge, September 22, 2016.

5. Concerning Wittgenstein's course lectures in the early 1940s, Wolfe Mays recalled that ". . . he read extracts from James' *Principles of Psychology* and discussed them critically" (Klagge, "The Wittgenstein Lectures, Revisited," 49).

6. Hänsel, *Begegnungen mit Wittgenstein*, 44–61.

7. Drury, "Conversations with Wittgenstein," 102.

8. Drury, "Conversations with Wittgenstein," 119.

9. MS 110, 177–299 (published in original German in WA3, 262–333).

10. This was labeled TS 211. Nedo writes: "According to the entries in his pocket diary he dictated regularly three or four hours each day, and often up to seven hours" (Nedo, "Introduction," in Wittgenstein, *Wiener Ausgabe*, vol. 8.1, p. x). Wittgenstein did not complete this set of dictations until he was in Vienna again the following summer, by which time he had filled two further manuscript notebooks.

11. Waismann, *Ludwig Wittgenstein and the Vienna Circle*, 166. See also Nedo, "Introduction," in Wittgenstein, *Wiener Ausgabe*, vol. 8.1, p. x, for the evidence that what Waismann saw was TS 211. Wittgenstein reported in a letter of August 23, 1931: "I've been very busy since I left Cambridge and have done a fair amount of work" (letter to Moore, WC, 193).

12. The so-called Big Typescript was 768 pages, and labeled TS 213. It was published in the original German as *Wiener Ausgabe*, vol. 11 and with an English translation, BT.

13. At some later point, 1936 or after, Wittgenstein returned to reflecting on Frazer, perhaps in connection with having received a gift of a one-volume abridged edition of Frazer from Raymond Townsend (Rhees, "Editorial Notes," 220). Wittgenstein left behind at Anscombe's house a second set of remarks on thirteen loose sheets of papers specifically focused on Frazer, found after his death. These have come to be called "Part II" of the remarks on Frazer. I will not be concerned with these.

14. Letter from Rhees to G. H. von Wright, September 4 or 5, 1962 (though the portion of the letter that is quoted is dated September 25), published in Erbacher, Jung, and Seibel, "The Logbook of Editing Wittgenstein's *Philosophische Bemerkungen*," 120.

15. Letter from Rhees to G. H. von Wright, February 10, 1963 (though the portion of the letter that is quoted is dated February 14), in Erbacher, Jung, and Seibel, "The Logbook of Editing Wittgenstein's *Philosophische Bemerkungen*," 128.

16. Letter from Rhees to Anscombe and von Wright, April 22, 1964, 142. In fact the remarks on Frazer in MS 110 were written about a year and a half after the "Ethics" lecture.

17. WLM, May 1–May 29, 1933, 316–365.

18. In our introduction to "Remarks on Frazer's *Golden Bough*," in PO, 115, we mistakenly state that the remarks were taken from TS 221. This was a typographical error and should read "TS 211" (noticed by Steen Brock).

19. What constitutes a "work" by Wittgenstein has been interestingly discussed by Joachim Schulte in his "What Is a Work by Wittgenstein?" I will be discussing only part I of Rhees's editing work and will not be considering part II or how parts I and II fit together.

20. Original German edition, with an introductory note on the text by Rhees, published as "Bemerkungen über Frazers *Golden Bough*," *Synthese*, 1967; English translation by A. C. Miles and Rush Rhees, with an extensive introductory discussion of the content by Rhees, published in *The Human World*, 1971; bilingual book edition, edited by Rhees and translated by A. C. Miles with revisions by Rhees, published by Brynmill Press, 1979; English translation by John Beversluis, published in *Wittgenstein: Sources and Perspectives*, 1979; German edition published in *Wittgenstein: Vortrag über Ethik und andere kleine Schriften*, edited by J. Schulte, 1989; and bilingual edition with an introductory note on the text by the editors and a slightly revised translation by Beversluis, published in PO, 1993, 115–155. The last-mentioned edition has been improved textually in the third printing issued in 2010 (this is not a new edition). I will use the text of this *Philosophical Occasions* edition, in its third printing, for my references. Note, however, that none of these published editions gives a fully accurate account of the source of the texts in part I.

Anthropologists have finally produced their own edition of Wittgenstein's remarks on Frazer: *The Mythology in Our Language: Remarks on Frazer's Golden Bough*, with a new translation by Stephan Palmié and a collection of seven new essays by anthropologists.

21. It is included by Wittgenstein in the so-called Big Typescript (TS 213) in the "Philosophy" chapter (PO, 178/179). A somewhat independent edition of Wittgenstein's remarks was compiled by Ketner and Eigsti in 1973 with an English translation. They were unable to get permission from the Wittgenstein executors to publish it. They had included this passage in their edition, and von Wright responded that it "does not really belong here, although the name 'Frazer' is mentioned" (Westergaard, "On the 'Ketner and Eigsti Edition,'" 137). Rhees then inserted it as a footnote in his later editions.

22. I would mark them in the text by adding "* * *" as follows: on PO, 132/133, insert asterisk breaks after the first paragraph and after the third paragraph; then on PO, 134/135, insert an asterisk break after the first paragraph. The other transitions are already marked by existing asterisk breaks in the text. Rhees included some such breaks himself, even explaining the transition to p. 250 of TS 211 by stating: "The remarks up to this point form the 'selection' Wittgenstein had typed as though forming a separate essay. The passages which follow were not included in this, although they come—at various points—in the same large manuscript and in the revision and the typing of it" (Rhees's editorial insertion in his bilingual book edition, p. 10/10e). However, this guidance actually applies even earlier, at the transition to p. 281 of TS 211. And when he moves to the hand-written material from MS 110, this is not indicated by anything more than a sort of asterisk break. Our own introduction to this material (in PO, 115) is no more helpful.

23. This is by no means unique in the published Wittgenstein corpus. The same can be said of part II of the *Philosophical Investigations* (now called "Philosophy of Psychology—A Fragment," in the 2009 fourth edition), *Remarks on the Foundations of Mathematics, Culture and Value, Remarks on Colour*, and *On Certainty*, not all of which Rhees edited. In each case, the editors have combined material not specifically combined and distinguished by Wittgenstein for publication.

24. A recently published letter from Rhees to Kenneth Ketner, April 10, 1973, reads in part, "When I was preparing this translation for publication I omitted one or two passages which had been published in the German text in *Synthese*, since they were less directly connected with the main theme than the others" (in Westergaard "On the 'Ketner and Eigsti Edition,'" 128). That really does not constitute much of an explanation, and it understates the amount that was cut.

25. There is a misprint on p. 139 of PO, among these bracketed sentences: in the fourth to the last sentence of part I, "rights" should be "rites" (*Riten*).

26. I do not wish to present Rhees as (intentionally) a pandering popularizer. He was very far from that. But while his editing work has served to make important

chunks of Wittgenstein accessible, not everyone has found this to be a virtue. Inevitably there is a trade-off between accessibility and scholarship. Denis Paul (in *Wittgenstein's Progress,* 17–20) has advocated studying Wittgenstein by reading straight through his manuscript notebooks from the time of his return to Cambridge in 1929. The first ten of these (MSS 105–114) have been published by Michael Nedo as the *Wiener Ausgabe,* vols. 1–5. They have not been translated into English, and it requires the time and commitment of a true scholar to read them. About his own editing, which I discuss further below, Rhees wrote that he wished "to make Wittgenstein's discussions available in readable form to those who were interested in philosophy. . . . But may it not be that Mr. Rhees [here he refers to himself in the third person] did *not* think of *Philosophische Grammatik* as a 'publication for purposes of serious scholarship'?" (italics added) (Rhees, "On Editing Wittgenstein," 56, 58).

27. Kenny, "From the Big Typescript to the *Philosophical Grammar,"* 41–53.

28. This chapter was eventually published by Heikki Nyman as "Philosophie," translated by Luckhardt and Aue as "Philosophy," and included as chapter 9 in PO.

29. Quotations from Kenny taken from pp. 47 and 52. TS 213 (the so-called Big Typescript), which formed the starting point for Rhees's edition, was eventually published in full, though in two somewhat different versions, as *Wiener Ausgabe,* vol. 11: *"The Big Typescript,"* edited by Michael Nedo; and with an English translation as *The Big Typescript* translated by C. Luckhardt and M. Aue. Denis Paul has offered a defense of Rhees's editing of *Philosophische Grammatik* in Paul, "Wittgenstein's Passages," 284–285.

30. "Editorial Preface," PO, ix. The expanded edition of "Notes for Lectures on 'Private Experience' and 'Sense Data'" was edited by David Stern. In an appendix to the volume, "Additions and Corrections to the Texts," we indicated (PO, 512–514) all the additions that were made to Rhees's published edition (amounting to some 30 percent). In our own editing of Rhees's lecture notes, "The Language of Sense Data and Private Experience," we noted (289) that Rhees had placed three of the lectures out of order.

In an unpublished letter to G. H. von Wright (January 23, 1977) concerning the "Notes for Lectures . . . ," Rhees wrote: "Where I have left out remarks, it is for the reasons I stated at the foot of page 274; and please note the phrase 'particularly in the first part'. I may have selected wrongly. But on the matter of making any selection at all, I am unrepentant. I will discuss this further with you, if you like. I am confirmed in my view by the attitude of Oxford scholars, for whom the writings of Wittgenstein 'or any other dead philosopher' should be studied as they study the Dead Sea Scrolls. (But I hope that those scholars who do study the Scrolls are not quite so ignorant or such charlatans.)" In the passage referred to, Rhees had written (Rhees, "I. Note on the Text," 274): "All that is printed here is a collection of rough notes or memoranda which Wittgenstein made for his own use. He would never have published them—he would not even have had them typed—without revising and rearranging them. . . . I have left out certain remarks, particularly in the first part. These are: (*a*) earlier versions of what is much better said later on in these notes; (*b*) jottings which are too sketchy to be intelligible; and (*c*) some remarks which do not seem closely connected with the main discussions."

31. Rhees, "On Editing Wittgenstein," 56. This letter of March 2, 1977, was in fact sent to Anthony Kenny in response to Kenny's criticisms (Kenny, "From the Big Typescript to the *Philosophical Grammar*") of Rhees's editing. (Thanks to Tommi Uschanov for this information.)

32. Rhees, "On Editing Wittgenstein," 57. I guess Rhees has followed Wittgenstein faithfully by creating "bewilderment" with some of his own editorial decisions!

33. LW1, §§923, 925, 927.

34. Perhaps the most egregious example of Rhees's editing is his attaching a "Foreword" to Wittgenstein's *Philosophische Bemerkungen*. While it is clear that the attached passage was meant as a Foreword for *some* work, Josef Rothhaupt has shown conclusively that it was not meant for that work, but for another work that Wittgenstein projected at that time but never collated, which Rothhaupt calls the "Kringel-Buch" (Rothhaupt, "Wittgenstein at Work," 54–59). This casts additional doubt on Rhees's authorial judgment.

Rhees's reason for publishing the preface where he did seems to be that he found it fascinating and wanted to publish it somewhere. He used the proximity of date without considering the relevance of content. In a letter to Anscombe and von Wright, dated January 14, 1964, "I found [it] so interesting when I read it, that I wanted to print that" (letter from Rhees to Anscombe and von Wright, April 22, 1964, 140).

35. The story of this edition is told in Peter K. Westergaard, "On the 'Ketner and Eigsti Edition' of Wittgenstein's *Remarks on Frazer's 'The Golden Bough.'*" A fuller 1975 edition of the Ketner and Eigsti work is available for loan from the Institute for Studies in Pragmatism, Texas Tech University. Two noteworthy characteristics: There are very extensive excerpts from Frazer placed in dialogue with the remarks by Wittgenstein, so that Westergaard is inclined to call it a "Frazer-Wittgenstein Dialogue" more than a "Wittgenstein-Frazer Dialogue" (138). And the edition includes all of §93 of the "Philosophy" chapter from the Big Typescript (PO, 196–199).

36. Hintikka, "An Impatient Man and His Papers," 198–199.

37. Wittgenstein's papers are now mostly freely available online at http://www.wittgensteinsource.org/. Wittgenstein's unpublished material had been available in microform since 1967—indeed, this is what Ketner and Eigsti used—but was not easily accessible and could not be quoted without permission.

38. PO p. 118/119, 5th paragraph (= MS 110, p. 178; published in WA3, 262 = TS 211, p. 313; published in *Wiener Ausgabe* vol. 8.2, p. 239).

39. Only in Beverlsuis's 1979 edition and translation are they not given or mentioned.

40. The newly affixed sentences come from MS 110, 58, 63 (WA3, 193, 195). They had been composed on February 10, 1931, while the core remarks on Frazer were composed beginning on June 19, 1931.

41. *The Golden Bough,* one-volume abridged edition, 264. Passage quoted in PO, 120–121. Frazer does not fault "our predecessors" for these errors. In fact, he recommends that "we shall do well to look with leniency upon" them, just as "we ourselves may one day stand in need of" such leniency from future generations. But Wittgenstein takes this to be a sort of false humility *and* he takes it to be a misdiagnosis of the situation.

42. PO, 123. While Frazer originally included discussion of Christianity among the religious practices (Frazer's 1900 edition, vol. 3, 186–198), in the 1935 third edition, he moved this discussion to a speculative appendix ("Note: The Crucifixion of Christ," vol. 9, 412–423), and he excluded it altogether from the abridged edition. When Drury and Wittgenstein read Frazer together in 1931, they only read the first volume (according to Drury), so they would not have reached Frazer's discussion of Christianity in volume 3.

43. PPO, 229, 231. "Help & Illuminate" was written in Wittgenstein's code. Wittgenstein has similar reflections about error earlier (February 19, 1937, 193: "there can be no talk of error here," and 199). In fact, the whole diary record of his religious/existential crisis (starting with the entry on January 27 and continuing through Easter and the return of the sun, 157–237) makes fascinating reading. Much of the diary record is written in code. See also much later (LW2, 38): "(Isn't belief in God an attitude?) . . . An opinion can be wrong. But what would an error look like here?"

44. PO, 121.

45. "Lectures on Freedom of the Will," (notes by Yorick Smythies), in PO, 433, 436. While we tentatively dated these lectures to Michaelmas term, 1939 (PO, 428), better and more recent evidence has identified them as coming from Lent term, 1941 (see *Wittgenstein's Whewell's Court Lectures*, 280).

46. I discuss Wittgenstein's views about the conceptual relevance of discoveries in neuroscience in several of my publications, most recently, "Wittgenstein, Science and the Evolution of Concepts." (Readers of that paper should be warned that the editors introduced faulty last-minute "corrections" to the citations. In endnotes 7 and 29, the reference to "Bennett and Hacker 2003" should be replaced with "Robinson 2007.")

47. Nevertheless, the practice continues even into the present. See "UK Water Firms Admit Using Divining Rods to Find Leaks and Pipes," *Guardian*, November 21, 2017, where it is reported that a dozen water companies in the United Kingdom continue to use the practice—Anglia Water being the most insistent. The reason seems to be

the difficulty of finding and locating underground water leaks and the apparent, even if slight, success of this method. Even so, this is not the sort of case that would get Wittgenstein's sympathy. The method is still used because of a lingering belief in the factual claim, not because of a claim that the practice has meaning or value apart from the factual claim.

Wittgenstein does mention the practice of divining water (BB, 9–11; Skinner, *Dictating Philosophy*, 243).

48. "An error arises only when magic [or another practice] is interpreted scientifically" (PO, 125). Wittgenstein admits there can be such cases, only they wouldn't then be magical practices: "Operations which depend on a false, overly simple idea of things and processes are to be distinguished from magical operations" (PO, 125)

49. In notes from a lecture that Wittgenstein gave (May 5, 1933) on Frazer in Easter term of 1933 (nearly two years later), according to G. E. Moore (WLM, 326; cf. PO, 106) Wittgenstein said, "Only in some cases do they thus entertain a false scientific belief."

50. In the 1933 lectures, Wittgenstein acknowledged that "there may be many reasons & not necessarily one predominating" (WLM, 326).

51. It is not in fact a simple matter to apply Wittgenstein's test for whether a practice may be in error. The Duhem-Quine thesis reminds us that any number of background assumptions can factor into the test of a hypothesis. In the case of gay conversion therapy, one could argue that the therapy hadn't been used long enough in each case, or the patient wasn't trying hard enough, for example.

52. PO, 121. Miles and Rhees translate the last clause as: "and what we have here is *not* an error." Recall the phrase Wittgenstein used about his own case, cited above in note 43 (PPO, 193; February 19, 1937: "there can be no talk of an error here").

53. Frazer, one-volume abridged edition, 264 (PO, 120): "Their errors were . . . simply hypotheses . . . which a fuller experience has proved to be inadequate."

54. PO, 119: "pieces of stupidity" and "sheer stupidity." Frazer does refer (Frazer abridged edition, 264; PO, 120–121) to the "opinions and practices of ruder ages and races," which leads Wittgenstein to object: "No *opinion* serves as the foundation for a religious symbol" (PO, 123); "ritualistic action is not at all a view, an opinion, whether true or false." (129); and "primitive man . . . does not act from *opinions* (contrary to Frazer)" (137). (Another possibility is that the practitioner is irrational.)

55. PO, 119, 121.

56. PO, 119, 127. In notes from the lectures that Wittgenstein gave on Frazer in Easter term of 1933, according to G. E. Moore (May 9, 1933, WLM, 328; PO, 106) Wittgenstein "said that the tendency to suppose that there was 'one motive which is *the* motive' was 'enormously strong.'" In Alice Ambrose's notes of the same lecture, we find the same words: "This tendency is enormously strong" (WLA, 33). What

Wittgenstein is calling in this lecture the "motive" seems to be analogous to what, in the written remarks, he calls the "explanation."

57. PO, 131.

58. PO, 133. Rhees's editing then interrupts the order of the typescript by introducing two remarks from fifty pages earlier that elaborate this notion. Their introduction here is justified by the fact that in the manuscript (MS 110, 256–257), they follow continuously. These remarks later become the core of PI §122. Credit is due to Baker and Hacker for first emphasizing the importance to Wittgenstein of this concept of a perspicuous representation, in Baker and Hacker, *Wittgenstein: Understanding and Meaning*, 1:531–545. The notion seems to first appear in Wittgenstein's work in the *Philosophical Remarks* 1930 typescript (p. 52; part I §1): "The chief trouble with our grammar is that we don't have a *bird's-eye view* [*Übersichtlichkeit*] of it."

59. PO, 121.

60. PO, 139. This comes from the final sentences in part I that Rhees deleted in 1971 and thereafter. It is possible that Wittgenstein's extended use of "explanation" here to cover even a perspicuous representation seemed to Rhees, on reflection, to be misguided. On the other hand, one is tempted to invoke Wittgenstein's remark (PI §79): "Say what you please, so long as it does not prevent you from seeing how things are." Wittgenstein's claim is that the perspicuous representation provides what is "wished for" and "resolves this particular difficulty."

In Malcolm's notes from Wittgenstein's lectures in 1946–1947, he reports that Wittgenstein said of the results of his synoptic method: "Thus your mental cramp is relieved" (*Memoir*, 43).

61. WLM, lecture on May 22, 1933, 352. And in an earlier lecture on May 15, after recounting a story from Frazer: "Now you are puzzled by this story. And you are puzzled less, if you have similar stories" (345). It is hard to see on what Wittgenstein bases this assertion (about your/my/our puzzlement), except his own experience.

62. And in the May 9 lecture cited above in note 56, he called this tendency "enormously strong."

63. *Zettel* §314 [*Halt zu machen*]. The full passage is worth reading and is discussed in chapter 4, but it derives directly from MS 115, 61, which is conjectured to have been written in 1933–1934 (PO, 493).

64. PO p. 119. First written February 10, 1931 in MS 110, 58 (published in WA3, 193); then included in TS 211, p. 313 (published in *Wiener Ausgabe*, vol. 8.2, 239). Although Wittgenstein claimed he had read no Aristotle (Drury, "Conversations with Wittgenstein," 158), compare: "We must, however, not only state the true view, but also explain the false view; for an explanation of that promotes confidence. For when we have an apparently reasonable explanation of why a false view appears true, that makes us more confident of the true view" (NE 1154a23–26).

See also Pascal, *Pensées*, I, 9: "When we wish to correct with advantage, and to show another that he errs, we must notice from what side he views the matter, for on that side it is usually true, and admit that truth to him, but reveal to him the side on which it is false. He is satisfied with that, for he sees that he was not mistaken, and that he only failed to see all sides. Now, no one is offended at not seeing everything; but one does not like to be mistaken, and that perhaps arises from the fact that man naturally cannot see everything, and that naturally he cannot err in the side he looks at, since the perceptions of our senses are always true." Wolfe Mays claims Wittgenstein had read Pascal, and Joachim Schulte finds an allusion to his *Pensées* at MS 116, 325 (Biesenbach, *Anspielungen und Zitate im Werk Ludwig Wittgensteins*, 389–390, 716).

65. On this issue, the translation by Miles and Rhees is a mess. They switch back and forth between "error" and "mistake" for what is consistently the German word *Irrtum* or its cognates. In the first dozen paragraphs they use "mistake" five times and "error" six times. While either of these might be acceptable translations, one or the other should be chosen, and used consistently.

Rhees explained the origin of this translation in a letter to von Wright, July 30, 1970: "One of the graduate students in the German Department at Swansea did a translation, which is tolerable, although it would need some corrections. I would undertake to put right any howlers in it, although I could not make it into something really good" (Westergaard, "A Note on Rhees, the *Bemerkungen über Frazers 'The Golden Bough'* and *Über Gewißheit*," 6). He certainly did not "make it into something really good," yet he stood by it in the face of the Ketner and Eigsti translation.

When we included Wittgenstein's remarks on Frazer in *Philosophical Occasions*, we opted to use the translation by John Beversluis. We were not aware of the Ketner-Eigsti translation at the time. The Beversluis translation was first published in 1979, as indicated in note 20 above, by which time Rhees and the other executors had finally given their permission (Luckhardt, "Editor's Introduction," 21) for a new translation based on the original 1967 German edition.

66. PO, 119, 121. In the first of these occurrences Miles and Rhees translate *verfehlt* as "wrong-headed," which I think is apt—it captures the notion of a mind-set. But cf. where Wittgenstein's criticism of Frazer and us is articulated in this way (124/125): "An error [*Irrtum*] arises only when magic is interpreted scientifically." The translation here is accurate, but to be consistent with his other uses (as I've tried to straighten them out), Wittgenstein should have labeled this *ein Fehler* [a blunder?] rather than *ein Irrtum*. In a lecture (WLM, 325; May 5, 1933), Wittgenstein put his point in English in this way: "In the *Golden Bough*, Frazer constantly makes one particular kind of mistake in explanation." "Mistake" could be an acceptable translation of *Fehler*. My point is that it is important to keep the kind of mistake Wittgenstein accuses Frazer and us of making—*ein Fehler*—distinct from the kind of mistake Frazer accuses primitive people of making—*ein Irrtum*. They operate at different levels.

67. MS 110, 193 (published in WA3, 270). This phrase appeared in a string of eleven manuscript pages that Wittgenstein cut out in creating TS 211, just above the last paragraph on PO, 124/125.

The difficulty of distinguishing between Frazer's (and our) errors and the primitive believers' errors was exacerbated by Wittgenstein's editing process. He moved the remarks from February about Frazer's (and our) errors into juxtaposition with his June remarks about Frazer's attribution of the supposed errors of primitive believers in the newly created typescript. But he never got around to doing any further editing of that material that might have led him to adjust his German terminology to make the distinction clearer.

68. PO, 125. Perhaps *überführen* does at least capture the notion of "leading" someone from one place to another, as in "transport." Miles and Rhees, in their 1979 book edition (p. 1), render *überführen* as "transform." Their earlier rendering (1971, p. 28) is hopeless: "We must begin with the mistake and *find out* the truth in it" (italics added).

These last three paragraphs well demonstrate, I think, the challenges of presenting draft material of any kind from Wittgenstein. Regardless of the work of editors, including the editing of Wittgenstein himself, it was *unfinished material.* Unfortunately, by his standards, virtually all of his work was unfinished. Therein, lies the dilemma of editing and studying Wittgenstein.

69. PO, 125.

70. Letter to Moore, August 23, 1931, in WC, 193. Moore confirms that Wittgenstein did not hold lectures during the three terms of 1931–32 (PO, 49). Interestingly, though, the *Cambridge University Reporter* issue for June 30, 1931, *already* announced (1285) that Wittgenstein would hold only "Informal discussions" in the Michaelmas term; then there was no listing for Wittgenstein at all for Michaelmas term in the October 2 issue (vol. 62, p. 85); then there was the announcement that he "will hold a Conversation class (no fee)" for both of the following terms (vol. 62, December 23, 1931, 449, and March 23, 1932, 754). Would that all of us professors could decide not to hold lectures . . . to reserve our strength for our work!

71. PPO, 131. We will examine this more closely in chapter 5.

72. CV, 62/71. Wittgenstein's concern with temperament is one of the main themes of my book *Wittgenstein in Exile,* especially 25–30, 36–39, 126–130, and 145–146. Wittgenstein's therapeutic approach is discussed in Fischer, *Philosophical Delusion and Its Therapy,* esp. chap. 9.

Chapter 4

1. WLL, 1; dated January 20, 1930.

2. WLM, 67–68; dated October 13, 1930.

3. Edwards, "Wittgenstein's Lectures."

4. LPP. Based on Shah's dated notes, Wittgenstein introduced the example on November 25.

5. Cf. Hertz (*The Principles of Mechanics*, 7–8): "When these painful contradictions are removed, the question as to the nature of force will not have been answered; but our minds, no longer vexed, will cease to ask illegitimate questions"; and Boltzmann ("On Statistical Mechanics," 167): "If therefore philosophy were to succeed in creating a system such that in all cases mentioned it stood out clearly when a question is not justified so that the drive toward asking it would gradually die away, we should at one stroke have resolved the most obscure riddles and philosophy would become worthy of the name queen of the sciences." These physicists, both well respected by Wittgenstein, anticipated what he sought.

6. *Zettel* §314 (MS 115, 61; 1933–1934).

7. Waismann, *Voices of Wittgenstein*, 309–311. The passage continues later: "And this is exactly what we are doing: we situate a linguistic form in its surroundings, we see the grammar of our language against a background of similar or related cases, and that banishes disquiet." In Waismann's later reworking of this material, *The Principles of Linguistic Philosophy*, this appears at p. 80. It is important to recall that these sentences come from the hand of Waismann, though we have reason to think that they express Wittgenstein's thoughts.

8. Skinner, *Dictating Philosophy*, 213. The phrase "the word which solves it" seems to be an allusion to Wittgenstein's search for *das erlösende Wort*. For more on this, see chapter 10 of my book *Wittgenstein in Exile*. Also, see Skinner, 110: "In notes, examples and similes are always useful. If I could give you enough of them, that would be all that would be necessary."

It is fascinating that Wittgenstein was dictating material to Waismann in Vienna, while at the same time he was dictating material to Skinner in Cambridge, in both cases with an eye to a joint product of some sort. There is a story here that remains to be told and awaits the publication of the Skinner material as well as further Waismann material (see Manninen, "Waismann's Testimony of Wittgenstein's Fresh Starts in 1931–1935," 244).

9. Anscombe, "Introduction," viii–ix; quoted more extensively in Klagge, "The Wittgenstein Lectures, Revisited," 53. Presumably the word and concept "painy" introduces an imaginary scenario in which we have a concept that applies to things that *cause* pain. Cf. PI §312.

10. Wittgenstein's reply to a paper by Smythies, Lent term 1940, in *Wittgenstein's Whewell's Court Lectures*, 196 (quoted and discussed more extensively in chapter 6, this volume). See also Plato, Phaedrus 271c–272a, for a similar point.

11. Skinner, *Dictating Philosophy*, 240; February 23, 1934.

12. CV, 56/64 (MS 134, 20; March 5, 1947).

13. Foot, *Natural Goodness*, 1. The discussion took place on May 14, 1947 (see Klagge, "The Wittgenstein Lectures, Revisited," 69). Much earlier, in a notebook that Wittgenstein kept during his first term of teaching at Cambridge (Lent term, 1930), Wittgenstein wrote: "One is often not allowed to start straight off with sense, but must often talk nonsense first since it is *this* which has to be overcome" (WA2, 184; MS 107, 266; January 30, 1930). In the 1933–1934 *Big Typescript* (§87; PO, 165) Wittgenstein takes it on himself (no doubt with the person's help) to articulate a person's confusion accurately: "One of the most important tasks is to express all false thought processes so characteristically that the reader says, 'Yes, that's exactly the way I meant it.'" After Wittgenstein had retired from teaching in 1948, he wrote, "When philosophizing you have to descend into the former [*alte*] chaos & feel at home there" (CV, 65/74; MS 136, 51a; January 3, 1948). The philosopher has to fully understand the (other person's or one's own earlier) confusions before effectively addressing them.

14. Kierkegaard, *Concluding Unscientific Postscript*, 264–265.

15. Wittgenstein's letter to Russell, dated November or December 1913, WC, 57/58.

16. CV, 77/88 (MS 137, 134b; December 25, 1948).

17. "Philosophy," from *Big Typescript*, §87, in PO, 165. And see comments noted by Skinner: "I want to talk about the difficulty in philosophy due to the fascination of certain words. If you say this to some people, they will say how queer! Philosophy must be a sort of psychoanalytic treatment. This is right in a way" (Skinner, *Dictating Philosophy*, 212; February 2, 1934).

As to the matter of speaking one's *own* mind, Socrates was emphatic: "Let us leave Gorgias out of it, since he is not here. But Meno, by the gods, what do you yourself say virtue is?" (*Meno* 71d); and "Right, but I am not asking [what is said by most people]. Rather, what do you say the courageous go toward with daring . . . ?" (*Protagoras*, 359d). In this positive sense, we can say that Socrates's (and Wittgenstein's) arguments were ad hominem—philosophy was directed at how an individual thought about something.

18. MS 158, 34r–34v (in English, apparently in connection with preparing for his class).

19. Malcolm, *Ludwig Wittgenstein: A Memoir*, 48.

20. Russell, *Autobiography of Bertrand Russell*, 2:137.

21. Bouwsma, *Wittgenstein: Conversations*, 69; November 28, 1950.

22. But see Diogenes Laertius, *The Lives of Eminent Philosophers*, book II, §29: "When Euthyphro had indicted his father for manslaughter, Socrates, after some conversation with him upon piety, diverted him from his purpose." There is no basis for

this claim in the Platonic dialogue; at best, we might imagine that Socrates shook Euthyphro's confidence.

23. Aristotle, *Nicomachean Ethics* 1179b4–18.

24. "Philosophy," PO, 161 (= BT §86). The sentence before the ellipsis has a source in MS 153b, 30r; probably 1931. The passage after the ellipsis first occurs at MS 110, 189; June 20, 1931.

25. CV, 20/17–18 (MS 154, 21v–22r; 1931).

26. MS 155, 42r (written in English). Von Wright conjectures that material in this notebook was composed in 1931 (PO, 488, 497). And, after all, Wittgenstein's aim in philosophy is not to convince the fly of any proposition, but to get it to leave the fly bottle (PI §309).

27. Dictations to Skinner in the so-called Pink Book, tentatively dated to 1933–1934 (Skinner, *Dictating Philosophy*, 134). Cf. Proust, *Swann's Way*, 151: "Facts do not find their way into the world in which our beliefs reside; they did not produce our beliefs, they do not destroy them; they may inflict on them the most constant refutations without weakening them, and an avalanche of afflictions or ailments succeeding one another without interruption in a family will not make it doubt the goodness of its God or the talent of its doctor."

28. The exceptions would be what I call "technical terms." See my discussion in *Wittgenstein in Exile*, 27, 88.

29. Drury, "Conversations with Wittgenstein," 157; Autumn 1948.

30. LC, 27. James Taylor's notes have an alternate last sentence: "I am saying I want you to look at things in a different way."

31. Explanation: PI §1, OC §34, Z §315; reasons: PI §326, Brown Book 143; justification: PI §485, OC §192; grounds: OC §§110, 204; doubting: PO, 377; OC §625; interpretation: RFM, 342.

32. And also LFM, 22; PPO, 382.

33. *Zettel* §314 (= MS 115, 61; 1933–1934).

34. Klagge, "The Wittgenstein Lectures, Revisited," 54.

35. Stephen Toulmin quoting John Wisdom, who reported a conversation with Wittgenstein in 1946 or 1947, in *Wittgenstein's Vienna*, 258.

36. "The Language of Sense Data and Private Experience," PO, 356–357; May 25, 1936. Wittgenstein had detected this error in 1930 (PR, 88): "The worst philosophical errors always arise when we try to apply our ordinary—physical—language in the area of the immediately given." But he later comes to see not just the error but a temptation toward this error.

37. LPP, 17; apparently November 1, 1946. Jackson's notes of the same point in the lecture put it (256): "There is perhaps an unavoidable wish to hypostatize a feeling here."

38. WLM: May term 1933, lecture 2b, 8:66, 313.

Ian Hacking summarizes the problem: "Our family of languages—traditionally called Indo-European—lends hypostasis more than a helping hand. We use sentences in which names for any old object, 'abstract' or 'concrete', serve as grammatical subjects. This leads to a point emphasized by Nietzsche long ago: European languages demand an existential presupposition for terms in the subject position. European grammars generate hypostasis. . . . Nietzsche thought this generated endless bad philosophy" (Hacking, *Why Is There Philosophy of Mathematics at All?* 255–256).

Chapter 5

1. McGuinness, "Wittgenstein and Literature," 258. In the mid-1930s Redpath inspected Wittgenstein's small bookcase full of books, noting that none were philosophical. Wittgenstein responded (Redpath, *Memoir*, 40), "I wonder what people would think. He calls himself a philosopher, but he has no philosophical books!"

2. PPO, 257–258.

3. Ludwig Hänsel, *Begegnungen mit Wittgenstein*, 51 (in the diary entry dated March 25–30, 1919). A survey of (all!) the references Wittgenstein makes to other people in his writings, letters and recorded conversations yields the following German-language poets and writers: Georg Trakl, Albert Ehrenstein, Rainer Marie Rilke, Karl Kraus, Johan Wolfgang Goethe, Wilhelm Busch, Gottfried Keller, Heinrich von Kleist, Johann Hebel, Eduard Mörike, Heinrich Heine, Friedrich Schiller, Count August von Platen, Gotthold Lessing, Franz Grillparzer, Georg Christoph Lichtenberg, Fritz Mauthner, Novalis, and Christian Hebbel; as well as non-German poets such as Lewis Carroll, Arthur Rimbaud, Edgar Allen Poe, Henry Wadsworth Longfellow, Samuel Johnson, John Milton, Dante, Shakespeare, Alexander Pushkin, Henrik Ibsen, Rabindranath Tagore and William Blake (Biesenbach, *Anspielungen und Zitate*). Of course, that does not cover Wittgenstein's lectures, which still need a complete index. But a perusal unearths, in addition to ones mentioned above, Friedrich Klopstock (LC, 4) and John Bunyan (*Wittgenstein's Whewell's Court Lectures*, 254).

4. Bouwsma, *Wittgenstein: Conversations, 1949–1951*, 62 (from notes dated September 14, 1950).

5. Hänsel, *Ludwig Hänsel—Ludwig Wittgenstein: Eine Freundschaft*, 39; letter dated November 30, 1920. Details about all these publications can be found in Beisenbach, *Anspielungen und Zitate im Werke Ludwig Wittgensteins*, 551, 557–561, 573–574, 582–583, 599, 601. Even during his teacher training, he wrote, "I sometimes read

fairy-tales [*Märchen*] to the children at school" (Engelmann, *Letters from Ludwig Wittgenstein*, 29; February 19, 1920).

6. Janik, "The Dichtung of Analytic Philosophy," 153 (personal communictation from Rudolf Koder, Vienna, 1969). Rothhaupt makes the case for Busch's influence on Wittgenstein in "Ludwig Wittgenstein and Wilhelm Busch." Wittgenstein expresses his affection for Mörike's work in a letter to Russell (WC, 65) and a letter to Engelmann (*Letters from Wittgenstein*, 5). Also see note 120 of chapter 6, this volume.

7. Feigl, "The Wiener Kreis in America," 638. Rabindraneth Tagore (1861–1941) was a Bengali polymath who won the Nobel Prize for Literature in 1913. Tagore was also a musical composer, with 2,230 songs to his credit, giving the lie to the claim that Bob Dylan was the first musical composer to win the Nobel Prize in Literature. Wittgenstein's ongoing interest in Tagore is indicated by the fact that in 1939, he and his friend Yorick Smythies drafted a modernized English translation of scene II of Tagore's play, *The King of the Dark Chamber* (see *Wittgenstein's Whewell's Court Lectures*, 325–333).

8. McGuinness, "Editor's Preface," 15. Personal communication from Feigl seems to be the source of this information: McGuinness, "Relations with and within the Circle," 189. McGuinness also adds that he would read to them from Wilhelm Busch, something of a nineteenth-century cartoonist.

9. This translation as well as German original in CV 1998 edition, p. 28. Winch's earlier translation reads, in part, "Philosophy ought really to be written only as a *poetic composition* [*dichten*]" (CV 1980 edition, 24).

10. Perloff, "Writing Philosophy as Poetry," 716 n. 3. The more colloquial one (which I have employed as the subtitle for this book) is from Antin, "Wittgenstein among the Poets," 161. See also Schulte's reflections on the translation of *Dichtung* in "Wittgenstein on Philosophy as Poetry," 352–353.

Equating "poetry" with a broader notion of what is fictional is supported directly by Wittgenstein's editing of his own remark in MS 109 (p. 31—August 22, 1930; published in WA3, 18). Wittgenstein writes: "We have in poetry [*Dichtung*] just the play of thoughts and ideas." And then he adds over the word *Dichtung* the variant *Erdichteten*, which means fictitious or imaginary. Allan Janik proposes a loose translation of the aphorism along these lines: "philosophy should only really be conceived as fiction (i.e., as a work of imagination)" ("The Dichtung of Analytic Philosophy," 145).

11. Schalkwyk, "Wittgenstein's 'Imperfect Garden,'" 57. His proposed translation, the one endorsed by Perloff, is on p. 56.

12. He had tried extensive explanations with Russell in December 1919 and with Ramsey in September 1923. We know he was disappointed in Russell's "Introduction" to his *Tractatus* (written soon after their extensive discussions): See Wittgenstein's letters to Russell, April 9, May 6, 1920, WC, 118–120.

Recall, in contrast, Wittgenstein's approval of the Uhland poem, quoted later and cited in note 89 for this chapter.

13. Monk, *Ludwig Wittgenstein: The Duty of Genius*, 255–257.

14. F. R. Leavis, "Memories of Wittgenstein," 66–67. Leavis's review of Empson's (and other) poems was published in the *Cambridge Review*, March 1, 1929, 317–318.

15. "Lecture on Ethics," PO, 36–44. This lecture was arranged by invitation from Empson (see chapter 2 above). While Leavis offers no conjecture about why Wittgenstein asked Leavis about Empson, it may be that the discussion with Leavis of Empson's poems had made Wittgenstein amenable to Empson's request.

16. *Venture*, no. 5 (February 1930): 208–215. Apparently the poem was originally addressed to Frank Ramsey, but Ramsey's sudden death on January 19, 1930, forced the last-minute change to Braithwaite before it was printed (Rosenbaum, "Appendix 1: Virginia Woolf among the Apostles," 161).

17. Letter to Lydia Lokopova Keynes, November 14, 1926, in Skidelsky, *John Maynard Keynes*, Vol. 2: *The Economist as Saviour*, 293.

18. Reprinted originally in *Whips and Scorpions: Specimens of Modern Satiric Verse, 1914–1931*, ed. S. Vines (London: Wishart, 1932), 21–30. More recently reprinted in Flowers and Ground, *Portraits of Wittgenstein* 2:498–504.

As far as I know, Bell did not attend any of Wittgenstein's course lectures. Among many other vague allusions and misrepresentations, Kimberley Cornish calls Bell one of Wittgenstein's "students," with no evidence (*The Jew of Linz*, 52). Cornish's claim (44) that "Julian Bell intended writing a PhD thesis on Wittgenstein" is also provided with no evidence. He says "as we shall later see," but there is nothing on that point later in the book.

19. Flowers and Ground, *Portraits of Wittgenstein*, 2:502.

20. Plato refers to the "ancient quarrel between philosophy and poetry" at *Republic* 607B.

Whether or not Wittgenstein was familiar with the poem, he was familiar enough with the poet to use "these Julian Bells" as a scornful characterization of young Cambridge aesthetes (Partridge, "Memories of Ludwig Wittgenstein," 475).

21. McGuinness, "Arthur MacIver's Diary," 237. MacIver's diary also notes that "Braithwaite's paper was one he had read to the Jowett [Society at Oxford] last term and was a muddled affair, though I liked it because he showed some understanding of the nature of Change. . . ."

The official minutes from this Cambridge Moral Sciences Club meeting are regrettably brief and read as follows: "The second meeting of the term was held in Mr Braithwaite's rooms on Friday February 7th at 8:30 pm. There were thirty members present. Prof. Moore was in the Chair. The minutes of the last meeting were read and adopted. Mr R. B. Braithwaite read a paper entitled 'Time'. A discussion followed." However, Fania Pascal notes in a memoir of Wittgenstein: "I remember a paper [at the Moral Sciences Club] given by Richard Braithwaite which Wittgenstein appeared to tear to pieces only to end up, to the amazement of all, by giving it his approval or maybe just letting it pass. . . . All this was in 1930–1" ("Wittgenstein: A Personal Memoir," 16).

The title and content, as reported by MacIver, make it sound very much like Braithwaite's paper "Time and Change," which was published in the *Aristotelian Society Supplementary Volume* (1928): 162–174, and presented at the 1928 joint meeting of the Aristotelian Society and the Mind Association, July 13–16, 1928, at the University of Bristol. However, the published version of Braithwaite's contribution to the symposium neither mentions nor quotes any poetry.

Francis Thompson (1859–1907) was an English poet and ascetic whose best-known poem was "The Hound of Heaven," which describes God's pursuit of the human soul. Pierre de Ronsard (1524–1585) was a French poet, known at the time as the "prince of poets."

22. CV, 6/8 (MS 109, 202; published in WA3, 109; November 5, 1930).

23. Richards, "Beginnings and Transitions: I. A. Richards Interviewed by Reuben Brower," 26–27. Also, Malcolm (*Memoir*, 56) reports Wittgenstein "had attended Moore's lectures . . . a few times, when he was a student at Cambridge before World War I. . . ."

24. Russo (*I. A. Richards: His Life and Work*, 143): "One day in fall 1931 Richards renewed acquaintance with Wittgenstein." This is based on "Beginnings and Transitions: I. A. Richards Interviewed by Reuben Brower," where Richards recalls, "I had one long session with Wittgenstein when I came back from one of our visits to China" (27). And see the letter from Richards to his wife, October 29, 1932 (in *Selected Letters of I. A. Richards*, 65).

25. Originally published in *New Statesman*, June 18, 1960, 900–901, and soon reprinted in Richards's poetry collection, *The Screens and Other Poems* (New York: Harcourt Brace, 1960). The poem is best known from its reprinting in Richards, *Internal Colloquies: Poems and Plays of I. A. Richards*, 183–186.

26. In an interview published in 1973, Richards mentions his interactions with Wittgenstein, and then says: "I wrote a poem much later . . . about his lectures in Trinity. I used to go to them occasionally" ("Beginnings and Transitions," 27).

27. *Selected Letters of I. A. Richards*, 160, 160n1.

28. Biographer John P. Russo writes: "The title 'Strayed Poet' refers to Arnold's 'The Strayed Reveller,' where after describing Tiresias's vision and the battle of the centaurs and the lapiths, the poet exclaims, 'such a price/the Gods exact for song:/

To become what we sing.' Wittgenstein became his limits, broke through them, 'beyond.' A 'poet' in Shelly's broad definition, he suffers the fate of the great poets: the struggle with language, and the anxiety of being continually misunderstood" (*I. A. Richards: His Life and Work*, 144). I'm not sure what I think about this.

29. Richards had sent a copy of the poem to Janet Adam Smith, at that time literary editor of *New Statesman*, on April 20. When she showed interest in the poem, he responded as above (in *Selected Letters of I. A. Richards*, 161–162). It was published in the June 18 issue. It does not seem to have provoked the sort of response he here anticipated. Richards seems not to have known of Julian Bell's 1930 poem or not to have remembered it (*Selected Letters of I. A. Richards*, 197).

30. Letter from Wittgenstein to Moore, August 23, 1931, WC, 193.

31. PPO, 131. Wittgenstein had also mentioned Kierkegaard in relation to philosophical style earlier this same year in his diary on May 6, 1931 (PPO, 83).

32. Walsh, "Kierkegaard the Poet," 154: "In his view, a genuine poetic work does not merely reproduce the life experiences of the author but transmutes that experience poetically so as not to identify the author with a particular character or perspective in the work."

33. "I cannot repeat enough what I so frequently have said: I am a poet, but a very special kind, for I am by nature dialectical, and as a rule dialectic is precisely what is alien to the poet" (Kierkegaard, *Journals and Papers*, IX A, §213 [1843]).

34. See Frede, "Plato's Arguments and the Dialogue Form," 201–219.

35. See Brickhouse and Smith, "Socrates' Claims Not to Know and the Irony Problem," 58–68.

36. Lee, "Wittgenstein: 1929–1931," 483; also Drury, "Some Notes on Conversations with Wittgenstein," 87.

37. Karl Menger reports the following remark from Moritz Schlick, who worked closely with Wittgenstein for several years: "Schlick was greatly impressed by Wittgenstein and deeply regretted his having given up work in philosophy [in the 1920s]. . . . The conversation turned to some philosopher or scientist who had stopped working and someone brought up Wittgenstein. 'There is a great difference, though,' said Schlick, 'Mr. (whoever it was) ceased working because of fatigue, whereas Wittgenstein has given up work because of *ressentiment*.' I remember Schlick using the French word" (Menger, "Wittgenstein, Brouwer and the Circle"). I'm not sure what Schlick might have meant by that.

38. Kierkegaard, *Point of View*, 53–54 (pt. 2, chap. IA5). And see Wittgenstein's remark: "Don't *for heaven's sake*, be afraid of talking nonsense! But you must pay attention to your nonsense" (CV, 56/64; MS 134, 20; March 5, 1947).

39. MS 110, 58 (February 10, 1931; published in WA3, 193)=TS 211, 313. Published with English translation in PO, 119.

40. MS 183, 122–123, published in "Movements of Thought: Diaries, 1930–1932 & 1936–1937," PPO, 130/131. See also CV, 29/34 (MS 118, 117v; September 24, 1937), where Wittgenstein worries about a *Gleichnis* (simile) that might lead you to "feel you were being cheated, that someone were trying to convince you by trickery." I illustrate this concern with trickery in chapter 6 in discussing Plato's Parable of the Cave.

41. MS 155, 42r (written in English). Von Wright conjectures that material in this notebook was composed in 1931 (PO, 488, 497). This passage was first quoted by Rhees, "The Philosophy of Wittgenstein," 43. Then later (1938) in MS 158, 34r–34v, Wittgenstein writes (again in English): "I'm not teaching you anything; I'm trying to persuade you to do something. What we do is much more akin to Psychoanalysis than you might be aware of. Schopenhauer: 'If you find yourself stumped trying to convince someone of something and not getting anywhere, tell yourself that it's the *will* and not the intellect you're up against.'" Schopenhauer says something close to this (in *The World as Will and Representation*, vol. 2, Supplements to the First Book: chapter 19, section 7, p. 226):

> Nothing is more tiresome and annoying than when we argue with a person with reasons and explanations, and take all the trouble to convince him, under the impression that we have to deal only with his *understanding*, and then finally discover that he *will* not understand; that we therefore had to deal with his *will*, which pays no heed to the truth, but brings into action willful misunderstandings, chicaneries, and sophisms, entrenching itself behind its understanding and its supposed want of insight. Then he is of course not to be got at in this way, for *arguments and proofs applied against the will* are like the blows of a concave mirror's phantom against a solid body.

In dictations to Skinner in the so-called Pink Book, tentatively dated to 1933–1934, Wittgenstein recalls this line: "Schopenhauer once said, 'If you try to convince someone and get to a certain resistance, you then know you are up against the will, not the understanding'. You are up against something else here. We have prejudices of thought" (Skinner, *Dictating Philosophy*, 134).

In students' notes from lectures on aesthetics that Wittgenstein gave in summer 1938, we find: "I am in a sense making propaganda for one style of thinking as opposed to another. . . . Nevertheless I'm saying: 'For God's sake don't do this.' [Taylor: . . . I persuade you to do something different.] . . . (Much of what we are doing is a question of changing the style of thinking.)" (LC, 28).

42. Emphasis on this phrase dates from July 2, 1931, where it appears in MS 110, 257 (published in WA3, 307). It is then used in TS 211, 281–282 (published in Wittgenstein, *Wiener Ausgabe*, vol. 8.1, 216). From there it becomes part of Rhees's edition of "Remarks on Frazer's *Golden Bough*," in PO, 132/133. A possible connection between this concept and poetry, broadly construed, appears a few months later (November 22, 1931; MS 112, 222): "The purpose of a good expression or a good simile is that it allows an instant synopsis. [*Der Zweck des guten Ausdrucks und des*

guten Gleichnisses ist, daß es die augenblickliche Übersicht erlaubt.]" That might suggest that poetry is not an alternative to synopsis, but a form of it or a means to it.

43. Pascal, "Wittgenstein: A Personal Memoir," 14. A letter from Bachtin to Wittgenstein (November 22, 1936) indicates that Bachtin was drafting a translation of Wittgenstein's work for him. McGuinness's footnote provides additional information about their relationship, including the fact that it was Bachtin to whom Wittgenstein referred in the Preface to *Philosophical Investigations* as the "someone" with whom Wittgenstein had recently reread the *Tractatus* (WC, 258, 239). Bachtin and Wittgenstein are two of the three main characters in Terry Eagleton's novel, *Saints and Scholars*. But there is little historical basis for Eagleton's characterization of Bachtin. He simply functions as a foil for Eagleton's Wittgenstein.

44. Bachtin, *Lectures and Essays*. Terry Eagleton calls this a "collection of rather unremarkable essays and lectures" (*Against the Grain*, 112), but in fact it contains some insights, and may well offer insight into aspects of Wittgenstein's thinking. Much of what we know about Bachtin comes from the "Biographical Introduction" by Francesca M. Wilson and A. E. Duncan-Jones. Nicholas Bachtin (Bachtin's own Anglicized spelling) was the brother of Mikhail Bakhtin, the Russian literary critic. For more about these brothers see Clark and Holquist, *Mikhail Bakhtin*, chap. 1.

45. Wilson, "Biographical Introduction," 3.

46. In chapter 10 of *Wittgenstein in Exile*, I trace Wittgenstein's search for the *erlösende wort*. This German phrase has been translated as "the key word" (Anscombe), "the liberating word" (Schulte and McGuinness; Luckhardt and Aue), "the word that breaks the spell" (Nedo), "the redeeming word" (Klagge), and could even be rendered as "the magic word." In that chapter, I offer "poetic" passages from the Book of Job and *Brothers Karamazov* as constituting a sort of redeeming word for urges of a sort that their authors (and Wittgenstein) oppose.

47. George Thomson, *The Greek Language*, xiii.

48. Bachtin analyzes the first half of the fourth verse of Pushkin's poem "Чем чаще празднует лицей . . ." ("The more often the Lyceum celebrates . . .") (1831):

> И мнится, очередь за мной,
> Зовет меня мой Дельвиг милый,
> Товарищ юности живой,
> Товарищ юности унылой
>
> And I feel it is now my turn,
> My dear Delvig calls for me,
> Comrade of my lively youth,
> Comrade of my melancholy youth.

http://ilibrary.ru/text/747/p.1/index.html It is an obscure poem for which I could find no other English translation than Bachtin's. Yet Bachtin, *Lectures and Essays*, claims all its worth is lost in translation (19).

In the back of the notebook MS 166, Wittgenstein transcribed five poems by Pushkin (PO, 458 n. 5). Pascal, "Wittgenstein: A Personal Memoir," recalls that "once he [Wittgenstein] quoted a Pushkin lyric to me. That he most certainly had from Bachtin, who adored reading Russian poetry out loud" (21).

49. "The Symbolist Movement in Russia," in Bachtin, *Lectures and Essays*, 39.

50. "Tolstoy's *War and Peace*," in Bachtin, *Lectures and Essays*, 29. Bachtin explains what he means here by poetry: "What poetry aims at is precisely to arouse, to maintain and intensify our conscious awareness of the verbal medium." That is not how I having been using the term, nor is it how Wittgenstein uses *Dichtung*.

51. "Tolstoy's *War and Peace*," in Bachtin, *Lectures and Essays*, 26–27. Wittgenstein's deep interest in and familiarity with *War and Peace* is attested to by Redpath, *Ludwig Wittgenstein: A Student's Memoir*, 49–50, 53.

52. PO, p. 160/161. The passage about Tolstoy originated in MS 112, p. 111v (November 22, 1931, and collected in CV, 17/25). This also resonates with what Bachtin later discussed.

53. Tolstoy, *What Is Art?* 79, 81. Wittgenstein's close friend Paul Engelmann wrote: "Wittgenstein had read with keen interest Tolstoy's book *What Is Art?* and agreed with some of its conclusions" (*Letters from Ludwig Wittgenstein: With a Memoir*, 91).

54. Tolstoy, *What Is Art?* 83. Schulte, in "Wittgenstein on Philosophy as Poetry," offers an interpretation of *dichten* that narrows its appeal through a kind of "parochialism" (367). But Wittgenstein's invocation of Tolstoy on the universal appeal of art seems to cause problems for Schulte's reading. Schulte does not mention Tolstoy in that essay.

55. Wittgenstein in fact has reservations about Tolstoy's "false" theory that art conveys the feelings of the *artist* (CV, 58/67; MS 134, p. 136; April 5, 1947): "That doesn't concern me *at all*."

56. See D. Z. Phillips, "Rush Rhees: A Biographical Sketch," 295.

57. The original reads in part:

> *Er spricht fortwährend in Gleichnissen (die nur teilweise eigentliche Beispiele sind), und sagt selbst, dass er immer in Gleichnissen denkt. Wenn etwas nicht klar wird, dann sucht er nicht, eine Erklärung in einfachen Sätzen zu geben, sondern er sucht nach ein neues Gleichniss. Diese Methode vereint sich allerdings mit seiner philosophischen Stellung, wonach die Antworte zu den wichtigsten philosophischen Fragen nicht durch Sätze und Theorien gegeben, sondern nur durch Gleichnisse oder "symbolische Formen" "gezeigt" werden können.*

Christian Erbacher discovered this letter in the Kastil Nachlass. Alfred Kastil (1874–1950) was a philosophy professor at the University of Innsbruck, where Rhees had attended in 1932–33, when they also became friends. It has been suggested by an anonymous reader for MIT Press that "symbolic forms" may be an allusion to Ernst

Cassirer's three-volume work, *The Philosophy of Symbolic Forms* (1923–1929). While there is no (other) evidence of Wittgenstein's familiarity with Cassirer, Rhees might have drawn a connection himself.

Cf. Rhees's account of Wittgenstein's use of *Gleichnisse* (parables) here with Matthew 13:34 (and see Mark 4:34), where we are told: "In all this Jesus spoke to the crowds in parables; indeed, he would never speak to them except in parables [*Gleichnisse,* in Luther's translation]."

58. See Klagge, "The Wittgenstein Lectures, Revisited," 36–39. During this term, Wittgenstein also began dictating his so-called Blue Book. Additional notes from this time period have recently come to light as part of the Francis Skinner Archive, but they have not yet been convincingly dated or sourced.

59. A search of the Bergen Electronic Edition of Wittgenstein's writings turns up 108 occurrences of *Gleichnis*, *Gleichnisse*, and *Gleichnissen* in his manuscripts and 122 occurrences in his typescripts.

60. For example, it is consistently translated in *The Big Typescript: TS 213* by Luckhardt and Aue as "simile." In *Culture and Value* Winch translates it sometimes as "comparison," sometimes as "simile." In the *Blue Book*, dictated by Wittgenstein in English in 1933–1934, he uses the word *parable* (BB, 45): "The . . . situation can be cleared up somewhat by looking at an example, in fact a kind of parable, illustrating the difficulty we are in, and also showing the way out of this difficulty."

In his wartime notebooks Wittgenstein discusses his "*Netz-Gleichnis der Physik,*" which Anscombe translates as "analogy of the net for physics" (NB, 38; January 17, 1915), looking forward to TLP 6.341ff. In TLP 4.01122 and 5.5563 Pears and McGuinness render *Gleichnis* as "likeness."

61. *Ludwig Wittgenstein: Dictating Philosophy*, 110. See also the notes by Ambrose and Margaret Masterman in the Yellow Book, dated 1933–1934: "Now you may question whether my constantly giving examples and speaking in similes is profitable. My reason is that parallel cases change our outlook because they destroy the uniqueness of the case at hand" (WLA, 50).

62. Johnson, "Parables," 125. Recollections from Hijab recorded October 9, 2002.

63. See, for example, Matthew 13:34, Mark 4:2, and John 10:6.

64. CV, 1998 edition, 42; taken from MS 162b, p. 63r (dated 1939–1940).

65. Eighty-six have been collected in *Parables of Kierkegaard*. Hundreds are listed in an appendix, 147–181.

66. Writing to his friend Ludwig Hänsel about a draft of a polemic lecture by Hänsel, Wittgenstein confesses: "I am barred from communicating my opinions to people in the form of polemic writings. I don't have the requisite *gift*; & must get my conviction, which is important to me, across in another, far less direct manner. . . . *For*

God's sake & for the sake of the good cause you must perhaps content yourself with a less direct one [i.e., path]. (This takes strength & courage.)" ("Ludwig Wittgenstein-Ludwig Hänsel: A Friendship, 1929–1940," PPO, 296/297, dated February 9, 1937).

67. Oden, "Introduction," in *Parables of Kierkegaard*, xiv.

68. This passage is published in CV, 24/28. The other two passages, as interesting as they are, were not collected in CV.

69. Bouwsma, *Wittgenstein: Conversations*, 11. We first hear of Wittgenstein's interest in the novel when it is one of the few personal items he takes with him to the front in the First World War. Then we hear that he read it aloud to the village priest when he was teaching in Lower Austria in the 1920's.

70. Dostoevsky, *Brothers Karamazov*, 213, as well as 214, 216, 228. The Grand Inquisitor story poem is told in book V, chapter 5. In connection with Wittgenstein's Russian lessons in 1934–1935 he certainly was able to read this in Russian.

71. MS 120, p. 145r, as translated by Schalkwyk, "Wittgenstein's 'Imperfect Garden,'" 72–73 n. 7. Presumably "the opinion" should be "*my* opinion." The passage is struck through by Wittgenstein with one diagonal line. Schulte ("Wittgenstein on Philosophy as Poetry," 349 n. 7) translates the passage as: "If what I want to teach is, not a more correct way of thinking, but a new movement of thought, then I am aiming for a 'revaluation of values' and come to resemble Nietzsche, also because in my view philosophers should be poets." Schulte then goes on to remark: "The more one thinks about this passage, the more one is tempted to despair of giving a convincing interpretation of the whole of it. And yet, the remark seems too evidently important to leave it alone" (350). I hope I have provided a plausible interpretation.

72. Nietzsche, *The Portable Nietzsche*, 656. When Wittgenstein was at the front in the First World War, he bought volume 8 of Nietzsche's collected works, which included among other things "The Antichrist" and Nietzsche's poems (GT, 49; December 8, 1914). "The Antichrist" was the first essay of a projected four-part work entitled *Unwertung aller Werte* [The Revaluation of All Values].

73. Redpath recalls (*Memoir*, 41; from the mid-1930s): "When I asked him what philosopher he thought *did* write impressively his immediate reply was 'Nietzsche.'"

74. Here are the occurrences I have found, in chronological order: MS 109, 30 (August 22, 1930): "*Weg der Gedankens*" (CV, 5/7; WA3, 18), and 207 (November 6, 1930): "*Denkbewegung*" (CV, 7/9; WA3, 112); "*Gedankenbewegung*" (MS 154, 15v; CV, 19/16, 1931); MS 183, 100 (October 13, 1931): "*Gedanken bewegung*" (PPO, 108/109), p. 125 (November 7, 1931): "*Denkbewegung*" (PPO, 132/133), 141 (January 28, 1932): "*Hauptdenkbewegung*" (PPO, 148/149); and MS 120, 145r (March 23, 1938) "*Gedankenbewegung*" (the passage under discussion). The phrase appears again in letters to Sraffa in English: "movements of thought" (February 21, 1934; published in Moira De Iaco, "Wittgenstein to Sraffa," 101), and much later: "movement of thought": (August 23, 1949; in WC, 450), which I discuss below.

75. Another passage that speaks of poets does not seem germane to the concerns under discussion. In 1939–1940, in MS 162b, Wittgenstein wrote (59r): "People nowadays think scientists are there to instruct them, poets, musicians etc. to entertain them. *That the latter have something to teach them*; that never occurs to them" (CV, 36/42). This sounds like poets and musicians might make a cognitive contribution. I don't dispute that, but I am more focused on their possible noncognitive contribution to philosophy. (On the other hand, perhaps what they have to teach is a new *way* of thinking, which would fit well with my point.)

76. MS 117, 193. Oddly this passage is not included in CV, even though other passages from MS 117 are. Schulte renders the second sentence as: "As a one-eyed man, though, I am a king among the blind" ("Wittgenstein on Philosophy as Poetry," 349 n. 6). Given what Wittgenstein said about Kierkegaard earlier, it seems he may have included him, along with himself, among the second-rate poets.

77. Nietzsche writes: "Whoever writes in blood and aphorisms does not want to be read but to be learned by heart" ("Thus Spoke Zarathustra," in *The Portable Nietzsche*, 152). In an undated and unpublished letter, apparently to Drury, Rhees wrote: "You may have to know a piece of music by heart on the way to understanding it. This does not mean that you have understood the piece of music if you know it by heart." It is not clear if he was quoting Wittgenstein.

78. Von Wright ("The Origin and Composition of the *Investigations*," 114) conjectures that this was 1945–1946.

79. Wittgenstein's reference to the ancient philosophers may be an allusion to Parmenides and his (mostly lost) poem, "On Nature," or Empedocles and his poems, or Heraclitus and his aphorisms. But Wittgenstein was quite familiar with Plato, who could be said to have written in a poetic fashion even as he attacked poetry. Recall Plato's reference to the "ancient quarrel between philosophy and poetry" (*Republic* 607B). And upon his return to philosophy in 1929, Wittgenstein took Heraclitus's aphorism "all is in flux" as a springboard for his own reflections (e.g., MS 107, 159, published in WA2, 92; MS 110, 34–39, published in WA3, 179–182; also Z §459).

80. "Wittgenstein's Philosophical Conversations with Rush Rhees," 62–63.

81. Murdoch's letter to Raymond Queneau, in *Living on Paper*, 104.

82. MS 133, 13r (written in code), as translated by Paul, *Wittgenstein's Progress*, 23, 268. However, Paul misdates the passage as November 2.

83. MS 134, 108, published in CV, 59/67. And see CV, 58/66: "If I had written a *good* sentence, & they were by accident two rhyming lines, this would be a *blemish*." Note that when Ivan calls his work "The Grand Inquisitor" a "poem," he specifically distinguishes it from "verse" (Dostoevsky, *Brothers Karamazov*, 228).

Wittgenstein seems to have forgotten the verses that he in fact did write more than twenty years earlier (see chapter 6). Paul Engelmann, Wittgenstein's close friend from the First World War, wrote: "Wittgenstein certainly never wrote a poem in his life—not even at the age when nearly all intellectually interested young people of his generation tended to try their hand at it—because no poem ever occurred to him spontaneously" (*Letters from Ludwig Wittgenstein,* 89).

84. MS 134, 147–148, in CV, 62/71.

85. Bouwsma, *Wittgenstein: Conversations,* 9 (conversation on August 5, 1949).

86. MS 137, 127a; published in CV, 76/87. The bracketed insert of Tolstoy's name is Wittgenstein's own insertion, not the editor's.

87. Published in WC, 450. The whole letter is of interest.

88. MS 173, 76r; CV, 85/96.

89. Engelmann, *Letters from Ludwig Wittgenstein,* 7, 82–84. Engelmann's letter to Wittgenstein, including the poem, dated April 4, 1917, in *Wittgenstein-Engelmann: Briefe, Begegnungen, Erinnerungen,* 22–24.

Chapter 6

1. The first is signed by Wittgenstein and dated Otterthal (where he was stationed as an elementary school teacher) 21.1.25. (Fillunger's seventy-fifth birthday would be January 27.) It is published in *Wittgenstein Familienbriefen* (104) and translated in *Wittgenstein's Family Letters* (138–139). The translator, Peter Winslow, has provided the following alternate translation, which he prefers:

> Song for Filu
> Dulcet is the quail's flutter
> Dulcet the bulbul's sweet lament
> But Filu's joyous melodies
> Your heart fill with bliss rent and bent.
> Soft is moss on the forest floor
> Zephyr's blest and fussy whispers
> Softer Filu's threads all woollen
> When under foot curled in twisters.
> The oak's trunk everlasting
> Quartz crested-mountain heights withal:
> Eternal, Filu's yarn enmeshed
> lifting strides, as if wing'd in sprawl!
>
> Ludwig Wittgenstein
> Otterthal, 21 January 1925

Winslow offers this interpretation of the poem:

> Wittgenstein—in obvious ways, it seems to me—styled his poem on Georg Trakl's poetry. I cannot say whether he did so wittingly or unwittingly, but there exist compelling similarities all the same; for instance, some word formations and images are strongly reminiscent of Trakl's. This is to say that, generally speaking, I read Wittgenstein's poem as being in line with expressionist poetry—and specifically expressionist poetry from Austria.

> The poem is a kind of compendium of metaphors and images—Schubert's quail, Filu's singing, a forest, Greek mythology, etc. But this last bit regarding Greek mythology is, as it were, not the whole truth. The word "Zephyr" is a translation of the German "Zephir"—which is not only one spelling of the German word for the west wind, but also, if I am not mistaken, the German word for muslin, a kind of cotton fabric. While the west wind seems to be the primary indication in this particular context (on account of the word "Säuseln"), I suspect that Wittgenstein smuggled in a verbal pun. I suspect the pun, because the most prominent image conveyed by the poem is hand-made socks. In a word, more than anything else, the poem is a playful ode to socks, presumably the ones Filu made for Wittgenstein (using muslin?).
>
> It seemed, indeed it seems, to me that Wittgenstein aimed to achieve tension between "high culture" and the simplicity of a kind gesture. It is not too far-fetched to say that Wittgenstein's poem intimates that high culture—classical music, song, leisurely walks in the woods—is made possible (anyway made easier) by the simple, even bare necessities of life such as clothing. At any rate, such an interpretation would mesh well with certain views Wittgenstein held around this time.
>
> In the event, Wittgenstein read this poem out loud at a celebration of Filu's 75th birthday, and I imagine he aimed to get a laugh out of the audience. I picture him, among other things, walking in place, as if on a walk in the woods and listening to and for the birds, and I like to imagine that, right at "lifting strides," he lifted his pants leg and exposed the socks Filu made him.

(Winslow has kindly allowed me to publish his alternate translation and his interpretation of the poem for the first time here.)

Georg Trakl (1887–1914) was one of the many beneficiaries of Wittgenstein's gift of 100,000 crowns for "Austrian artists who are without means [*unbemittelte*]" before the war. When Wittgenstein discovered Trakl was serving on the Eastern Front in his vicinity, he determined to visit him, only to find that he had died just days before. When Wittgenstein later had a chance to read some of his poems, he commented, "I do not understand them but their *tone* makes me happy. It is the tone of the true genius" ("Letters to Ludwig von Ficker," 86–88; and see also Janik, "Wittgenstein, Ficker, and *Der Brenner*," 163–169).

Wittgenstein's second poem has been labeled "Ein Gedicht/A Poem" and is published with a translation in the 1998 edition of CV, 100 (with a bit of information on p. xiii). McGuinness adds this: "It is in fact a mock-poetic form of thanks for a pair of socks knitted for him by a family friend, the singer Marie Fillunger, at a time when he was working as a gardener," presumably in 1926 ("Wittgenstein and Biography," 21 and n. 32). The poem is undated, but 1926 seems a plausible conjecture, when Wittgenstein was working as a gardener outside Vienna. McGuinness claims the last line of the poem, which was crossed out in the original and not included in the publication, clinches his interpretation: "And the gardener nods: 'tis Filu's troth."

Apparently, these poems are not well known, even among Wittgenstein scholars. Janik recently asserted, "The fact remains that there are not even hints of any attempts to write poetry in the sense of *Lyrik* anywhere in Wittgenstein's corpus" ("The Dichtung of Analytic Philosophy," 156). Granted, these were not written when Wittgenstein was trying to do philosophy. Speaking of the 1926 poem, Schulte claims: "These lines are obviously not a serious attempt at writing poetry" ("Wittgenstein on

Philosophy as Poetry," 363 n.29). No—but they do seem to be a humorous attempt at writing poetry. In any case, they are an attempt at writing poetry.

2. The German original of this letter is given in note 57 in chapter 5 above. An English translation of the letter has been published in Erbacher and Schirmer, "On Continuity: Rush Rhees on Outer and Inner Surfaces of Bodies," 6. The translation in the body of this chapter is my own. As far as the translation of *Gleichnis* is concerned, among the leading dictionaries we find:

Oxford-Duden German Dictionary: *Gleichnis*—(*Allegorie*) allegory; (*Parabel*) parable
New Cassell German Dictionary: *Gleichnis*—image, simile, similitude; comparison; allegory; parable; (the parables of Christ)
Langenscheit's Standard Dictionary: *Gleichnis*—image; *rhet.* simile; *biblical*: parable.

Schulte also has an extended reflection on the meanings of the term as Wittgenstein uses it in "Wittgenstein on Philosophy as Poetry," 365–366.

3. Eighty-six have been collected in *Parables of Kierkegaard*; hundreds are listed in an appendix, 147–181. Kierkegaard does not seem to have a single term that he uses to identify these vignettes. He uses *Billede* [=image] (*Concluding Unscientific Postscript*, 55, 241) and *Fortællingen* [=story or narrative] (*Johannes Climacus*, 117, *Works of Love*, 294) to refer to them.

4. Presumably, "Half a moment." In Hardy, *In Search of Isaiah Berlin*, 5, and also PI §133.

5. Nietzsche, "Thus Spoke Zarathustra," *The Portable Nietzsche*, 152).

6. G. H. von Wright ("The Origin and Composition of the *Investigations*," 114) conjectures that this was 1945–1946.

7. Bouwsma reports on a conversation with Wittgenstein in 1950: "W[ittgenstein] reads Plato—the only philosopher he reads. But he likes the allegories, the myths. They're fine" (Bouwsma, *Wittgenstein: Conversations*, 61; September 14, 1950). Hallett reports that Wittgenstein had a five-volume edition of Plato's dialogues in German at his death ("Appendix: Authors Wittgenstein Knew or Read," 771).

8. "Wittgenstein's Philosophical Conversations with Rush Rhees," 62–63.

9. MS 133, 13r (written in code).

10. Johnson, "Parables," 124. Johnson interviewed Hijab on October 9, 2002. When Hijab told me this same story in 1999, he referred to it as "the allegory of the wall."

11. "Agrammaticality," 168. An anonymous reader for MIT Press suggested that Anscombe's book *Intention* comes close to Wittgenstein's style. In chapter 7, I try to do a bit of philosophy in "his heterodox literary style" and after the fashion of "the poetic discourse he suggests."

12. Geach's notes in LPP, 90; then Edwards's unpublished version in "Wittgenstein's Lectures," 128–129. Malcolm, presumably reporting on the same lecture, writes (*Dreaming*, 87): "In a lecture Wittgenstein once said that it is an important thing in philosophy to know when to *stop*." Also, Kanti Shah: "We must know where to stop" (LPP, 220); Jackson: "In philosophy an important thing is to know when to stop" (LPP, 321).

13. See especially chapter 8 of *Wittgenstein in Exile*, and most recently my book review of two editions of Wittgenstein's lectures, "Review of Wittgenstein," in *Philosophy: Journal of the Royal Institute of Philosophy*. For a biblical parable that echoes aspects of this, see Mark 4:26–29, where we need have no concern with how the seed grows. And see also Wittgenstein's comment from 1942 (MS 125, 44r; collected in CV 42/48): "You cannot draw the seed up out of the earth. You can only give it warmth, moisture & light & then it must grow. (You mustn't even touch it except with care.)"

14. And cf. this recollection from Denis Paul (*Wittgenstein's Progress*, 26): "A twinned pair of typescripts . . . appear to have contributed to the final version of Part I of *Investigations*. . . . Elizabeth Anscombe showed them to me in 1952. . . . Her story about them was what Wittgenstein had told her. They were housed in identical file boxes and consisted of roughly identical paragraphs arranged in different orders, and his interest in them was that they demonstrated the different ways in which philosophical ideas can connect with one another." No more information about this has come down to us. It is just possible that Paul was confusedly recalling the box of index cards that was published as *Zettel*. See the "Editors' Preface" (Z, v–vi), which recounts a file box of cuttings that Peter Geach *rearranged* according to *his* judgment of subject matter! (This reminds one of the "authorial stance" that Rhees took as an editor of Wittgenstein's work, discussed in chapter 3 above.)

15. As with the Sermon on the Mount (Matthew 5) and the Sermon on the Plain (Luke 6:17–49). See also Jesus's image of the mustard seed, the smallest seed of all, which becomes a large shrub in Mark (4:32) but a tree (*sic*) in Luke (13:19). Matthew (13:32) tries to have it both ways: "It is the biggest of shrubs, and becomes a tree"!

16. As does the parable of the wedding feast (Matthew 22:1–14; Luke 14:15–24).

17. While this line is best known from its appearance in *Zettel*, that collection was, of course, compiled from clippings of material from other sources. In fact, this line first appears in MS 115, 61, which was probably composed in 1933–1934 (see von Wright's dating in PO, 486, 493).

18. MS 155, 42r (written in English), quoted in chapter 4 above. Von Wright conjectures that material in this notebook was composed in 1931 (PO, 488, 497).

19. *Confessions*, bk. XI, chap. xii (14). The problem with pleading ignorance is that it implies there is an answer after all. For more on this see Wittgenstein's discussion of sleep walking in the text accompanying note 24. Eric Heller misremembers (or has one of his characters misremember) Augustine's reply as being the "joke" reply, in

"Investigations of a Dog and Other Matters," 106. In fact, Augustine goes on to explain (chap. xiii, 15) that God created time as well, so there was no time before creation.

20. Based on a letter of November 22, 1970, from Rush Rhees, Hallet reports: "Among the few books in [Wittgenstein's] possession when he died there was both a Latin edition . . . and a German translation" of the *Confessions* ("Appendix: Authors Wittgenstein Knew or Read," 761). And, of course, Wittgenstein quotes or cites several passages from the *Confessions* in the *Philosophical Investigations*.

21. *Martin Luther's Tabletalk*, §67. Cf. Drury, "Conversations with Wittgenstein," 143; 1939: "Wittgenstein: I have been reading Luther recently. Luther is like an old gnarled oak, as strong as that. That isn't just a metaphor." The crack about Hell has also been attributed, probably apocryphally, to John Calvin: "God was not idle but was creating hell for curious questioners!"

22. Kierkegaard, *Early Polemical Writings*, 105.

23. Cf. the Copenhagen interpretation of quantum mechanics, which responds to the question whether light is waves or particles with: "Don't ask!" One is simply not allowed to ask what happened in a situation where no measurement was made.

24. Edwards, "Wittgenstein's Lectures," 34. Cf. similar notes of the same point in the lecture by three other note takers in LPP, 44/169/287.

In spring 1914, Russell gave a course at Harvard on logic (Philosophy 21: Advanced Logic). Harry T. Costello, Russell's assistant for the lectures that term, reports, "[Albert Perley] Brogan wanted to know whether there were simples, and why not infinite divisibility. . . . Were there then atomic propositions? Russell so frowned on this that he scared Brogan into temporary silence" (Costello, "Logic in 1914 and Now," 254–255). The mathematician Mark Kac referred to this style of response as "proof by intimidation" (quoted in Rawls, "Afterword," 419).

25. I discuss this story in *Wittgenstein in Exile*, 132–135. The passages quoted are from the book of Job 40:4, 42:2, 6. The commentator is Peter Scherer, "The Book of Job: Exposition," 1192–1193. A more recent commentator explains: "The exploration of the problem of theodicy in the Book of Job and the 'answer' it proposes cannot be separated from the poetic vehicle of the book, . . . one misses the real intent by reading the text, as has too often been done, as a paraphrasable philosophical argument merely embellished or made more arresting by poetic devices" (Alter, *The Art of Biblical Poetry*, 93). Alter explains the operation of the poetic devices at pp. 116–138.

When Wittgenstein had a discussion with Drury in 1951 about suffering and morality, Wittgenstein ends the conversation in a way reminiscent of God from the whirlwind: "You don't understand, you are quite out of your depth" (Drury, "Conversations with Wittgenstein," 170). In a similar vein, we read in Ecclesiastes 7:10, "Do not ask why the past was better than the present, for this is not a question prompted by wisdom."

26. Tolstoy, *Walk in the Light and Twenty-Three Tales*, 187.

27. King, "Recollections of Wittgenstein," 72: "He went on to recommend Tolstoy, and encouraged me to read the *Twenty Three Tales*; and when I had bought a copy he marked those which he thought most important. These were 'What Men Live By,' 'The Two Old Men,' 'The Three Hermits,' and 'How Much Land Does a Man Need?' 'There you have the essence of Christianity!' he said." And see Malcolm, *Memoir*, 45: "Once when we were conversing Wittgenstein was delighted to learn that I knew Tolstoy's *Twenty-three Tales*. He had an extremely high opinion of these stories." And Drury reports Wittgenstein as saying ("Conversations with Wittgenstein," 86), "Those short stories of Tolstoy will live forever. They were written for all peoples." See also Paul Engelmann's discussion of "Two Old Men" (*Letters from Ludwig Wittgenstein*, 80–81) as one of Wittgenstein's favorites. When ordering books for his elementary students in 1920, he ordered one containing Tolstoy's "Three Questions" and "What Men Live By" (*Ludwig Wittgenstein—Ludwig Hänsel: Eine Freundschaft*, 39; letter dated November 30, 1920, quoted in chapter 5 above).

28. I discuss this story in *Wittgenstein in Exile*, 135–138. Dostoevsky's comments about his approach can be found in "Dostoevsky's Letters," 761–762; August 24, 1879.

29. Jourdain, "The Paradoxes of Logic," 77. I'm not sure that Jourdain's characterization of Poincaré (and, later, Schoenflies) is accurate, but I am more interested here in these proposed kinds of responses than their accuracy.

Poincaré remarks about Russell's suggested responses to the paradoxes: "The true mathematics, the mathematics that is of some use, may continue to develop according to its own principles, taking no heed of the tempests that rage without, and step by step it will pursue its wonted conquests, which are decisive and have never to be abandoned" (*Science and Method*, 189). This may be the basis of Jourdain's remark.

30. The quoted passage is from Russell, "Mathematical Logic as Based on the Theory of Types," 63. Russell makes this remark in discussing the difficulty of saying what one cannot say. This is reminiscent of Frank Ramsey's comment about "the absurd position of the child in the following dialogue: 'Say breakfast.' 'Can't.' 'What can't you say?' 'Can't say breakfast.'" ("Philosophy," 268).

31. Lewis Carroll, *Alice's Adventures in Wonderland*, chaps. 7 and 9. The relevant passages are provided by Jourdain in appendix Q, 93–94.

32. Drury, *The Danger of Words*, 257. And also Rhees, "Wittgenstein's Philosophical Conversations with Rush Rhees," 25–26.

Wittgenstein was not always impressed by humor. Reflecting in his diary on his lectures in 1930, he wrote, "In my lectures I often seek to gain favor with my audience through a somewhat comic turn; to entertain them so they will willingly hear me out. That is certainly something bad" (PPO 21; May 2, 1930). But note that this was before his "evangelical" turn, as I call it in chapter 1.

33. Kafka, *The Complete Stories and Parables,* 442.

34. I have discussed this previously in *Wittgenstein in Exile,* 44–45. The revised translation in the fourth edition by Hacker and Schulte renders this as "we wouldn't be able to understand it." Anscombe's original and literal translation strikes me as clearly preferable. There seems to me to be a difference between "wouldn't be able to" (which I hear as "wouldn't now be able to" or "wouldn't, as things stand, be able to") and "couldn't" (which I hear as more permanent, or deep). Perhaps others hear them differently. In any case, I see no reason to deviate from Anscombe's literal translation.

35. Are there ways to identify talking without understanding? Perhaps we could identify talking by its symptoms, so to speak—the lions would seem to pay attention to one another, or have some point of attention in common, react to each other's sounds, and so forth. Just as we, for example, could recognize that people are talking in a foreign country in which we do not understand the language. In a 1939 lecture (LFM, 203; May 3, 1939), Wittgenstein mentions, for example, "What we call language is characterized . . . by certain other signs too: a criterion [I think "symptom" would be the better term here] of talking is that they make articulated noises. For instance, if you see me and Watson at the South Pole making noises at each other, everyone would say we are talking, not making music, etc."

36. Notes from Alice Ambrose and Margaret Masterman, "Yellow Book (1933–1934)," in WLA, 43.

Wittgenstein contradicts this in a remark just two paragraphs above his remark about the lion (PI, part ii, section xi, 223 = PPF §325):

> One human being can be a complete enigma to another. One learns this when one comes into a strange country with entirely strange traditions; and, what is more, even though one has mastered the country's language. One does not *understand* the people.

But I also don't understand this remark. The scenario he describes leads me to doubt the assertion that the visitor "has mastered the country's language." In fact, Wittgenstein himself made the appropriate reply about ten years earlier. In a manuscript from 1937–1938, in regard to the woodcutters who sell wood by its footprint rather than by volume: "We should presumably say in this case: they simply do not mean the same by 'a lot of wood' and 'a little wood' as we do . . ." (RFM, 94 = MS 117, 48). They make sounds that are the same as those English phrases, but it doesn't follow that they are expressing those phrases. It seems that we have to take a stance of radical translation with regard to the woodcutters, as with the lion. If there is not enough evidence to understand what the lion is saying, we are not yet in a position to suppose that it is doing anything more than roaring. That is, we have to go back and question our interpretation of their utterances when that interpretation defies understanding. Understanding is a necessary fulcrum for interpretation.

37. Moore, "Moore's Paradox," 207.

38. WC, 365; October 1944.

39. Malcolm, *Memoir*, 56. Actually, Malcolm says Wittgenstein remarked that it was "the only work of Moore's that greatly impressed him."

40. This is suggested by the elaboration in the manuscript: "He becomes a mystery to us by a certain behavior, enigmatic." Perhaps the behavior of a predator would be enigmatic to us.

41. Emojis would seem to count as semasiographic language. It seems possible that Wittgenstein invented emojis (LC, 4; summer 1938): "If I were a good draughtsman I could convey an innumerable number of expressions by four strokes—" and he then draws and describes three simplified faces, which can only be called emojis! "Doing this, our descriptions would be much more flexible and various than they are as expressed by adjectives." (This circulated as a meme on social media in 2019.)

42. Our preference for a sequential view of the world is reflected in our tendency to use hypotaxis in narration, in which clauses are subordinated by temporal, causal, or logical ordering. This is contrasted with parataxis in narration, in which clauses are presented without such subordination. Robert Alter, in his account of his translation of the Hebrew Bible, emphasizes the prominence there, but oddity to modern ears, of paratactic narration (*The Art of Bible Translation*, 29): "Parataxis is above all a device of narrative concatenation. Instead of stipulating causal relations and so showing how one element in the narrative report qualifies or complicates or is a consequence of another, it marches us steadily from one point to the next in the narrative sequence." Parataxis describes how Heptapod B functions. Banks characterizes a heptapod lecture on heptapod history as "filled with apparent non sequiturs" (142), which is exactly how paratactic history would sound to us.

43. Actually, as I said in *Wittgenstein in Exile* (63), I think "form of life" (like "language game" or "possible world") is a heuristic device for discussing scenarios. There is no objective sense in which something *is* or *is not* a form of life or in which two circumstances are or are not *different* forms of life. This approach suggests that we might take the question whether the lion talks as a matter of "seeing as"—do we *see* the lion *as* talking? Or, to use Dennett's terminology, should we take the "intentional stance" with respect to the lion? There is clear precedent for this approach in Wittgenstein (PI, part ii, p. 178 = PPF §22): "My attitude towards him is an attitude towards a soul. I am not of the *opinion* that he has a soul." And (PPO, 225; March 15, 1937), "My faith is too weak. I mean my belief in providence, my feeling: 'everything happens through the will of God.' And this is no opinion—also not a conviction, but an attitude toward the things & what is happening." (Also, see LW2, 38.)

Lem touches on the matter of stance when the narrator discusses another scientist (189): "Not willing to give up treating the Universe as a purely physical object, devoid of 'meanings,' Lerner acted like a man prepared to study a handwritten letter as if it were a seismograph. In the final analysis, handwriting, like a seismograph, has a lot of complicated curved lines."

44. MS 167, 12v; MS 137, 96b; MS 144, 97; and LW1 §190.

And why didn't Wittgenstein write: If lions could talk, we couldn't understand them? Why did he use the singular: *lion*?

45. See also Malcolm's account of a tribe that unreliably measures fields by strides (*Memoir*, 41–42), recounted in notes from other note takers in LPP, 24 and 142.

46. In both MS 117, 49, and TS 222, 118, which was the direct source for the published edition of RFM, this remark about Gotham *follows* the next remark about Frege. I know of no reason why the editors reversed them.

47. Frege, *The Basic Laws of Arithmetic*, XVI. Frege was imagining that "beings were even found whose laws of thought directly contradicted ours, so that their application often led to opposite results." So, the woodsellers might be imagined to be an example of what "this would really be like."

48. LFM, 202, 204; May 3, 1939.

49. That Wittgenstein found himself at odds with the habits and practices of his neighbors in Skjolden is documented in Åmås and Larsen, "Ludwig Wittgenstein in Norway: 1913–1950." See especially conflicting attitudes about timeliness (30) and cursing (26). (I recount these events in my book *Simply Wittgenstein*, 70–71.) Then there is Wittgenstein's own account of his troubles with Anna Rebni, a neighbor in Skjolden (MS 119, 119r–121r; November 1937) where he finally asks after her coldness toward him only to find it was due to her (understandable) misunderstanding of his shaking his walking stick at her in a seemingly threatening way—apparently meant by him to be an expression of affection. (!!?)

50. Taken from Blount's *Tenures of Land*, 133.

Kierkegaard also relates a story about "the wise men of Gotham" in *Concluding Unscientific Postscript*, 337, but it is a different story with a different point unrelated to Wittgenstein's parable here.

51. The Jerusalem Talmud: Berakhoth, 2:3c.

52. Cf. the parable of the lost sheep (Matthew 18:10–14; Luke 15:4–6) in which a shepherd leaves ninety-nine sheep unattended to go in search of one lost sheep: "Which one of you with a hundred sheep, if he lost one, would fail to leave the ninety-nine in the desert and go after the missing one till he found it?" (Luke 15:4). I would. But if we really try to think or feel our way into the view of this shepherd, it does seem possible after all. Would the motivation have something to do with comforting fright, or perhaps being motivated by Rawls's difference principle? This parable has in fact been marshaled on social media in connection with the current tension between the slogans "Black Lives Matter" and "All Lives Matter." To show a special concern for the one missing sheep does not mean to deny the importance of the rest.

53. And for the same reason, I am somewhat unimpressed by Wittgenstein's line (PI §217): "Once I have exhausted the justifications, I have reached bedrock, and

my spade is turned. Then I am inclined to say: 'This is simply what I do.'" I'm more impressed by this answer if there is a community of diggers whose spades are turned.

54. Presumably there could be signs (perhaps there are, in connection with an elevator) designed to get you to look (or go) up or down. Perhaps this would be understood from the context—"beware of the low-hanging electric-lines above you" or "beware of the land mines in the ground right here." There is, after all, even ambiguity in the left- or right-pointing arrows, as anyone who drives can attest. Does the arrow mean turn right *immediately* (i.e., in the very two-dimensional plane of the sign) or (very?) soon? How soon? "Is *that* where I was supposed to turn?"

55. Hultgren, *The Parables of Jesus*, 40 n.31.

56. Janik and Toulmin, *Wittgenstein's Vienna*, 228. Toulmin attended Wittgenstein's lectures from Lent 1946 through Easter 1947. Since this parable never occurs in the four sets of lecture notes we have from the academic year 1946–47, it is plausible to suppose this comes from Lent or Easter terms of 1946. (There are no other known lecture notes from those terms.)

57. See Guthrie, *The Sophists*, 58.

58. And see Wittgenstein's comments along the same line in a lecture of January 31, 1947, in LPP, 57 and 181.

59. On pp. 61–65 of my little introductory book *Simply Wittgenstein*, I have made this point and applied it to debates about the "meaning" of the Confederate battle flag and various sports mascots.

60. Klagge, "The Meanings of Symbols." A reader questioned this dialogue because it puts kneeling and the Confederate battle flag on a par with one another. Certainly they are not on a par morally, but they seem to me to be on a par logically or semantically.

61. Wittgenstein here mentions as examples "a feeling of ardent love or hope" and "felt deep grief." That seems to me to be different from the *feelings associated with* ardent love or hope or deep grief, which you could perhaps experience momentarily. Would it have been clearer if Wittgenstein had instead doubted whether one could *have* ardent love or hope or deep grief only for one second?

While taking a heart rhythm medication, amiodarone, a few years ago, I occasionally experienced phantosmia—smell hallucinations. (While I'm sure it was a side effect, it is not a medically recognized one.) And associated with these hallucinations I would experience a feeling of doom, for only a brief time. Does this contradict Wittgenstein's claims? Could one have a feeling of doom for one second—no matter what preceded or followed this second? I would say, Yes. Perhaps that shows doom is more like violent pain. But isn't doom the same as hopelessness? And presumably Wittgenstein thinks you can't have (feelings of) hopelessness for one second—no matter what preceded or followed this second.

62. Putnam, "The Meaning of 'Meaning,'" 223–227. Putnam makes no reference to Wittgenstein in this paper, but to me, the parallel between temporal context (Wittgenstein's case) and spatial context (Putnam's case) seems striking.

63. Written in the last month of his life, this passage may well represent Wittgenstein's own situation toward the end of his life. During Wittgenstein's visit to Malcolm in the United States in 1949, Malcolm reported: "More than once, Wittgenstein said to me that it was a problem for him as to what to do with the remainder of his life. 'When a person has only one thing in the world—namely, a certain talent—what is he to do when he begins to lose that talent?' he asked" (*Ludwig Wittgenstein: Memoir*, 76).

64. PO, 258 = MS 149, 67.

65. Gasking and Jackson, "Ludwig Wittgenstein," 1038. The preface to the parable, "It is as if," sounds just like the preface of one of Jesus' parables, "To what then shall I compare . . . ?" (Luke 7:31) or "It is like . . ." (Mark 13:34) or "For it is as when . . ." (Matthew 25:14).

66. On the ad hoc nature of countering temptations and obsessions, see also Wittgenstein's comment from a 1942 notebook (CV, 43/49): "At present we are combatting a trend. But this trend will die out, superseded by others. And then people will no longer understand our arguments against it; will not see why all that needed saying." See also CV, 65/74, and PPO, 383.

This perhaps speaks to the relative unpopularity of Wittgenstein's work in the twenty-first century. On this, see my book *Wittgenstein in Exile*, especially chap. 11: "Wittgenstein in the Twenty-First Century." The key question is whether Wittgenstein provides or suggests tools to combat contemporary trends.

67. There seems to be an allusion to the parable of the cave in a lecture by Wittgenstein in 1946 (LPP, 32).

68. Redpath's *Ludwig Wittgenstein: A Student's Memoir*, 28.

69. See also Gregory and Wallace, *Recovery from Early Blindness: A Case Study*.

70. PPO, 130/131. Quoted and discussed in chapter 5 above.

71. Findlay, "My Encounters with Wittgenstein," 681; alluding to Gellner, *Words and Things*, 152.

72. Johnson, "Parables," 125. Recollections from Hijab recorded October 9, 2002. Wittgenstein also uses the English word *parable* in this sort of context at BB, 45.

For an earlier use of the idea of "keys" in Wittgenstein, see Moore's lecture notes from October 27, 1930 (WLM, 75); and also MS 155, 1931 (published in WA3, vii): "What I should like to get you to do is not to agree with me in particular opinions but to investigate the matter in the right way. To notice the interesting kind of things (i.e. the things which will serve as keys if you use them properly."

73. Here is Hijab's written account, from section 217: "Wittgenstein and his Students," in an unpublished typescript "Philosophy Revisited: A Personal Exposition of Wittgenstein."

> This brings us to the parable of the "Mystery Wall", which Wittgenstein used to illustrate what he thought of other people's reaction to his ideas. He told me one day, and I believe Miss Anscombe was there too, the following parable to explain what his ex-students did: *Once upon a time, there was a village with a high wall on one side of it. The wall bore markings, which seemed to be possible gates, but no one was ever able to open any of these gates. One day, someone found tiny and shining golden keys near the wall. After he put a selection of these keys, in the right order, in a set of holes in one of the gates, he discovered that the gate was opened with surprising ease. After that, some people exclaimed, "All the gates in the wall have been opened!" Others who checked and saw there were still so many closed gates, exclaimed, "No gate has been opened!" Still others, who came to the wall in order to open the gates, were fascinated by the shining golden keys, and started playing with these keys, forgetting why they came to the wall in the first place.*
>
> In Wittgenstein's intriguing parable, the "gates" are the age-old problems of philosophy: What is Time? What is space? What is truth? What is Reality? What is Existence? Is Reality the same thing as Existence? What is knowledge? What is Science? How do we know the Truth? What is Mind? What is Good? What is God? What is Faith? What is Meaning? What is Free Will? And so on. The 'tiny and shining golden keys' are the tools of Wittgenstein's Socratic method (or, as Miss Anscombe once called them, Wittgenstein's heavy machinery of demolition).

Or, as I call them, Wittgenstein's artillery.

74. CV, 11/13–14; MS 153a, 35v; 1931.

75. See also Plato's parable about seeds at *Phaedrus* 276b–e.

76. MS 162b, 59v–60r; 1939–1940; quoted in Rhees, "Correspondence and Comments," 157.

77. Drury, "Conversations with Wittgenstein," 121.

78. CV, 42/48–49 (MS 125, 58v; May 15, 1942).

79. Recall Jesus's puzzling comment that he spoke in parables "so that they may look and look but never perceive; listen and listen but never understand" (Mark 4:12). I think, instead, that the gospel writer put these words in Jesus's mouth to account for the apparent failure of his message to move people.

80. The last quoted remark is prefaced by: "And the word 'behavior,' as I use it, is generally misleading, for it includes in its meaning also the external circumstances of behavior in the narrower sense."

81. Dostoevsky, *Brothers Karamazov*, pt. I, bk. III: The Sensualists; Chapter 2: Stinking Lizaveta: 86–87. It is important to see that Dostoevsky's point is *not* that she had nothing to be proud of, but that she didn't have the conceptual capacity for pride.

82. Bouwsma, *Wittgenstein: Conversations*, 5; July 1949. Here in Bouwsma's account Wittgenstein speaks (in English) of "patterns of life." In PPF §1 (quoted above) he wrote, "The phenomena of hope are modes of this complicated form of life."

83. See *Wittgenstein's Family Letters.*

84. Hermine Wittgenstein, *"Ludwig sagt . . ."* 69, dated February 1917. Wittgenstein mentions Rembrandt in other places later on, showing a familiarity with his paintings (RC, 9, 27; BB, 183). Cf. also Wittgenstein's letter to Engelmann expressing his frustration with a publisher (*Letters from Wittgenstein,* 15, October 22, 1918): "The devil knows what he is doing with my manuscript. Perhaps he is examining it chemically as to its fitness."

85. See my paper "Wittgenstein and von Wright on Goodness," 291–303.

86. WLM, 332 (May 9, 1933). And see Alice Ambrose's notes of presumably the same lecture (WLA, 34): "very like talk of looking for the *ingredients* in a mixture, as though qualities were ingredients of things."

87. See my paper "An Unexplored Concept in Wittgenstein," 473–475.

88. "Movements of Thought," in PPO, 159–161.

89. LC, 24 (lecture apparently given during summer 1938). In his memoir, Redpath later remarked about this: "I believe it may have been one of the times when he thought I was 'playing the devil' that made him take a verbal revenge in one of his [lectures] by saying 'Suppose we boil Redpath' (which some people have said will earn me immortality—I hope it will not be the eternity of the damned!)" (*Ludwig Wittgenstein: A Student's Memoir,* 81–82).

90. As for religion, William James made the case most persuasively in *The Varieties of Religious Experience,* lecture II: Circumscription of the Topic. Bouwsma reports a conversation with Wittgenstein (*Wittgenstein: Conversations,* 55; August 28, 1950): "Religion takes many forms, there are similarities, but there is nothing common among all religions."

91. Saddam Hussein was faced with this challenge in 2002: How to show that his country did NOT have weapons of mass destruction? While he was unable to satisfy the warmongers in the United States and United Kingdom of the truth of the negative existential, the subsequent invasion came as close to proving it as one could: despite a tremendous desire to justify the invasion by showing that Iraq *did* have weapons of mass destruction and an extremely careful search, none were ever found.

While that challenge was deadly serious, a more comical example comes from Russell. In his obituary for Wittgenstein in 1951, he relates the following anecdote from their early encounters: "This was in a lecture room, and I invited him to consider the proposition: 'There is no hippopotamus in this room at present'. When he refused to believe this, I looked under all the desks without finding one; but he remained unconvinced" ("Obituary—Ludwig Wittgenstein," 297). Russell told various versions of this anecdote, but this version suits my purpose here.

92. Suits, *The Grasshopper,* 55. His more elaborate definition is, "To play a game is to engage in activity directed towards bringing about a specific state of affairs, using

only means permitted by rules, where the rules prohibit more efficient in favor of less efficient means, and where such rules are accepted just because they make possible such activity" (48–49).

93. Drury, "Conversations with Wittgenstein," 116.

94. Malcolm, *Ludwig Wittgenstein: A Memoir*, 57–58. Unfortunately, I have not been able to find any date for this incident. It must have happened in between 1929 and 1931, but it would be nice to know more precisely when. Around this time Wittgenstein was reading (or re-reading) Spengler's book *The Decline of the West*. In the chapter "Peoples, Races, Tongues" Spengler considers "gesture-language" in addition to "word-language" and references "the work of Jorio on the gestures of the Neapolitans" (vol. II, 140, n.1).

Another friend of Wittgenstein, von Wright, tells a somewhat different version of the Sraffa anecdote, which Malcolm relates in a footnote (58 n.3). Mauro Engelmann (*Wittgenstein's Philosophical Development*, 152) has made the case that von Wright's version is the correct one. However, my purposes here are not biographical or scholarly; my interest is in how the gesture could serve a certain noncognitive purpose. As Alfred Nordmann has said ("The Sleepy Philosopher," 158), "even apocryphal or false stories about Wittgenstein [sometimes] do the job."

95. Von Wright, "A Biographical Sketch," 15.

96. Austin, "Performative Utterances," 234.

97. Klagge, "The Wittgenstein Lectures, Revisited," 15–16; and MS 133, 13r, dated November 1, 1946. See also Wittgenstein's letter to Moore, dated December 3, 1946, and the editor's comments (WC, 405). "Nondescription" may in fact have been an early draft of "Performative Utterances."

98. And more generally see McGuinness, *Wittgenstein: A Life*, 34–35: "To say what Wittgenstein admired in Goethe would almost be to say what he found remarkable or worthwhile in life, so many are the themes and attitudes from Goethe that recur in his thought."

99. Drury, "Conversations with Wittgenstein," 157 (Autumn 1948): "Wittgenstein: . . . Hegel seems to me to be always wanting to say that things which look different are really the same. Whereas my interest is in showing that things which look the same are really different."

100. While Wittgenstein regularly rejects explanations in the standard sense in his methodological remarks, recall from chapter 3 that he was also willing to use the term, in presumably a slightly different sense, in connection with his own method: "Once such a phenomenon is brought into connection with an instinct which I myself possess, this is precisely the explanation [*Erklärung*] wished for, that is, the explanation which resolves this particular difficulty" (MS 110, 298, July 6, 1931; WA3, 332; PO, 139). And also: "Various disquiets of the mind are calmed by various

means (all of them we call problems and speak of looking for and finding their solution). Some of your explanations [*Erklärungen*] through similes [*Gleichnisse*] make some simplifications" (MS 154, 31v; 1931).

101. Goethe, "The Metamorphosis of Plants," in *Goethe: Scientific Studies*, 96–97 (§§113, 114, 119, 120, 122).

102. Goethe, "Excerpt from 'Studies for a Physiology of Plants' [A Schematic Fragment]," 73. And also: "Let us not seek for something behind the phenomena—they themselves are the theory" (#575, in "Selections from Maxims and Reflections," 307).

103. About Goethe's "Metamorphosis," a commentator has written, "It seems . . . to be written out of a spirit of opposition to Linnaeus' great achievement in marking off species from one another by precisely defined, and often countable features" (Boyle, *Goethe: The Poet and the Age,* 1:595). This makes it sound as though we could say that Wittgenstein stands to Austin as Goethe stands to Linnaeus. Linnaeus is known as the "father of modern taxonomy." That could be an apt characterization of Austin.

104. Waismann, *The Voices of Wittgenstein,* 311. I have not been able to find this alleged aphorism of Goethe, though it resembles §119 of "The Metamorphosis of Plants." Cf. also Goethe's July 31, 1787, letter to Charlotte von Stein: "From first to last, the plant is nothing but leaf [*Blatt*]."

Interestingly, when Waismann rewrites this passage in 1936 for *Logik, Sprache, Philosophie*, he leaves off the claim that it "banishes disquiet" (128 = *Principles of Linguistic Philosophy*, 81). It seems that this can only be an indication of some new hesitation on this point.

105. Miller, "Introduction," in Goethe, *The Metamorphosis of Plants*, xxiv.

106. Goethe, "The Metamorphosis of Plants," in *Goethe: Selected Verse*, 147–151. In fact, Wittgenstein quotes from this very passage—"thus the whole chorus of them suggests a secret law"—in his "Remarks on Frazer" (PO, 133; and quoted in chapter 3 above).

107. Boyle, *Goethe: The Poet and the Age*, 2:638, 2:676. Goethe's friend Karl von Knebel was working on a translation of Lucretius's poem, *On the Nature of Things*. See also my mention of Lucretius's poem in chapter 7.

108. MS 112, 222; November 22, 1931.

109. Malcolm, *Ludwig Wittgenstein: A Memoir*, 75, 84.

110. Wittgenstein, LW1 §913 (MS 138, 24b; February 22, 1949). And also Z §173 (= RPP2 §504): "(Only in the stream of thought and life do words have meaning.) [(*Nur in dem Fluß der Gedanken und des Lebens haben die Worte Bedeutung.*)]"

111. Tolstoy, *War and Peace*, bk. 1, pt. 4, chap. 13.

112. TS 219, 11; probably 1932 or 1933. See also: "The task of philosophy is to soothe the mind about meaningless questions. Whoever doesn't tend to such

questions doesn't need philosophy" (PPO, 73; February 8, 1931); and: "Someone who must fight (against) (swarms of) mosquitoes finds it an important matter to have chased some away. But that is quite unimportant to those who are not concerned with mosquitoes. When I solve philosophical problems I have a feeling as though I had done something of utmost importance for all of humanity & don't think that these matters appear so immensely important to me (or shall I say: *are* so important to *me*) because they plague me" (PPO, 133–135; November 7, 1931).

113. This book was completed during the time of the COVID-19 pandemic, when the value of an acquired immunity or a cure for an illness became quite clear.

114. Tolstoy, *A Confession*, 65–66, 63; chap. 12. Compare this with Wittgenstein's attitude toward G. E. Moore (Letter from Wittgenstein to Malcolm, February 18, 1949, in Malcolm, *Memoir*, 116): "There is also a certain *innocence* about Moore. . . . For you aren't talking of the innocence a man has fought for, but of an innocence that comes from a natural absence of temptation." In this respect, Moore is rather like Platon.

For another expression of critical naiveté, see the well-known first four lines of the penultimate paragraph of T. S. Eliot's poem "Little Gidding," the last of his *Four Quartets* (1942), where he comes to "know the place for the first time."

115. Taken from MS 129, 40; 1944(?).

116. Z §433 (= RPP1 §444; and originally from MS 132, 69, September 26, 1946).

117. PPO, 393; September 22, 1941. (After a lengthy illness, Wittgenstein's mother passed away on June 3, 1926.)

Not long after this 1941 conversation, Wittgenstein had his gall bladder removed in 1942 (Rhees, "Editorial Notes," 223). Dorothy Emmet related in 1943 or 1944 that (Flowers and Ground, *Portraits of Wittgenstein*, 2:733) "[Wittgenstein] remembered coming to after an operation and 'My soul was a black ghost in the corner of the room, and it came nearer and took possession of my body.'" In the conversations with Thouless, in their next meeting (PPO, 394; September 25, 1941) Thouless asks whether "such a word as 'sensation' stood for a mere ghost" and Wittgenstein replies: "Yes, that is right. It is a ghost word."

118. PO, 447, 451.

119. Gopnik, "Broken Kingdom."

120. Wittgenstein's friend Paul Engelmann, whose acquaintance dated from the First World War, recalled Wittgenstein's affection for another story, which describes the sound of a trombone:

> Wittgenstein was enraptured by Mörike's immortal story, *Mozart's Journey to Prague*, and in it especially by the passages describing musical effects in words: 'Coming from remotest starry worlds, the sounds fall from the mouth of silvery trombones, icy cold, cutting through marrow and soul; fall through the blueness of the night,' he would recite with a shudder of awe. (Engelmann, *Letters from Wittgenstein*, 86)

The difference here is that the sounds, while described, are not hypostatized.

121. Letter from Dr. Edward Bevan to Sister Mary Elwyn McHale, August 30, 1966, on deposit at Cornell University Library.

122. Apparently Joan Bevan offered her recollections orally, more than once. In 1983 Michael Nedo published what seem to be excerpts from her (oral?) recollections in *Wittgenstein: Sein Leben in Bildern und Texten*, 346. And she is interviewed in Christopher Sykes's 1989 BBC "Horizon" film/documentary, *Wittgenstein: A Wonderful Life*, at 47:48 (available on YouTube). Since Nedo does not quote the same lines leading up to the sentence in question, it seems to stem from a different interview. In Nedo's transcription, he renders her report as: "Tell them I've had a wonderful life." And in Sykes's interview, her report of the statement slightly emphasizes "Tell them" and merits no exclamation mark at the end.

I have discussed this line in a few places: Klagge, "Editor's Preface," x–xii; *Wittgenstein in Exile*, 153–154; and *Simply Wittgenstein*, 98–99. Being a friend to Wittgenstein was notoriously difficult. In William Lyons's dramatic presentation of portions of Wittgenstein's life, he ends by having Russell recount Wittgenstein's dying words to his paramour, to which she replies: "But what about *them*?" (*Wittgenstein—The Crooked Roads*, 82).

123. Malcolm, *Memoir*, 81 (in the 1984 edition; 100 in the 1958 edition).

124. See Derek Jarman, "Wittgenstein" (1993), and the script in *Wittgenstein: The Terry Eagleton Script and the Derek Jarman Film*, 69–144. The review is no longer online, but was once posted on PopcornQ: The Ultimate Home for the Queer Moving Image, at Planetout.com.

125. John, "Wittgenstein's Wonderful Life," 510. Peter was murdered under tragic circumstances in 2014. I want to express my debt to our conversations in 1984–1985 at UCSD.

126. Russell, *The Philosophy of Leibniz*, 220. In the Preface, Russell says that he has translated all the passages, and he thanks "Mr. G.E. Moore . . . for the serious labour of revising all the translations from the Latin" (xiv–xv). Also, Boswell, in his *Life of Johnson*, which Wittgenstein read as recently as 1948 (Drury, "Conversations with Wittgenstein," 155), regularly uses "wonderful" in this sense as well.

127. Anscombe, "Wittgenstein's Two Cuts," 186.

Chapter 7

1. "Philosophy," PO, 161 (= BT §86). The passage after the ellipsis first occurs at MS 110, 189; June 20, 1931.

2. MS 155, 42r (written in English). Von Wright conjectures that material in this notebook was composed in 1931 (PO, 488, 497).

3. Dictations to Skinner in the so-called Pink Book, tentatively dated to 1933–1934 (Skinner, *Dictating Philosophy*, 134).

4. MS 158, 34r–34v (in English, apparently in connection with preparing for his class, 1938). And according to student notes from a class in summer 1938 (LC, 27): "What I'm doing is also persuasion. If someone says: 'There is not a difference', and I say: 'There is a difference' I am persuading." And also from a lecture in 1939 (LFM, 103; February 27, 1939): "You are inclined to put our difference in one way, as a difference of opinion. But I am not trying to persuade you to change your opinion."

5. See chapter 1 (and my book *Wittgenstein in Exile*, 25) for an overview of the range of over one hundred points in (part I of) the *Philosophical Investigations* where Wittgenstein addresses these sorts of noncognitive concerns.

6. Cf. J. P. Stern, *A Study of Nietzsche*, 201: "What Nietzsche teaches us is not to read philosophy as literature, let alone literature as philosophy, but to read both as closely related forms of life." Stern knew Wittgenstein during the Second World War (Klagge, "The Wittgenstein Lectures, Revisited," 66–68).

7. Gardner, *Reader's Companion for Thomas Gardner's* Poverty Creek Journal. The passage quoted is from section 2: On Reading, 7. The essay by Burke that he quotes is "Symbolic Action in a Poem by Keats," 447, originally published in autumn 1943.

8. There is, of course, in philosophy the contrast between justification and discovery. A philosopher may well offer an argument by way of justification for a position arrived at. And a philosophical historian may well offer an account of how a position was in fact arrived at. But the question here is: What it would take to get the reader, what did it take to get the author, to hold (or, arrive at) the position in question?

Wittgenstein's parable of the seeds, as I called it in chapter 6, is unsatisfying to me as it stands because it "speaks from a position of arrival." It simply presents to us as fact that the seeds have no (contemporary) differences. Other versions of the parable show us more "in the act of finding" (see Klagge, *Wittgenstein in Exile*, chap. 8; and "Review of *Wittgenstein: Lectures*").

9. Carnap, "Intellectual Autobiography," 25.

10. Helping readers to reenact that process is the purpose of my book *Tractatus in Context*. Comparing the dialogical style of the *Investigations* with the *Tractatus*, we find only one proposition in the *Tractatus*, 5.633, where Wittgenstein addresses another: "You will say that . . . ," presumably addressing (one who agrees with) Schopenhauer. And while he does occasionally mention Frege and Russell, it hardly suffices to allow one to reenact his movements of thought.

What I have just said holds on a straightforward reading of all but the end of the *Tractatus*. However, the ladder metaphor of 6.54 offers an instance of "the act of getting there."

11. PO, 119. First written February 10, 1931 in MS 110, 58 (published in WA3, 193); then included in TS 211, 313. I discuss this passage more fully in chapter 3.

12. The quotations in this paragraph come from an unpublished draft for use in the classroom, "Reading Poetry" by Thomas Gardner, dated August 29, 2013, 2–3.

13. *Whewell's Court Lectures*, 196; Lent term, 1940.

14. CV, 43/49 (MS 126, 64r; December 15, 1942).

15. For more on Wittgenstein in relation to his time and ours, see my book *Wittgenstein in Exile*, especially chapters 4 and 11. This suggests that the value in Wittgenstein's work is not so much what he said to address the concerns of his students and imagined readers, but what we might say using Wittgenstein's tools ("keys," according to the parable that Hijab recounted) to address the concerns of ourselves, our students, and imagined readers *now*.

See my recent paper, "Wittgenstein, Science and the Evolution of Concepts," for a study of how Wittgenstein's own view changed on an important issue and how that might affect the application of his views to contemporary issues.

16. It is this reputation, I think, that led Schulte to suppose that doing philosophy as poetry would narrow, to what he calls "parochialism," rather than broaden its appeal ("Wittgenstein on Philosophy as Poetry," 367). And it was this practice, by my high school Honors English teacher, that drove me away from poetry for many years.

17. These passages are from CV, 34/40 (MS 121, 35v; June 11, 1938); 57/65 (MS 134, 76; March 28, 1947); 66/75 (MS 136, 80a; January 8, 1948); 68/77 (MS 136, 128b; January 18, 1948); and 80/91 (MS 138, 9a; January 24, 1949). Perloff addresses this issue in "The Right Tempo," the last section in her essay "Writing Philosophy as Poetry," 725–727.

18. Gardner, *Reader's Companion*, 8.

19. CV, 77/88 (MS 137, 134b; December 25, 1948).

20. My reading of the *Phaedo* is influenced by the seminar I took on Plato from William S. Cobb as an undergraduate at the College of William and Mary in 1976, as well as my own experience teaching the dialogue dozens of times since then. Cobb's work was published as "Plato's Treatment of Immortality in the *Phaedo*."

21. As shown, for example, in Martha Nussbaum's influential reading of the *Symposium* in *The Fragility of Goodness*, chap. 6.

In this discussion of the *Phaedo* when I say "Socrates," I mean the character in the dialogue, not the historical person.

22. It is noteworthy that Socrates is willing to discuss whether the soul is immortal without first inquiring after the definition of "soul"! Yet given the time constraints, if he had first addressed the nature of the soul, the sun might well have set and

the execution commenced without their having reached what is weighing on his friends. Socrates had to judge "what medicine" they needed here *and now*.

23. We should also remember what positions on immortality are presented by Plato in other Middle Dialogues. While he apparently endorses immortality in the *Republic*, we get a very different story from Diotima, who appears as the teacher of Socrates in the *Symposium* (207d, 208b): "Mortal nature seeks as far as possible to live forever and be immortal. And this is possible in one way only: by reproduction, because it always leaves behind a new young one in place of the old. . . . In that way everything mortal is preserved, not, like the divine, by always being the same in every way, but because what is departing and aging leaves behind something new, something such as it had been." We should be very careful about ascribing any particular view about immortality to Plato or Socrates.

24. The Roman philosopher-poet Lucretius (99–55 BCE) understands this concern and uses the poetic form of his *On the Nature of Things* to address it, "For obviously my actual technique does not lack a motive." He employs a different childhood analogy to explain his approach (bk. I, lines 936–951):

> Doctors who try to give children foul-tasting wormwood first coat the rim of the cup with the sweet juice of golden honey; their intention is that the children, unwary at their tender age, will be tricked into applying their lips to the cup and at the same time will drain the bitter draught of wormwood—victims of beguilement, but not of betrayal, since by this means they recover strength and health. I have a similar intention now since this philosophy of ours often appears somewhat off-putting to those who have not experienced it, and most people recoil back from it, I have preferred to expound it to you in harmonious Pierian poetry and, so to speak, coat it with the sweet honey of the Muses. My hope has been that by this means I might perhaps succeed in holding your attention concentrated on my verses, while you fathom the nature of the universe and the form of its structure.

I am not saying Plato and Lucretius employ their poetry in the same way, but to the same end.

25. Bouwsma, *Wittgenstein: Conversations*, 61; September 14, 1950. Also, Findlay recalls Wittgenstein's rooms in 1939 ("My Encounters with Wittgenstein," 679): "There were hardly any books, though some Platonic dialogues were on the shelves."

26. Dimensions that are usually lost on contemporary readers. For example, see Gifford's article, "Dramatic Dialectic in *Republic* Book I," for the dramatic and philosophical significance of Cephalus and Polemarchus. And, more generally, see Nails, *The People of Plato*, for background information on the interlocutors.

27. Cf. BB, 1.

28. PI, §374.

29. Cf. BB, 27–28.

30. "A Lecture on Ethics," PO, 39.

31. Cf. Foot, "Moral Beliefs," 111.

32. Tolstoy, *A Confession*, chap. 3.

33. Last sentence: BB, 7. See also PPO, 97 (May 6, 1931): "There is only one remedy against this seduction: to listen to the soft voices that tell us that things here are not the same as there."

34. Bob Dylan plays with an entitative conception of dignity in his song "Dignity" (1989/1994).

35. Cf. BB, 1.

36. Cf. PO, 161 (= BT §86): "Philosophy . . . lead[s] me to . . . abandon a certain combination of words as senseless."

37. CV, 39/44; MS 117, 156; February 2, 1940; translation from 1980 edition.

38. Tolstoy, *A Confession*, chaps. 3 and 4.

39. PPO, 225; March 15, 1937.

40. Tolstoy, *A Confession*, chap. 10. The four tales by Tolstoy that Wittgenstein valued the most—"Three Hermits," "What Men Live By," "How Much Land Does a Man Need?" and "Two Old Men"—were all written in 1885 and published shortly thereafter. See note 27 in chapter 6 above.

41. It was an interesting and different experience to write these remarks in Wittgenstein's style. There was a lot of cutting, pasting, and rearranging involved. The ideas I worked with mostly came from the first part of a talk I have given at club meetings and in classes dozens of times since 1985: "From the Meaning of Life to a Meaningful Life" http://jamesklagge.net/downloads/pdf/meaning.pdf. I was also helped by comments from Reza Hosseini and his *Wittgenstein and Meaning in Life*.

Fans of the *Investigations* will have noted that it (i.e., part I) ends at remark 693, where these remarks then pick up. A humorous continuation of the *Investigations* was composed by Michael Frayn in 1964: "Fog-Like Sensations" (§§694–708). Then this was continued by Jerry Fodor, "Further Meteorological Addenda to PI" (§§709–727), which can be found online: http://alexdunn.info/fodor/.

42. Douay-Rheims translation, 1610.

43. Recall Wittgenstein's own concern in 1946 about an upcoming Joint Session of the Mind Association and the Aristotelian Society meeting. Karl Britten described how Wittgenstein "railed against professional philosophers, mourned the present state of philosophy in England and asked: 'What can one man do alone?'" (see chapter 1 above).

44. A Jewish version of this joke appears in Cohen, *Jokes*, 19–20.

45. Malcolm, *Ludwig Wittgenstein: A Memoir*, 28. On three occasions Wittgenstein offered advice on the writing of polemical pieces in the press. Generally his point was to focus on the key issue and not add distracting material that is only tangentially relevant (letter to Victor Gollancz, September 4, 1945—extracts in Monk, *Ludwig Wittgenstein: The Duty of Genius*, 481–482; and Rush Rhees, "Postscript," 203). But in an extended response to two pieces by Ludwig Hänsel, Wittgenstein wrote (PPO, 297; February 9, 1937), "I am barred from communicating my opinions to people in the form of polemic writings. I don't have the requisite *gift*; & must get my conviction, which is important to me, across in another, far less direct manner. . . . *For God's sake* & for the sake of the good cause you must perhaps content yourself with a less direct [approach]. (This takes courage & strength.)" This is reminiscent of his comments on Kierkegaard (PPO, 131), quoted and discussed in chapter 5 above.

Bibliography

Alter, Robert. *The Art of Bible Translation*. Princeton: Princeton University Press, 2019.

Alter, Robert. *The Art of Biblical Poetry*, new and rev. ed. New York: Basic Books, 2011.

Åmås, Knut Olav, and Rolf Larsen. "Ludwig Wittgenstein in Norway: 1913–1950." In *Wittgenstein in Norway*, ed. K. Johannesen, R. Larsen, and K. Åmås. Oslo: Solum Forlag, 1994.

Ambrose, Alice. *Wittgenstein's Lectures: Cambridge, 1932–1935*. Totowa, NJ: Rowman and Littlefield, 1979.

Anscombe, G. E. M. Introduction to *Metaphysics and the Philosophy of Mind*, vol. 2 of *Collected Philosophical Papers of G.E.M. Anscombe*. Minneapolis: University of Minnesota Press, 1981.

Anscombe, G. E. M. "The Simplicity of the Tractatus." In *From Plato to Wittgenstein: Essays by G.E.M. Anscombe*, ed. M. Geach and L. Gormally. Exeter: Imprint Academic, 2011.

Anscombe, G. E. M. "Wittgenstein's 'Two Cuts' in the History of Philosophy." In *From Plato to Wittgenstein: Essays by G. E. M. Anscombe*, ed. M. Geach and L. Gormally. Exeter: Imprint Academic, 2011.

Antin, David. "Wittgenstein among the Poets." *Modernism/Modernity* 5, no. 1 (1998): 149–166.

Austin, J. L. "Performative Utterances." In *Philosophical Papers*, 3rd ed. New York: Oxford University Press, 1979.

Bachtin, Nicholas. *Lectures and Essays*. Ed. A. E. Duncan-Jones. Birmingham: University of Birmingham, 1963.

Baker, Gordon. "Preface." In *The Voices of Wittgenstein: The Vienna Circle*, ed. Gordon Baker. New York: Routledge, 2003.

Baker, Gordon, and P. M. S. Hacker. *Wittgenstein: Understanding and Meaning*. Vol. 1 of *An Analytical Commentary on the Philosophical Investigations*. Chicago: University of Chicago Press, 1980.

Baker, Gordon, and P. M. S. Hacker. *Wittgenstein: Rules, Grammar and Necessity*. Vol. 2 of *An Analytical Commentary on the Philosophical Investigations*, 2nd ed. Oxford: Wiley-Blackwell, 2009.

Bartley, William. *Wittgenstein*, 2nd ed. La Salle, IL: Open Court, 1985.

Bell, Julian. "An Epistle on the Subject of the Ethical and Aesthetic Beliefs of Herr Ludwig Wittgenstein (Doctor of Philosophy) to Richard Braithwaite, Esq., M.A. (Fellow of King's College)." *Venture* 5 (1930): 208–215.

Biesenbach, Hans. *Anspielungen und Zitate im Werk Ludwig Wittgensteins*, exp. new ed. Sophia: St. Kliment Ohridski University Press, 2014.

Bilder, James G. *Artillery Scout: The Story of a Forward Observer with the U. S. Field Artillery in World War I*. Havertown, PA: Casemate, 2014.

Black, Max. *A Companion to Wittgenstein's Tractatus*. Ithaca: Cornell University Press, 1964.

Black, Max. *Max Black: A Memoir*. Ed. Susanna Eve. King of Prussia, PA: ModinoUSA, 2014.

Blount, Thomas. *Tenures of Land and Customs of Manors*, ed. W. Carew Hazlitt. London: Reeves and Turner, 1874.

Boltzmann, Ludwig. "On Statistical Mechanics (1904)." In *Theoretical Physics and Philosophical Problems*, ed. B. McGuinness. Dordrecht: D. Reidel, 1974.

Bouwsma, O. K. *Wittgenstein: Conversations, 1949–1951*. Indianapolis: Hackett, 1986.

Boyle, Nicholas. *Goethe: The Poet and the Age*, vol. 1: *The Poetry of Desire, 1749–1790*. New York: Oxford University Press, 1991.

Boyle, Nicholas. *Goethe: The Poet and the Age*, vol. 2: *Revolution and Renunciation, 1790–1803*. New York: Oxford University Press, 2000.

Braithwaite, Richard. "Time and Change." *Proceedings of the Aristotelian Society, Supplementary Volume* 8 (1928): 162–174.

Brickhouse, T., and N. Smith. "Socrates' Claims Not to Know and the Irony Problem." In *The Philosophy of Socrates*, sec. 2.1.2. Boulder, CO: Westview Press, 2000.

Britton, Karl. "Portrait of a Philosopher." In *Portraits of Wittgenstein*, exp. ed., vol. 2, ed. F. Flowers and I. Ground. London: Bloomsbury Academic, 2016.

Burke, Kenneth. "Symbolic Action in a Poem by Keats." *A Grammar of Motives*. New York: Prentice Hall, 1945.

Calendar section. *Cambridge Review* 51, no. 1248 (1929).

Carnap, Rudolf. "Intellectual Autobiography." In *The Philosophy of Rudolf Carnap*, ed. P. Schilpp. La Salle, IN: Open Court, 1963.

Carnap, Rudolf. "Wittgenstein and the Vienna Circle." In *Portraits of Wittgenstein*, exp. ed., vol. 1, ed. F. Flowers and I. Ground. London: Bloomsbury Academic, 2016.

Carroll, Lewis. *Alice's Adventures in Wonderland*. 1865.

Cavell, Stanley. "The Availability of Wittgenstein's Later Philosophy." In *Must We Mean What We Say?* New York: Cambridge University Press, 1976.

Chiang, Ted. "Story of Your Life." In *Stories of Your Life and Others*. New York: Macmillan, 2002.

Clark, Katerina, and Michael Holquist. *Mikhail Bakhtin*. Cambridge, MA: Belknap Press of Harvard University Press, 1984.

Cobb, William S. "Plato's Treatment of Immortality in the *Phaedo*." *Southern Journal of Philosophy* 15 (1977): 173–188.

Cohen, Ted. *Jokes: Philosophical Thoughts on Joking Matters*. Chicago: University of Chicago Press, 1999.

Cornforth, Maurice. "Recollections of Cambridge Contemporaries." In *David Guest: A Scientist Fights for Freedom (1911–1938)*, ed. Carmel Haden Guest. London: Lawrence & Wishart, 1939.

Cornish, Kimberley. *The Jew of Linz: Wittgenstein, Hitler and Their Secret Battle for the Mind*. London: Century, 1998.

Costello, Harry T. "Logic in 1914 and Now." *Journal of Philosophy* 54 (1957): 245–264.

De Ioca, Moira. "A List of Meetings between Wittgenstein and Sraffa." *Nordic Wittgenstein Review* 7, no. 1 (2018): 83–99.

De Iaco, Moira. "Wittgenstein to Sraffa: Two Newly-Discovered Letters from February and March, 1934." *Nordic Wittgenstein Review* 8. nos. 1–2 (2019): 209–223.

de Saint-Exupéry, Antoine. *The Little Prince*. Trans. Katherine Woods. New York: Harcourt Brace, 1971.

Dostoevsky, Fyodor. *Brothers Karamazov: Norton Critical Edition*. 2nd ed. Ed. S. Oddo and trans. C. Garnett, and revised by R. Matlaw and S. Oddo. New York: Norton, 2011.

Dostoevsky, Fyodor. "Dostoevsky's Letters." In *Brothers Karamazov: Norton Critical Edition*, 2nd ed., ed. S. Oddo, 653–665. New York: Norton, 2011.

Drury, M. O'C. "Conversations with Wittgenstein." In *Recollections of Wittgenstein*, rev. ed., ed. Rush Rhees. New York: Oxford University Press, 1984.

Drury, M. O'C. *The Danger of Words*. In *The Selected Writings of Maurice O'Connor Drury: On Wittgenstein, Philosophy, Religion and Psychiatry*, ed. John Hayes. London: Bloomsbury, 2017.

Drury, M. O'C. "Some Notes on Conversations with Wittgenstein." In *Recollections of Wittgenstein*, rev. ed., ed. Rush Rhees. New York: Oxford University Press, 1984.

Dummett, Michael. *Elements of Intuitionism*. Oxford: Oxford University Press, 1977.

Du Val, Patrick. "On a Philosopher Dying (F. P. R.)." *Cambridge Review*, February 14, 1930, 262.

Eagleton, Terry. *Saints and Scholars*. London: Verso, 1987.

Eagleton, Terry. "Wittgenstein's Friends." In *Against the Grain: Essays, 1975–1985*. London: Verso, 1986.

Edwards, Gilbert Harris. "Wittgenstein's Lectures, 1946–1947." Unpublished notes (510). Wren Library, Trinity College, Cambridge.

Empson, William. *Selected Letters of William Empson*, ed. John Haffenden. Oxford: Oxford University Press, 2006.

Engelmann, Mauro. *Wittgenstein's Philosophical Development: Phenomenology, Grammar, Method, and the Anthropological View*. New York: Palgrave Macmillan, 2013.

Engelmann, Paul. *Letters from Ludwig Wittgenstein: With a Memoir*. Oxford: Basil Blackwell, 1967.

Engelmann, Paul. *Wittgenstein—Engelmann: Briefe, Begegnungen, Erinnerungen*, ed. Ilse Somavilla. Innsbruck: Haymon Verlag, 2006.

Erbacher, C., J. Jung, and A. Seibel. "From the Archives—The Logbook of Editing Wittgenstein's *Philosophische Bemerkungen*: Rush Rhees' Letters to Georg Henrick von Wright, 1962–1964." *Nordic Wittgenstein Review* 6, no. 1 (2017): 105–147.

Erbacher, Christian, and Tina Schirmer, "On Continuity: Rush Rhees on Outer and Inner Surfaces of Bodies." *Philosophical Investigations* 40, no. 1 (2017): 3–30.

Feigl, Herbert. "The 'Wiener Kreis' in America." In *The Intellectual Migration: Europe and America, 1930–1960*, ed. D. Fleming and B. Bailyn. Cambridge, MA: Belknap Press of Harvard University Press, 1969.

Findlay, J. N. "Introductory." In *Wittgenstein: A Critique*. London: Routledge & Kegan Paul, 1984.

Findlay, J. N. "My Encounters with Wittgenstein." In *Portraits of Wittgenstein*, exp. ed., vol. 2, ed. F. A. Flowers III and Ian Ground. London: Bloomsbury, 2016.

Findlay, J. N. *Plato: The Written and Unwritten Doctrines*. London: Routledge & Kegan Paul, 1974.

Fischer, Eugen. *Philosophical Delusion and Its Therapy: Outline of a Philosophical Revolution*. New York: Routledge, 2011.

Flowers III, F. A., and Ian Ground, eds. *Portraits of Wittgenstein*, exp. ed. London: Bloomsbury, 2016.

Foot, Philippa. "Moral Beliefs." In *Virtues and Vices and Other Essays in Moral Philosophy*. Berkeley: University of California Press, 1978.

Foot, Philippa. *Natural Goodness*. New York: Oxford University Press, 2001

Frayn, Michael. "Fog-Like Sensations." In *Collected Columns*. London: Methuen, 2007.

Frazer, Sir James. *The Golden Bough: A Study in Magic and Religion*, abr. ed. London: Macmillan, 1922.

Frazer, Sir James. *The Golden Bough: A Study in Magic and Religion*. London: Macmillan, 2nd edition, 1900; 3rd edition, 1935.

Frede, Michael. "Plato's Arguments and the Dialogue Form." In *Methods of Interpreting Plato and His Dialogues*, ed. J. Klagge and N. Smith. Oxford: Clarendon Press, 1992.

Frege, Gottlob. *The Basic Laws of Arithmetic*, trans. P. Ebert and M. Rossberg. New York: Oxford University Press, 2013.

Frege, Gottlob. "Frege-Wittgenstein Correspondence," trans. B. Dreben and J. Floyd. In *Interactive Wittgenstein: Essays in Memory of Georg Henrik von Wright*, ed. E. De Pellegrin. Dordrecht: Springer, 2011.

Gardner, Thomas. *John in the Company of Poets: The Gospel in Literary Imagination*. Waco, TX: Baylor University Press, 2011.

Gardner, Thomas. *Reader's Companion for Thomas Gardner's* Poverty Creek Journal. North Adams, MA: Tupelo Press, 2014.

Gasking, D. A. T., and A. C. Jackson. "Ludwig Wittgenstein." In *Portraits of Wittgenstein*, exp. ed.,vol. 2, ed. F. A. Flowers III and Ian Ground. London: Bloomsbury, 2016.

Gellner, Ernest. *Words and Things: An Examination of, and Attack on, Linguistic Philosophy*. London: Victor Gollancz, 1959.

Gifford, Mark. "Dramatic Dialectic in *Republic* Book I." In *Oxford Studies in Ancient Philosophy*, vol. 20. Oxford: Clarendon Press, 2001.

Goethe, Johann Wolfgang von. "Excerpt from 'Studies for a Physiology of Plants' [A Schematic Fragment]." In *Goethe: Scientific Studies*, ed. Douglas Miller. New York: Suhrkamp, 1983.

Goethe, Johann Wolfgang von. "The Metamorphosis of Plants." In *Goethe: Scientific Studies*, ed. Douglas Miller. New York: Suhrkamp, 1983.

Goethe, Johann Wolfgang von. "The Metamorphosis of Plants." In *Goethe: Selected Verse*, ed. and trans. D. Luke. New York: Penguin, 1986.

Goethe, Johann Wolfgang von. "Selections from Maxims and Reflections." In *Goethe: Scientific Studies*, ed. Douglas Miller. New York: Suhrkamp, 1983.

Gopnik, Adam. "Broken Kingdom: Fifty Years of 'The Phantom Tollbooth.'" *New Yorker*, October 17, 2011.

Grattan-Guinness, I. "Russell and Karl Popper: Their Personal Contacts." *Russell* 12, no. 1 (1992): 3–18.

Gregory, R. L., and J. G. Wallace. *Recovery from Early Blindness: A Case Study*. Experimental Psychology Society Monograph, no. 2, 1963.

Guthrie, W. K. C. *The Sophists*. Cambridge: Cambridge University Press, 1971.

Hacker, P. M. S. *Wittgenstein, Meaning and Mind*. Vol. 3 of *An Analytical Commentary on the Philosophical Investigations, Part II—Exegesis §§243–427*, 2nd ed. Hoboken, NJ: Wiley Blackwell, 2019.

Hacking, Ian. *Why Is There Philosophy of Mathematics at All?* New York: Cambridge University Press, 2014.

Hallett, Garth. "Appendix: Authors Wittgenstein Knew or Read." In *A Companion to Wittgenstein's "Philosophical Investigations."* Ithaca, NY: Cornell University Press, 1977.

Hänsel, Ludwig. *Begegnungen mit Wittgenstein: Ludwig Hänsels Tagebücher 1918/1919 und 1921/1922*. Ed. Ilse Somavilla. Innsbruck: Haymon Verlag, 2012.

Hänsel, Ludwig. *Ludwig Hänsel-Ludwig Wittgenstein: Eine Freundschaft: Briefe, Aufsätze, Kommentare*. Ed. Ilse Somavilla. Innsbruck: Haymon Verlag, 1994.

Hardy, Henry. *In Search of Isaiah Berlin: A Literary Adventure*. New York: I. B. Tauris, 2018.

Hayes, John. "Drury and Wittgenstein: Kindred Souls." In *The Selected Writings of Maurice O'Connor Drury: On Wittgenstein, Religion and Psychiatry*, ed. John Hayes. New York: Bloomsbury, 2017.

Heal, Jane. "Wittgenstein and Dialogue." In *Philosophical Dialogues: Plato, Hume, Wittgenstein*. Oxford: Oxford University Press, 1995.

Heller, Erich. "Investigations of a Dog and Other Matters: A Literary Discussion Group in an American University." In *The World of Franz Kafka*, ed. J. P. Stern. New York: Holt, 1980.

Hertz, Heinrich. *The Principles of Mechanics: Presented in a New Form*. 1894. Trans. D. Jones and J. Walley. New York: Dover, 1956.

Hijab, Wasfi. "Philosophy Revisited: A Personal Exposition of Wittgenstein." Unpublished manuscript, November 1995.

Hintikka, Jaakko. "An Impatient Man and His Papers." *Synthese* 87 (1991): 183–201.

Hintikka, Jaakko. "Intellectual Autobiography." In *The Philosophy of Jaakko Hintikka: Library of Living Philosophers,* ed. R. Auxier and L. Hahn. Chicago: Open Court, 2006.

Hodges, Andrew. *Alan Turing: The Enigma*. New York: Simon & Schuster, 1984.

Hosseini, Reza. *Wittgenstein and Meaning in Life: In Search of the Human Voice*. New York: Palgrave Macmillan, 2015.

Hultgren, Arland J. *The Parables of Jesus: A Commentary*. Grand Rapids, MI: William B. Eerdmanns, 2000.

James, William. *The Varieties of Religious Experience: A Study in Human Nature*. 1902. Reprint, New York: Penguin, 1982.

Janik, Allan. "The Dichtung of Analytic Philosophy: Wittgenstein's Legacy from Frege and Its Consequences." In *New Essays on Frege: Between Science and Literature*, ed. G. Bengtsson, S. Säätelä, and A. Pichler, New York: Springer, 2018.

Janik, Allan. "Wittgenstein, Ficker, and *Der Brenner*." In *Wittgenstein: Sources and Perspectives*, ed. C. G. Luckhardt. Ithaca, NY: Cornell University Press, 1979.

Janik, Allan, and Stephen Toulmin, *Wittgenstein's Vienna*. New York: Simon & Schuster, 1973.

Johnson, Charles W. "Parables." In *Time and History: Papers of the 28th International Wittgenstein Symposium,* ed. Friedrich Stadler and Michael Stöltzner. Kirchberg am Wechsel: Austrian Ludwig Wittgenstein Society, 2005.

Jourdain, Philip. *The Philosophy of Mr. B*rtr*nd R*ss*ll*. London: Allen & Unwin, 1918.

Juster, Norton. *The Phantom Tollbooth*. New York: Random House, 1961.

Kafka, Franz. *The Complete Stories and Parables*. Ed. Nahum N. Glatzer. New York: Quality Paperback Book Club, 1983.

Kenny, Anthony. "From the Big Typescript to the *Philosophical Grammar*." *Acta Philosophica Fennica* 28, nos. 1–3 (1976): 41–53.

Kenny, Anthony. *Wittgenstein*, rev. ed. Oxford: Blackwell, 2006.

Kierkegaard, Søren. *Concluding Unscientific Postscript*. Trans. D. Swenson and W. Lowrie. Princeton: Princeton University Press, 1941.

Kierkegaard, Søren. *Early Polemical Writings*. Trans. Julia Watkin. Princeton: Princeton University Press, 1990.

Kierkegaard, Søren. *Johannes Climacus*. Trans. T. Croxall. Stanford, CA: Stanford University Press, 1958.

Kierkegaard, Søren. *Parables of Kierkegaard*. Ed. T. Oden. Princeton: Princeton University Press, 1978.

Kierkegaard, Søren. *The Point of View*. Ed. H. Hong and E. Hong. Princeton: Princeton University Press, 1998.

Kierkegaard, Søren. *Søren Kierkegaard's Journals and Papers*, vol. 6: *Autobiographical, Part 2: 1848–1855*. Ed. H. Hong and E. Hong. Bloomington: Indiana University Press, 1978.

Kierkegaard, Søren. *Works of Love*. Trans. H. Hong and E. Hong. New York: Harper & Row, 1962.

King, John. "Recollections of Wittgenstein." In *Recollections of Wittgenstein*, rev. ed., ed. Rush Rhees. New York: Oxford University Press, 1984.

Klagge, James C. "2002 Addendum." In *Public and Private Occasions*, ed. J. Klagge and A. Nordmann. Totowa, NJ: Rowman and Littlefield, 2003.

Klagge, James C. "Editor's Preface." In *Wittgenstein: Biography and Philosophy*. New York: Cambridge University Press, 2001.

Klagge, James C. "From the Meaning of Life to a Meaningful Life." 2000. http://jamesklagge.net/downloads/pdf/meaning.pdf.

Klagge, James C. "The Meanings of Symbols." *Roanoke Times*, September 15, 2018.

Klagge, James C. "Review of *Wittgenstein: Lectures, Cambridge, 1930–1933, From the Notes of G. E. Moore*, and *Wittgenstein's Whewell's Court Lectures: Cambridge, 1938–1941, From the Notes by Yorick Smythies*." *Philosophy: Journal of the Royal Institute of Philosophy* 93, no. 365 (2018): 471–475.

Klagge, James C. *Simply Wittgenstein*. New York: Simply Charly, 2016.

Klagge, James C. *Tractatus in Context: The Essential Background for Appreciating Wittgenstein's* Tractatus Logico-Philosophicus. New York: Routledge, forthcoming 2022.

Klagge, James C. "An Unexplored Concept in Wittgenstein." *History of Philosophy Quarterly* 12 (1995): 469–486.

Klagge, James C. "Wittgenstein and His Audience: Esotericist or Evangelist?" In *The Textual Genesis of Wittgenstein's Philosophical Investigations*, ed. N. Venturinha. New York: Routledge, 2013.

Klagge, James C. *Wittgenstein in Exile*. Cambridge, MA: MIT Press, 2011.

Klagge, James C. "The Wittgenstein Lectures, Revisited." *Nordic Wittgenstein Review* 8, nos. 1–2 (2019): 11–82.

Klagge, James C. "Wittgenstein, Science and the Evolution of Concepts." In *Wittgenstein and Scientism*, ed. J. Beale and I. Kidd. New York: Routledge, 2017.

Klagge, James C. "Wittgenstein and von Wright on Goodness." *Philosophical Investigations* 41 (2018): 291–303.

Krämer, Hans Joachim. *Plato and the Foundations of Metaphysics: A Work on the Theory of the Principles and Unwritten Doctrines of Plato with a Collection of the Fundamental Documents*. Trans. John R. Catan. Albany: SUNY Press, 1990.

Leavis, F. R. "Memories of Wittgenstein." In *Recollections of Wittgenstein*, rev. ed., ed. Rush Rhees. New York: Oxford University Press, 1984.

Lee, Desmond. "Wittgenstein:1929–1931." In *Portraits of Wittgenstein*, exp. ed., vol. 2, ed. F. Flowers and I. Ground. London: Bloomsbury, 2016.

Lem, Stanisław. *His Master's Voice*. Trans. Michael Kandel. Cambridge, MA: MIT Press, 1968/2020.

Lemoine, Roy E. *The Anagogic Theory of Wittgenstein's "Tractatus."* The Hague: Mouton, 1975.

Levy, Paul. *Moore: G. E. Moore and the Cambridge Apostles*. New York: Oxford University Press, 1979.

Lewy, Casimir. *Meaning and Modality*. New York: Cambridge University Press, 1976.

Luckhardt, C. G. "Editor's Introduction." In *Wittgenstein: Sources and Perspectives*, ed. C. G. Luckhardt. Ithaca, NY: Cornell University Press, 1979.

Lyons, William. *Wittgenstein—The Crooked Roads*. London: Bloomsbury Methuen Drama, 2015.

Malcolm, Norman. *Dreaming*. New York: Humanities Press, 1959.

Malcolm, Norman. *Ludwig Wittgenstein: A Memoir*, new ed. New York: Oxford University Press, 1984.

Malcolm, Norman. *Math Notes by Ludwig Wittgenstein*. San Francisco, 1954. Bootleg printing of Malcolm's notes from the 1939 lectures.

Manninen, Juha. "Waismann's Testimony of Wittgenstein's Fresh Starts in 1931–1935." In *Friedrich Waismann: Causality and Logical Positivism* ed. B. F. McGuinness. New York: Springer, 2011.

Manninen, Juha. "Wittgenstein's Virtual Presence in the Vienna Circle, 1931–1935." https://www.academia.edu/13589910/Wittgensteins_Virtual_Presence_in_the_Vienna_Circle. Unpublished, expanded edition of Manninen, "Waismann's Testimony of Wittgenstein's Fresh Starts in 1931–1935."

Marjanović, Alexandra. "Introduzione alla vita e alle carte di Raffaello Piccoli: un racconto." *Cartevive Periodico dell'Archivio Prezzolini* 16, no. 1 (2005): 26–84.

Maslow, Alexander. *A Study in Wittgenstein's Tractatus*. Berkeley: University of California Press, 1961.

McGuinness, Brian. "Arthur MacIver's Diary: Cambridge (October 1929—March 1930)." *Wittgenstein-Studien* 7 (2016): 201–256.

McGuinness, Brian. "Editor's Preface." In *Wittgenstein and the Vienna Circle*, ed. Brian McGuinness Oxford: Basil Blackwell, 1979.

McGuinness, Brian. "In the Shadow of Goethe: Wittgenstein's Intellectual Project." *European Review* 10 (2002): 447–457.

McGuinness, Brian. "Relations with and within the Circle." In *Approaches to Wittgenstein*. New York: Routledge, 2002.

McGuinness, Brian. "Waismann: The Wandering Scholar." In *Friedrich Waismann: Causality and Logical Positivism*, ed. B. McGuinness. New York: Springer, 2011.

McGuinness, Brian. *Wittgenstein: A Life, Young Ludwig (1889–1921)*. Berkeley: University of California Press, 1988.

McGuinness, Brian. "Wittgenstein and Biography." In *The Oxford Handbook of Wittgenstein*, ed. O. Kuusela and M. McGinn. New York: Oxford University Press, 2011.

McGuinness, Brian. "Wittgenstein and Literature." In *Language and World, Part Two: Signs, Minds and Actions: Proceedings of the 32nd International Ludwig Wittgenstein Symposium*, ed. V. Munz, K. Puhl, and J. Wang. Frankfurt: Ontos Verlag, 2009.

Melzer, Arthur M. *Philosophy between the Lines: The Lost History of Esoteric Writing*. Chicago: University of Chicago Press, 2014.

Menger, Karl. *Reminiscences of the Vienna Circle and the Mathematical Colloquium*. ed. L. Golland, B. McGuinness, and A. Sklar. Dordrecht: Kluwer, 1994.

Miller, Gordon L. "Introduction." In *The Metamorphosis of Plants* by Johann von Goethe. Cambridge, MA: MIT Press, 2009.

Monk, Ray. *Ludwig Wittgenstein: The Duty of Genius*. New York: Free Press, 1990.

Moore, G. E. "Moore's Paradox." In *G. E. Moore: Selected Writings*, ed. T. Baldwin. New York: Routledge, 1993.

Moore, G. E. "Wittgenstein's Lectures in 1930–1933." In *Philosophical Occasions: 1912–1951*, ed. J. Klagge and A. Nordmann. Indianapolis: Hackett, 1993. (PO)

Murdoch, Iris. *Living on Paper: Letters from Iris Murdoch, 1934–1995*, ed. A. Homer and A. Rowe. Princeton, NJ: Princeton University Press, 2016.

Nails, Debra. *The People of Plato: A Prosopography of Plato and Other Socratics*. Indianapolis: Hackett, 2002.

Natali, Carlo. *Aristotle: His Life and School*. Princeton: Princeton University Press, 2013.

Nedo, Michael. "Ludwig Wittgenstein: Life and Work." In *Wiener Ausgabe: Einführung*, ed. M. Nedo. Vienna: Springer-Verlag, 1993.

Nedo, Michael, and M. Ranchetti, eds. *Wittgenstein: Sein Leben in Bildern und Texten*. Frankfurt am Main: Suhrkamp Verlag, 1983.

Nietzsche, Friedrich. *The Basic Writings of Nietzsche*, ed. W. Kaufmann. New York: Modern Library, 1992.

Nietzsche, Friedrich. *The Portable Nietzsche*, ed. W. Kaufmann. New York: Penguin, 1976.

Nordmann, Alfred. "The Sleepy Philosopher: How to Read Wittgenstein's Diaries." In *Wittgenstein: Biography and Philosophy*, ed. J. Klagge. New York: Cambridge University Press, 2003.

Nordmann, Alfred. *Wittgenstein's* Tractatus*: An Introduction*. New York: Cambridge University Press, 2005.

Nussbaum, Martha. *The Fragility of Goodness*. Rev. ed. New York: Cambridge University Press, 2001.

Ortner, M. Christian. *The Austro-Hungarian Artillery from 1867–1918: Technology, Organization and Tactics*. Vienna: Verlag Militaria, 2007.

Partridge, Frances. "Memories of Ludwig Wittgenstein." In *Portraits of Wittgenstein*, exp. ed., vol. 2, ed. F. Flowers and I. Ground. London: Bloomsbury, 2016.

Pascal, Fania. "Wittgenstein: A Personal Memoir." In *Recollections of Wittgenstein*, rev. ed., ed. Rush Rhees. New York: Oxford University Press, 1984.

Paul, Denis. "Wittgenstein's Passages." In *Wittgenstein's Enduring Arguments*, ed. E. Zamuner and D. Levy. New York: Routledge, 2009.

Paul, Denis. *Wittgenstein's Progress: 1929–1951*. Bergen: Wittgenstein Archives at the University of Bergen, 2007.

Perloff, Marjorie. "Writing Philosophy as Poetry: Literary Form in Wittgenstein." In *The Oxford Handbook of Wittgenstein*, ed. O. Kuusela and M. McGinn. New York: Oxford University Press, 2011.

Phillips, D. Z. "Rush Rhees: A Biographical Sketch." In *Wittgenstein and the Possibility of Discourse*. New York: Cambridge University Press, 1998.

Plato. *Plato: Complete Works*. Ed. John Cooper. Indianapolis: Hackett, 1997.

Poincaré, Henri. *Science and Method.* New York: Thomas Nelson & Sons, 1908.

Popper, Karl. *The Open Society and Its Enemies*, vol. 2: *The High Tide of Prophecy*. Princeton: Princeton University Press, 1945.

Proust, Marcel. *Swann's Way: In Search of Lost Time*, vol. 1. Trans. Lydia Davis. New York: Penguin, 2004.

Putnam, Hilary. "The Meaning of 'Meaning.'" In *Mind, Language and Reality: Philosophical Papers*, vol. 2. New York: Cambridge University Press, 1975.

Ramsey, Frank. "Philosophy." In *Foundations of Mathematics and Other Logical Essays*, ed. R. Braithwaite. London: Routledge & Kegan Paul, 1931.

Rawls, John. "Afterword: A Reminiscence." In *Future Pasts: The Analytic Tradition in Twentieth-Century Philosophy*, ed. Juliet Floyd and Sanford Shieh. New York: Oxford University Press, 2001.

Redpath, Theodore. *Ludwig Wittgenstein: A Student's Memoir*. London: Duckworth, 1990.

Rhees, Rush. I. "Note on the Text." *Philosophical Review* 77 (1968): 271–275.

Rhees, Rush. "Correspondence and Comments." *Human World* 15–16 (1974): 153–162.

Rhees, Rush. "On Editing Wittgenstein." *Philosophical Investigations* 19, no. 1 (1996): 55–60.

Rhees, Rush. "Editorial Notes." In *Recollections of Wittgenstein*, rev. ed., ed. Rush Rhees. New York: Oxford University Press, 1984.

Rhees, Rush. "The Philosophy of Wittgenstein." In *Discussions of Wittgenstein*. New York: Schocken, 1970.

Rhees, Rush. "Postscript." In *Recollections of Wittgenstein*, rev. ed., ed. Rush Rhees. New York: Oxford University Press, 1984.

Richards, I. A. "Beginnings and Transitions: I. A. Richards Interviewed by Reuben Brower." In *I. A. Richards: Essays in His Honor*, ed. R. Brower, H. Vendler, and J. Hollander. New York: Oxford University Press, 1973.

Richards, I. A. *Selected Letters of I. A. Richards*. Ed. John Constable. Oxford: Clarendon Press, 1990.

Richards, I. A. "The Strayed Poet: Ludwig Wittgenstein." In *Internal Colloquies: Poems and Plays of I. A. Richards*. New York: Harcourt, 1972.

Rosenbaum, S. P. "Appendix 1: Virginia Woolf among the Apostles." In *The Bloomsbury Group Memoir Club*, ed. James M. Haule. London: Palgrave Macmillan, 2014.

Rosenbaum, S. P. "Wittgenstein in Bloomsbury." In *Portraits of Wittgenstein*, exp. ed., vol. 2, ed. F. Flowers and I. Ground. London: Bloomsbury, 2016.

Rothhaupt, Josef. "Ludwig Wittgenstein and Wilhelm Busch: 'Humour Is Not a Mood, But a "Weltanschauung."'" In *Wittgenstein Reading*, ed. S. Bru, W. Huemer, and D. Streuer. Berlin: de Gruyter, 2013.

Rothhaupt, Josef. "Wittgenstein at Work: Creation, Selection and Composition of "Remarks." In *Wittgenstein after His Nachlass*, ed. N. Venturinho. New York: Palgrave, 2010.

Russell, Bertrand. *The Autobiography of Bertrand Russell: 1914–1944*, vol. 2. London: Allen & Unwin, 1968.

Russell, Bertrand. *A Critical Exposition of the Philosophy of Leibniz*. 1900. Reprint, London: Routledge, 1992.

Russell, Bertrand. "The Limits of Empiricism." *Proceedings of the Aristotelian Society* n.s. 36, no. 1 (1935–1936): 131–150.

Russell, Bertrand. "Mathematical Logic as Based on the Theory of Types (1908)." In *Logic and Knowledge: Essays, 1901–1950*, ed. R. Marsh. London: Allen & Unwin, 1956.

Russell, Bertrand. "Obituary—Ludwig Wittgenstein." *Mind* 60 (1951): 297–298.

Russell, Bertrand. *The Philosophy of Logical Atomism*. Ed. D. Pears. 1918. Reprint, La Salle, IL: Open Court, 1985.

Russo, John. *I. A. Richards: His Life and Work*. Baltimore: Johns Hopkins University Press, 1989.

Sacks, Oliver. *An Anthropologist on Mars: Seven Paradoxical Tales*. New York: Knopf, 1995.

Schalkwyk, David. "Wittgenstein's 'Imperfect Garden': The Ladders and Labyrinths of Philosophy as *Dichtung*." In *The Literary Wittgenstein*, ed. J. Gibson and W. Huemer. New York: Routledge, 2004.

Scherer, Peter. "The Book of Job: Exposition." In *The Interpreter's Bible*, vol. 3. Nashville: Abingdon Press, 1954.

Schmidt, Alfred. "Wittgenstein and World War I: Some Additional On-Line Sources." *Nordic Wittgenstein Review* 3 (2014): 181–185.

Schopenhauer, Arthur. *The World as Will and Representation*, vol. 2. Trans. E. Payne. New York: Dover, 1966.

Schulte, Joachim. "What Is a Work by Wittgenstein?" In *Wittgenstein: The Philosopher and His Works*, ed. A. Pichler and S. Säätelä. Working Papers from the Wittgenstein Archives at the University of Bergen 17 (2005): 356–363.

Schulte, Joachim. "Wittgenstein on Philosophy as Poetry." In *Morphology: Questions on Method and Language*, ed. M. Molder, D. Soeiro, and N. Fonseca. Bern: Peter Lang, 2013.

Silone, Ignazio. *Bread and Wine*. 1936. Reprint, New York: Signet, 1963.

Skidelsky, Robert. *John Maynard Keynes*, vol. 2: *The Economist as Saviour, 1920–1937*. London: Macmillan, 1992.

Skinner, Francis. *Ludwig Wittgenstein: Dictating Philosophy to Francis Skinner, The Wittgenstein-Skinner Papers*. Ed. Arthur Gibson and Niamh O'Mahony. New York: Springer, 2020.

Sloan, Pat. *John Cornford: A Memoir*. London: Jonathan Cape, 1978.

Stern, David. *Wittgenstein's Philosophical Investigations: An Introduction*. New York: Cambridge University Press, 2004.

Stern, J. P. *A Study of Nietzsche*. New York: Cambridge University Press, 1979.

Sturgeon, Nicholas, and Stuart Brown Jr. "Memorial Minutes for Max Black." In *Proceedings of the American Philosophical Association* 64, no. 5 (1991): 61–62.

Suits, Bernard. *The Grasshopper: Games, Life and Utopia*. Ontario: Broadview Press, 2005.

Thomson, George. *The Greek Language*. Cambridge: W. Heffer and Sons, 1960.

Tolstoy, Leo. *A Confession and Other Religious Writings*. Trans. Jane Kentish. New York: Penguin, 1987.

Tolstoy, Leo. *Walk in the Light and Twenty-Three Tales* (1934). Walden, NY: Plough Publishing, 1998.

Tolstoy, Leo. *War and Peace*. Trans. L. and A. Maude. Oxford: Oxford University Press, 1923.

Tolstoy, Leo. *What Is Art?* Trans. R. Pevear and L. Volokhonsky. New York: Penguin, 1995.

Tranøy, Knut. "Wittgenstein in Cambridge: 1949–1951, Some Personal Recollections." In *Portraits of Wittgenstein*, exp. ed., vol. 2, ed. F. Flowers and I. Ground. London: Bloomsbury, 2016.

Trevelyan, Julian. *Indigo Days*. London: Macgibbon & Kee, 1957.

Venturinha, Nuno. "Agrammaticality." In *New Essays on Frege: Between Science and Literature*, ed. G. Bengtsson, S. Säätelä, and A. Pichler. Berlin: Springer, 2018.

von Wright, G. H. "A Biographical Sketch." In *Ludwig Wittgenstein: A Memoir*, 2nd ed. New York: Oxford University Press, 1984.

von Wright, G. H. "The Myth of Progress." In *The Tree of Knowledge and Other Essays*. New York: E. J. Brill, 1993.

von Wright, G. H. "The Origin and Composition of the *Investigations*." In *Wittgenstein*. Minneapolis: University of Minnesota Press, 1982.

von Wright, G. H. "The Wittgenstein Papers." In *Philosophical Occasions: 1912–1951*, ed. J. Klagge and A. Nordmann. Indianapolis: Hackett, 1993.

von Wright, G. H. "Wittgenstein and the 20th Century." In *The Tree of Knowledge and Other Essays*. New York: E. J. Brill, 1993.

Waismann, Friedrich. *Logik, Sprache, Philosophie*. Ed. G. Baker and B. McGuinness. Stuttgart: Reclam, 1976.

Waismann, Friedrich. *Ludwig Wittgenstein and the Vienna Circle*. Ed. Brian McGuinness. Oxford: Blackwell, 1979.

Waismann, Friedrich. *The Principles of Linguistic Philosophy*. Ed. R. Harré. London: Macmillan, 1965.

Waismann, Friedrich. *Voices of Wittgenstein: The Vienna Circle*. Ed. G. Baker. New York: Routledge, 2003.

Walsh, Sylvia. "Kierkegaard the Poet." *Enrahonar: Quaderns de Filosofia* 29 (1998): 153–156.

Watson, W. H. *On Understanding Physics*. Cambridge: Cambridge University Press, 1938.

Westergaard, Peter K. "On the 'Ketner and Eigsti Edition' of Wittgenstein's *Remarks on Frazer's 'The Golden Bough.'*" *Nordic Wittgenstein Review* 4, no. 2 (2015): 117–142.

Westergaard, Peter K. "A Note on Rhees, the *Bemerkungen über Frazers 'The Golden Bough'* and *Über Gewißheit*." In *The Philosophy of Perception and Observation: Contributions to the 40th International Wittgenstein Symposium*, ed. C. Limbeck-Lilienau et al., 288–291. Neulengbach: Austrian Ludwig Wittgenstein Society, 2017.

Wilson, Francesca M., and A. E. Duncan-Jones. "Biographical Introduction." In Nicholas Bachtin, *Lectures and Essays*, ed. A. E. Duncan-Jones. Birmingham: University of Birmingham, 1963.

Wittgenstein, Hermine. *Familienerinnerungen*. Ed. Ilse Somavilla. Innsbruck: Haymon, 2015.

Wittgenstein, Hermine. *"Ludwig Sagt . . ." Die Aufzeichnungen der Hermine Wittgenstein*. Ed. Mathias Iven. Berlin: Parerga Verlag, 2006.

Wittgenstein, Hermine. "Mein Bruder Ludwig." In *Ludwig Wittgenstein: Porträts und Gespräche*. Ed. Rush Rhees. Frankfurt am Main: Suhrkamp, 1987.

Wittgenstein, Hermine. "My Brother Ludwig." In *Recollections of Wittgenstein*, ed. Rush Rhees. New York: Oxford University Press, 1984.

Wittgenstein, Ludwig. "Appendix II: Wittgenstein's 1938 Preface." In *Wittgenstein after His Nachlass*, ed. Nuno Venturinha. New York: Palgrave Macmillan, 2010.

Wittgenstein, Ludwig. "Bemerkungen über Frazers *The Golden Bough.*" *Synthese* 17 (1967): 233–253.

Wittgenstein, Ludwig. *Bemerkungen über Frazers* Golden Bough/*Remarks on Frazer's* Golden Bough. Ed. Rush Rhees, trans. A. C. Miles, and revised by Rush Rhees. Herefordshire: Brynmill Press, 1979.

Wittgenstein, Ludwig. "Bemerkungen über Frazers *The Golden Bough.*" In *Vortrag über Ethik und andere kleine Schriften*, ed. Joachim Schulte. Frankfurt am Mein: Suhrkamp, 1989.

Wittgenstein, Ludwig. *The Big Typescript: TS 213*. Trans. C. G. Luckhardt and M. Aue. Oxford: Blackwell, 2005.

Wittgenstein, Ludwig. *The Blue and Brown Books: Preliminary Studies for the "Philosophical Investigations."* Oxford: Blackwell, 1958. (BB)

Wittgenstein, Ludwig. *Familienbriefen*. Ed. B. McGuinness, M. Ascher, and O. Pfersmann. Vienna: Verlag Hölder-Pichler-Tempsky, 1996.

Wittgenstein, Ludwig. *Geheime Tagebücher: 1914–1916*. Ed. W. Baum. Vienna: Turia & Kant, 1991. (GT)

Wittgenstein, Ludwig. *Gesamtbriefwechsel* (Innsbruck Electronic Edition). Charlottesville, VA: Intelex Corp., 2011.

Wittgenstein, Ludwig. *Last Writings on the Philosophy of Psychology*, vol. 1. Ed. G. H. von Wright and H. Nyman, trans. C. G. Luckhardt and M. Aue. Chicago: University of Chicago Press, 1982. (LW1)

Wittgenstein, Ludwig. *Last Writings on the Philosophy of Psychology: The Inner and the Outer*, vol. 2. Ed. G. H. von Wright and H. Nyman, trans. C. G. Luckhardt and M. Aue. Oxford: Blackwell, 1992. (LW2)

Wittgenstein, Ludwig. *Lecture on Ethics*. Ed. E. Zamuner, E. V. Di Lascio and D. K. Levy. Oxford: Wiley Blackwell, 2014.

Wittgenstein, Ludwig. *Lectures and Conversations on Aesthetics, Psychology and Religious Belief.* Ed. C. Barrett. Berkeley: University of California Press, 1972. (LC)

Wittgenstein, Ludwig. *Letters to C.K. Ogden*. Ed. G. H. von Wright. Oxford: Basil Blackwell, 1973.

Wittgenstein, Ludwig. "Letters to Ludwig von Ficker." In *Wittgenstein: Sources and Perspectives*, ed. C. G. Luckhardt. Ithaca, NY: Cornell University Press, 1979.

Wittgenstein, Ludwig. "Ludwig Wittgenstein-Ludwig Hänsel: A Friendship, 1929–1940." In *Public and Private Occasions*, ed. J. Klagge and A. Nordmann. Totowa NJ: Rowman & Littlefield, 2003.

Wittgenstein, Ludwig. *The Mythology in Our Language: Remarks on Frazer's Golden Bough*. Ed. Giovanni da Coland S. Palmié. Trans. S. Palmié. London: HAU Books, 2018.

Wittgenstein, Ludwig. *On Certainty*. Ed. G. E. M. Anscombe and G. H. von Wright. Oxford: Blackwell, 1969. (OC)

Wittgenstein, Ludwig. *Philosophical Grammar*. Ed. R. Rhees, trans. A. Kenny. Oxford: Blackwell, 1974.

Wittgenstein, Ludwig. *Philosophical Investigations*, rev. 4th ed. Ed. and trans. P. M. S. Hacker and J. Schulte. Oxford: Wiley-Blackwell, 2009. (PI)

Wittgenstein, Ludwig, *Philosophical Occasions: 1912–1953*. Ed. James Klagge and Alfred Nordmann. Indianapolis: Hackett, 1993. (PO)

Wittgenstein, Ludwig. *Philosophical Remarks*. Ed. R. Rhees, trans. R. Hargreaves and R. White. Oxford: Blackwell, 1975. (PR)

Wittgenstein, Ludwig. Philosophie. Edited by H. Nyman. In *Revue Internationale de Philosophie* 43 (169) (1989): 175–203.

Wittgenstein, Ludwig. *Philosophische Bemerkungen*. Ed. R. Rhees, Oxford: Blackwell, 1964.

Wittgenstein, Ludwig. *Philosophische Untersuchungen: Kritisch-Genetische Edition*. Ed. J. Schulte. Frankfurt am Main: Suhrkamp, 2001.

Wittgenstein, Ludwig. "Philosophy." Trans. C. G. Luckhardt and M. Aue. *Synthese* 87, no. 1 (1991): 3–22.

Wittgenstein, Ludwig. *Public and Private Occasions*. Ed. J. Klagge and A. Nordman. Totowa, NJ: Rowman & Littlefield, 2003. (PPO)

Wittgenstein, Ludwig. *Remarks on Color*. Trans. L. McAlister and M. Schätte. Berkeley: University of California Press, 1977. (RC)

Wittgenstein, Ludwig. *Remarks on the Foundations of Mathematics*, rev. ed. Cambridge, MA: MIT Press, 1978. (RFM)

Wittgenstein, Ludwig. "Remarks on Frazer's 'Golden Bough.'" Trans. A. C. Miles and Rush Rhees. *Human World* 3 (May 1971): 18–41.

Wittgenstein, Ludwig. "Remarks on Frazer's *Golden Bough*." Trans. John Beversluis. In *Wittgenstein: Sources and Perspectives*, ed. C. Luckhardt. Ithaca, NY: Cornell University Press, 1979.

Wittgenstein, Ludwig. *Remarks on the Philosophy of Psychology*, vol. 1. Ed. G. E. M. Anscombe and G. H. von Wright, trans. G.E.M. Anscombe. Chicago: University of Chicago Press, 1980. (RPP1)

Wittgenstein, Ludwig. *Remarks on the Philosophy of Psychology*, vol. 2. Ed. G. H. von Wright and H. Nyman, trans. C. G. Luckhardt and M. A. E. Aue. Chicago: University of Chicago Press, 1980. (RPP2)

Wittgenstein, Ludwig. *Wiener Ausgabe*, vol. 1. Ed. M. Nedo. New York: Springer-Verlag, 1994. (WA1)

Wittgenstein, Ludwig. *Wiener Ausgabe*, vol. 2. Ed. M. Nedo. New York: Springer-Verlag, 1994. (WA2)

Wittgenstein, Ludwig. *Wiener Ausgabe*, vol. 3. Ed. M. Nedo. New York: Springer-Verlag, 1995. (WA3)

Wittgenstein, Ludwig. *Wiener Ausgabe*, vol. 7: *Synopse der Manuskiptbände I bis IV*. Ed. M. Nedo. Frankfurt am Main: Vittorio Klostermann, 2020.

Wittgenstein, Ludwig. *Wiener Ausgabe*, vol. 8.1: *Synopse der Manuskriptbände V bis X*. Ed. M. Nedo. New York: Springer-Verlag, 2000.

Wittgenstein, Ludwig. *Wiener Ausgabe*, vol. 8.2: *Synopse der Manuskriptbände V bis X*. Ed. M. Nedo. Frankfurt am Main: Vittorio Klostermann, 2019.

Wittgenstein, Ludwig. *Wiener Ausgabe*, vol. 11: "*The Big Typescript*." Ed. M. Nedo. New York: Springer-Verlag, 2000.

Wittgenstein, Ludwig. *Wittgenstein in Cambridge: Letters and Documents, 1911–1951*. Ed. Brian McGuinness. Oxford: Blackwell, 2008. (WC)

Wittgenstein, Ludwig. *Wittgenstein: Lectures, Cambridge 1930–1933: From the Notes of G. E. Moore*. Ed. D. Stern, B. Rogers, and G. Citron. New York: Cambridge University Press, 2016. (WLM)

Wittgenstein, Ludwig. *Wittgenstein und die Musik: Ludwig Wittgenstein—Rudolf Koder Briefwechsel*. Ed. M. Alber. Innsbruck: Haymon-Verlag, 2000.

Wittgenstein, Ludwig. *Wittgenstein's Family Letters: Corresponding with Wittgenstein*. Trans. Peter Winslow. London: Bloomsbury Academic, 2019.

Wittgenstein, Ludwig. *Wittgenstein's Lectures on the Foundations of Mathematics: Cambridge, 1939*. Ed. Cora Diamond. Ithaca, NY: Cornell University Press, 1976. (LFM)

Wittgenstein, Ludwig. *Wittgenstein's Lectures: Cambridge, 1932–1935, from the Notes of Alice Ambrose and Margaret MacDonald*. Ed. A. Ambrose. Totowa, NJ: Rowman and Littlefield, 1979. (WLA)

Wittgenstein, Ludwig. *Wittgenstein's Lectures: Cambridge, 1930–1932, from the Notes of John King and Desmond Lee*. Ed. Desmond Lee. Chicago: University of Chicago Press, 1980. (WLL)

Wittgenstein, Ludwig. *Wittgenstein's Lectures on Philosophical Psychology: 1946–47*. Ed. Peter Geach. Chicago: University of Chicago Press, 1988. (LPP)

Wittgenstein, Ludwig. *Wittgenstein's Nachlass: The Bergen Electronic Edition.* CD-ROM. Oxford: Oxford University Press, 2000. (MS or TS)

Wittgenstein, Ludwig. "Wittgenstein's Philosophical Conversations with Rush Rhees (1939–1950): From the Notes of Rush Rhees." Ed. G. Citron. *Mind* 124, no. 493 (2015): 1–71.

Wittgenstein, Ludwig. *Wittgenstein's Whewell's Court Lectures: Cambridge, 1938–1941, from the Notes by Yorick Smythies.* Ed. Volker Munz and Bernhard Ritter. Oxford: Wiley-Blackwell, 2017.

Wittgenstein, Ludwig. *Word Book.* Trans. Bettina Funcke. Intro. Désirée Weber. New York: Badlands Unlimited, 2020.

Wittgenstein, Ludwig. *Zettel.* Trans. G. E. M. Anscombe. Oxford: Blackwell, 1967. (Z)

Wood, Alan. *Bertrand Russell: The Passionate Skeptic, A Biography.* New York: Simon & Schuster, 1958.

Wünsche, Konrad. *Der Volksschullehrer Ludwig Wittgenstein: Mit neuen Dokumenten und Briefen aus den Jahren 1919 bis 1926.* Frankfurt am Main: Suhrkamp, 1985.

Index